Women Among the Brethren

Stories of 15 Mennonite Brethren and Krimmer Mennonite Brethren Women

Katie Funk Wiebe, Editor

The Board of Christian Literature
of the General Conference of Mennonite Brethren Churches
Hillsboro, Kansas
1979

Acknowledgments

Chapter 3, ''She Passed on the Faith'' is adapted from Chapter 4 of *Full Circle: Stories of Mennonite Women*, edited by Mary Lou Cummings, Newton, Kansas: Faith and Life Press, 1978. Used by permission.

Chapter 12, ''A Time of Terror'' is a translation of pp. 98-103 of *Sagradowka*, Historische Schriftenreihe, Book 4, by Gerhard Lohrenz. Rosthern, Saskatchewan: 1947. Used by permission of the author and the Bargen family.

Chapter 13, ''A Flight in Winter'' is a translation of pp. 116-120 in *Das Ende von Chortitza* edited by Gerhard Fast, Selbstverlag: 1973. Used by permission of Mrs. Gerhard Fast and Mrs. Anna (Julius) Loewen.

Library of Congress Number 79-54802
International Standard Book Number 0-935196-00-S
Printed in the United States of America

Cover design by John Hiebert

Printing by Mennonite Brethren Publishing House, Hillsboro, Kansas 67063

To my mother

Anna Janzen Funk

Table of Contents

. . . WAITING AND PRAYING

. . . AS WAYFARERS

. . . IN WOMANLY WORK

. . . WEEPING, AGAIN

. . . WORKING WITH WORDS

Introduction

Six years ago, I wrote a series of skits for my girl's Sunday school class. The skits portrayed significant events in the story of the Mennonite Brethren Church. I based these skits on readily available literature of the church. Because that literature focused on the male leadership of the church, most of the girls in the final dramas played male roles. I asked myself, "Do these skits encourage the girls to be participants in, or spectators of the work of the church?"

In this book, *Women Among the Brethren*, Katie Funk Wiebe brings together stories of women of God who were part of the Mennonite Brethren and Krimmer Mennonite Brethren church story. In doing so, Katie preserves a heritage that includes both women and men. It is a heritage that calls girls, as well as boys, to lives of significant faith and service.

I hope this book is only a beginning. Perhaps it will cause readers to recall almost-forgotten journals or once-heard stories kept within the family. Perhaps it will inspire readers to begin preserving today's stories for future reading. Hopefully, *Women Among the Brethren* will inspire future stories of God's work among the women of the Mennonite Brethren and Krimmer Mennonite Brethren churches. Meanwhile, readers should let this book encourage them to be participants in God's work among his people.

Karen Neufeld
Hillsboro, Kansas

Preface

Frequently persons who have followed God's call have at some time in their lives come face to face with a person or an image which embodied the concept of discipleship. It may have been a teacher, a friend, or a distant acquaintance. That person's spirit called forth something in their spirit, and they accepted the challenge of that life.

In earlier decades in the life of the church, such role models were as close as the next-door neighbor, when orphans found a permanent home there; or the church pulpit, when foreign missionaries came home to report the working of the Spirit in another land. In the small, closely-knit communities, children watched these models and heard their parents talking about them: Schellenberg's Katharina had left the community to become a doctor; Brother Wiebe from China had proclaimed the power of the Gospel in that country at the missions festival; Anna Baerg had written another poem for a silver wedding anniversary; Sister Hiebert had delivered her three hundredth baby last night.

Today, in our more widely dispersed congregations, such models have to come in other forms as well to be visible. We have to read about them. One educator has said, "To destroy a civilization you do not need to burn its records in a single fire. Leave those records unread for a few generations and the effect will be the same." Aspects of the corporate life of the church are in danger of being destroyed when the records of the past are neglected and forgotten.

Though we have a great heritage of courage, vision, sacrifice, and faith on the part of women, their stories have rarely been recorded so today's generation can read them. Aware of this gap in the story of the church, the Board of Christian Literature asked me to develop a book of biographies about women of the church and their contribution to it.

I sensed at once the assignment would be difficult because women in past years have not been part of the formal decision-making process of the church. Therefore, their contribution in other areas has largely remained undocumented as well. Yet the story of the church is the story of how God uses men and women to glorify him. So this book attempts to add to this story, not to change it, and to show how the gifts of women of Mennonite Brethren and Krimmer Mennonite Brethren congregations contributed to its development.

I asked the writers to consider several factors in selecting their subjects. We were not necessarily looking for firsts, nor for women in position places. We were looking for women who had a clear dedication to Christ and the church with a story to tell. We wanted to show the vision and spirit of these women and the struggles and victories they encountered in bringing that vision to fruition. We wanted to include a variety of women with regard to marital status, vocation, and time period in which they lived. We wanted to recognize many kinds of women in addition to the single missionary, whose story appears most often in church literature.

A factor we had to consider as the project progressed was the availability of research material. Women who should have been included in this volume had to be omitted because they had left few written records and gathering information about them was too difficult for the resources of this project. The fifteen biographies in this book represent hundreds of hours spent researching archives, personal files, libraries, and conducting oral interviews, as well as in writing. Admittedly, the task of the writers was difficult and they are to be commended for their diligence. For some it was the first attempt at this type of writing.

Several conclusions can be made at the end of the project. Women have contributed much to the life and work of the church. They have an interesting and exciting story to tell. The records show they were women of strong character, vital and courageous. When they saw a task that needed doing and they knew they had the skills to do it, they didn't ask whose job it was. They simply moved in and did it.

Frequently their contribution outside the home was an extension of familial roles — feeding, caring, teaching children and young women, or looking after the sick. How these women, some with families of eight to ten children, found time for extensive hospitality, midwifery, teaching or missionary activity, in addition to their home responsibilities in difficult pioneer times, may be mystifying to today's busy homemaker with her many laborsaving devices.

The book traces the story of Mennonite Brethren and Krimmer Mennonite Brethren women from a historical perspective to a limited degree. The first biographies deal with women involved in the founding of churches in Russia. Their story, like those which follow, is a story of births, sickness, and deaths; hard work and travel; waiting and praying. Their contribution was often mostly patient endurance.

Then the story moves across the ocean to Canada and United States where an interest in and opportunity for mission to people beyond the church constituency developed. Creative expression through the arts and higher education for women were natural accompaniments.

To have omitted the story of women during World Wars 1 and 2 because these accounts are mostly in Geman would have left the record incomplete. Extended periods of separation from their men and suffering have always been the lot of women. It is also a large part of the story of women among brethren who were looking for a place to live out their religious beliefs in peace and freedom. War increased this burden of pain and suffering.

In this volume you will not find women who had close personal ties with the institutional church. The book includes no soapbox orators. No church planners. No leaders in science or technology. But you will find leaders in the art of living and loving. These women gave liberally of themselves to others. These short glimpses of their lives reveal that God does not limit himself to the kinds of persons he uses to glorify himself. His ways are multitudinous.

My sincere appreciation goes to the writers of these biographies, to all who encouraged the project, especially the Board of Christian Literature, and to Malinda Nikkel, Karen Neufeld, Becky Basinger, and Millie Kroeker who read and critiqued the manuscripts.

Katie Funk Wiebe
Hillsboro, Kansas
May, 1979

Intertwined in the account of the origin of the Mennonite Brethren Church is the story of a Russian sister who was converted and baptized by a Mennonite Brethren minister. Her clear testimony of faith brought others into the kingdom of God. Efrosinia Morozowa probably was born about 1850. After the trial of Heinrich Huebert, who was accused of having baptized her, she is not mentioned again in the history books.

1

THE RUSSIAN SISTER

Efrosinia Morozowa (c. **1850-?**)

By Katie Funk Wiebe

Efrosinia stood a respectful three to four feet behind her uncle as he talked to the strange man. Her eyes wandered about the yard. The hard dirt by the front door had been swept smooth. Stones daubed with white paint edged the flower garden nearby. Behind her in the apple orchard she could hear children shrieking in play.

She heard her name and turned to look at the man. Not very tall. Nor heavy. Bearded. A little gray. And tired looking. But his eyes looked kind, almost sad-kind. A Mennonite, her uncle had said. She knew about them. When her mother and father were still alive, Efrosinia often had seen Mennonites in the marketplace buying nuts and dried fish and bolts of cloth.

The thought of her mother and father made her swallow hard. Because they were gone, she was here.

"The girl's name?"

"Efrosinia Morozowa. Her parents died of black pox several

months ago. She'll make a good nursemaid for your children. She works fast and obeys well. You should have no trouble.'' Her uncle spoke rapidly, pushing the words out before him.

The older man's eyes dropped to the young dark-haired girl in the polka-dotted cotton shirt and blouse. Her eyes fell to the ground, but her ears caught her uncle's next words.

''I would like to leave her with you — her work in exchange for food and lodging and perhaps some small items of clothing your wife can spare. Sinia's been with us for several months, but she's old enough now to work — a very good worker.''

''How old is she?''

''Nearly ten.''

''Where do you live?''

''In Ostrikow — across the river.''

''Oh yes, I know the place well.'' The voice did sound kind. Efrosinia listened for a gentle tone. The man looked at her again. Efrosinia pulled her small bundle of clothing closely to her thin body. The matter of her future would soon be decided. A fly lit on her instep and she rubbed one bare foot over the other.

''All right, leave her here,'' said the man, his eyes still on her. ''My wife needs help. I would call her but she's not feeling well. She's lying down.''

''Good,'' said her uncle, his face broadening into a smile. ''Thank you, thank you.''

He turned to the young girl. ''*Wirt* Huebert has agreed to keep you. It is as we had hoped. You will like it here. Do your work well.'' He patted her bony shoulder briefly, then turned to climb back onto his wagon waiting on the road under the acacia trees. He whipped the horses briskly and the wagon rolled down the street. He never looked back. The transaction had been made.

Efrosinia stood there in the mid-afternoon sun, not knowing what to do next. She bit her lip, wishing she had said good-bye once more to her aunt. Her uncle's house was too full with his family. She knew that. They had no room for orphans, even though she had slept on a mat in the children's room. A tear rolled down her cheek. If she worked hard, she would get along well, her uncle had told her. She watched the chickens scratching for food in the hard dirt near the house. They were busy — as she would be soon.

She swallowed hard at the lump in her throat and blinked till her eyes cleared. On the rooftop of the house, beside a large untidy nest built on an old wagon wheel fastened to the peak, stood a large white stork, tall, motionless, watching her. A stork was always a good omen, her mother had once told her. She hitched her bundle a little closer. Maybe she would like this place.

So began Efrosinia's life with the Heinrich Hueberts of Liebenau as household servant and nursemaid. She grew up with the children she took care of, rocking the baby when it cried, minding the younger ones, and playing with the older children as time allowed.

Both the Hueberts were often sickly, which meant that added responsibilities fell on the young girl. Yet it did not take her long to realize that something was very different in this home. The family members did not bow to icons, nor did they cross themselves before they prayed. They never went to confession. They read from the Bible, a book her parents had not owned, for they could neither read nor write. She listened from a silent distance as Mr. Huebert explained Bible stories to his children about Abram and Isaac, David and Goliath, and Jesus and the boy who was raised from the dead. If she found herself thinking too much about the stories as she went about her work, she crossed herself quickly to erase the thoughts.

Her uncle rarely visited her and she soon almost forgot the family who had had no room for her in their home. Efrosinia found herself strangely attracted to her employer, this gentle man with the retiring ways and clear peaceful gaze, and the weak voice, which he rarely raised against either human beings or animals.

Often he sat deep in thought over his books in the evenings after the day's work at his treadmill was finished. She noticed he particularly enjoyed his Bible. Friends listened carefully when he explained what certain passages meant. He also liked to study a book of astronomy — about the stars, he told her. He had other books, arranged carefully on his desk, which he said were poetry. Sometimes when she was dusting the furniture in that room, she sneaked a look briefly. What were those strange marks on the pages which meant so much to him?

After she climbed upstairs to her featherbed in the attic room, she often heard the low mumble of men as they talked deep into the night. The large clock hanging on the wall in the front room, with its shining round gold pendulum and weights suspended by a fine chain, struck 11 or 12 before they left. Sometimes after she had been asleep, she was awakened suddenly by very animated conversation. Then again, all would be quiet. Before she drifted off again, she thought about the long conversations of the men. She knew Mrs. Huebert would be irritable in the morning when she went down to help with the morning meal.

One day in late November of 1859, on St. Martin's Day, she overheard Mr. Huebert tell his wife that he and some other men who were dissatisfied with the spiritual life of the Mennonite church had celebrated their first private communion in a home in Elizabethtal. They refused to eat at the Lord's table with people who called themselves Christians yet lived sinful lives. Efrosinia wasn't sure how they could have had communion with no priest present, but she didn't dare ask.

Mr. Huebert's voice grew unusually firm as he spoke about the communion. "No one should accept the cup and the bread unless they repent of ungodly conduct, are born again and feel conviction concerning their former sins, and are convinced they should live righteously." His voice was almost loud. Sinia didn't know what the words meant, but she noticed Mrs. Huebert looked troubled as she returned to the bedroom to lie down.

After that, for a while, the evening callers increased considerably. Efrosinia was often sent upstairs early after the children had been put to sleep. She lay awake in the darkness recalling what her mother had said before she died about believing in Christ. Mr. Huebert had told them one morning that 18 family heads had signed a document stating they were withdrawing from the Mennonite church because the people in it were not "born again." The Orthodox catechism, of which Efrosinia knew very little, mentioned believing in Christ and fearing God. Her mother had encouraged her to be a good girl and to pray. But she did not know she could be saved from eternal damnation. "If a man is not born again, he cannot enter the kingdom of heaven," Mr. Huebert had said. No one had ever told her Christ had died for her sins, or that she could know she was eternally saved. Her mother had said to keep seeking God.

One day as Mr. Huebert was ready to go back to the mill, the 12-year-old housemaid asked him if he thought she could be born again too. She wanted to know if her sins were forgiven.

Mr. Huebert looked startled at the young girl's request. Then a quiet smile lit up his face. He assured her she, too, could have forgiveness of sins. Salvation was for all people. Sometime later that week, Efrosinia accepted this salvation and told her employers her decision.

In May 1860 Huebert was elected first teaching minister of the new church and Jacob Bekker associate minister. Johann Claassen, who later made many trips to Petersburg and Odessa to get permission for the new group to be recognized as a Mennonite church under the original charter with the Russian government, came to the house often when he was in Liebenau.

But Efrosinia's newfound joy and peace hardly knew how to understand the pain and agony her employer was facing. One day he and Benjamin Bekker were ordered by the mayor of the village of Liebenau to appear before the district government on June 9, 1860, to explain their actions. When he returned late that evening, he told the family what had happened.

''After we got there Benjamin Bekker and I were handed some paper and a pen by the officials and sent to the lower floor of the building to write an explanation of what our new group intended to do. You know that's the floor the clerks of the Mennonite churches use in slack season to do their work.''

His wife nodded. Efrosinia knew she should go to the kitchen, but she waited.

''Before we began to write, we knelt to pray to ask for God's wisdom. At that, the clerks rushed from the room. They had probably never seen anyone kneel in prayer — yet they are clerks of the church.'' Mr. Huebert had that sad-kind look again. She went to the kitchen to get more bread.

Efrosinia knew she had been forgiven. And almost daily she sifted through her child-woman heart and mind the information about the newly formed Mennonite Brethren Church. Jakob Bekker and Heinrich Bartel had baptized each other at the river and then Bekker had baptized three others. This was a troubling bit of information for Efrosinia. How could adults be baptized? Children were the ones who were baptized. By a priest. With a little water sprinkled over them. She listened carefully that evening when Mr. Huebert told his wife how the Brethren (as the new group was called) had been called before the five elders and five preachers of the church. The elders and preachers had done their utmost to bring Huebert and his friends over to their point of view with all kinds of arguments.

"Finally one of the elders said, 'We will give you one week to think the matter over. If you do not return to the church after that time, we will take serious action against you, and the church will disenfranchise you as colonists and exile you from our midst.' "

"And what did you say, Heinrich?" asked his wife. Efrosinia waited. She wanted to hear too.

"I was standing close to the mayor. I said, 'Honorable Mayor, you cannot do more than God permits you to do. For God it is a simple matter to deliver us from your hands. Jesus said, "The very hairs of your head are numbered; not one shall fall from your head without God's will." ' I took a lock of hair between my fingers." He showed them how he had done it and grasped a few strands of thinning hair. "I told him that I have only a few hairs left on my head, but he couldn't pluck a single one without God's will. God was able to deliver us out of his hand, but if he did not do so, he should know we would not return to the church for we fear God. We would rather fall into the hands of men than into the judgment of God. Efrosinia, bring the *Prips*," he said, holding out his cup to her to fill with the cereal beverage.

Efrosinia had been listening so hard she had forgotten her work. *We would rather fall into the hands of men than into the judgment of God.* Would she ever have that kind of faith? But she was only a Russian peasant girl. *Wirt* Huebert was a highly educated minister, a leader, a deep thinker. She thanked God for her own assurance of salvation. She thought of the men who had been imprisoned in Chortitza and even treated cruelly, confined in semi-dark cells for several weeks without adequate clothing or food, and forced to work at hard labor outdoors. Mr. Huebert's weak voice had trembled when he had told the family about these men. "For the faith we must do it," he had said. "To prison if need be."

For the faith. But God expected suffering only of leaders, not poor Russian girls. She plunked a dish into the dishpan. *For the faith.*

One day Gerhard Wieler, the village school teacher who frequently visited the Huebert home, called when Mr. Huebert was not at home. Efrosinia liked it when he came. He always had a word or smile for her. He often asked her how she was getting along in her Christian walk, for he had learned about her commitment from the Hueberts. As he waited for Huebert to return from work in the mill, Wieler asked the girl if she would like to learn to read.

To read? Unbelievable! Efrosinia's face brightened. To read like Mr. Huebert? To understand what the marks on the paper meant? Her beaming smile was his answer. Wieler took a slate and wrote her name.

"EFROSINIA — your name. It is a long one. See if you can copy it." Efrosinia carefully followed his markings, but her letters looked awkward and stumbled over each other.

"Tomorrow we will try again," Wieler said as Mr. Huebert entered.

Efrosinia nodded. She was going to learn to read. The Bible. And other books. She carried the slate upstairs so no one would erase the letters. She would practice hard and show him she could do it. He was an important teacher from the Chortitza district who had taught in this area for six years and was recognized as one of the best teachers. For him she would do anything.

Whenever Wieler came to the Huebert house thereafter, even in later years when he was hiding from church and government officials for having joined the Brethren, he took a few minutes to help her read and write.

In spring, Efrosinia heard that the new group, which had officially begun with a communion service in November of 1859, by New Year's 1861 had 102 adult members, with some 40 family heads. Mr. Huebert had told his wife, "Our task is to keep spreading the good news. We must always witness to our faith."

That spring the Brethren often had services on the north side of the village of Liebenau across the brook from Ostrikow, Efrosinia's former home. The Russian peasants who worked for the Mennonites, often attracted by good wages, were invited to attend prayer and Bible study periods in their homes. When Mrs. Huebert could spare her, Efrosinia put on her best dress and attended also. She was glad when the meetings were at the Huebert home, for then she was sure to go.

At times the harness room was so full some people had to stand outside even though no seats were provided. Efrosinia loved the singing, the Bible study and the prayer-time. Mr. Wieler, who spoke Russian well and preached powerfully, was often the speaker. One day he asked if anyone wanted to say something for the Lord. Efrosinia found her heart beating wildly. She listened to the testimony of one man who spoke of seeking God and never finding him. He had even considered becoming a monk. Then he had met Christ at these meetings.

I have something to say also, decided Efrosinia. She had never told anyone outside the Huebert family how she had become a Christian. She spoke up, her clear youthful voice carrying to everyone in the full room, telling them how she had been seeking after God and had found peace in Christ. If they wanted to find him in the magnificence of the temples or the pomp and solemnity of the Orthodox services, they would never find him. Only the words of the Bible would supply them with answers to their questions. She was surprised at her own words. Then some other persons, both men and women, spoke. All knelt for prayer. She thanked God silently for the opportunity to tell others. From then on she always took part openly in the services. If only Russians were present, she prayed in Russian. If only Mennonites, she prayed in German at these *Stundist* (meaning hour for worship and fellowship) meetings.

But the Huebert family was in difficulty. One day Mr. Huebert came home to tell them the church ban had been placed on the seceding families. The next step would be banishment from the village and loss of citizenship. He was weary, and his voice sounded faint. Many evenings, Efrosinia knew, he sat up late working at his books, especially his accounts.

One day in 1861 Mr. Huebert announced to the family he had sold the treadmill business because of the economic ostracism of the community. The members of the church would not bring their business to him. He could not continue. The patience of his creditors was running out. He had sold the mill for 925 rubles and the house and lot for 3,300. He talked about moving to the Kuban, where new land was being acquired for the Brethren.

In May 1861 Huebert was baptized by immersion. The same year Efrosinia decided she did not need to cross herself so often. And she knew she, too, wanted to be baptized as it was taught in the New Testament, which she read every evening. But she knew also that the government did not allow her, a Russian Orthodox, to join another church.

Wieler did not come as often during these trying days, for his teaching position was in jeopardy. In December he arrived at the Hueberts' late one evening to tell them he had been released from his teaching position in the Liebenau school. Although his work had always been very satisfactory, he was not allowed to do private tutoring either.

"Mayor Peters told me the citizens do not want to send their children to my school. The school society said if I broke my connections with the Brethren I could keep on teaching. But how can I do that when Christ calls us to his work?" He had been offered a job in Einlage in Chortitza, he said. He would have to move his sick wife and child now, in the dead of winter. He did not know how he would survive if that job fell through.

Efrosinia felt sad. Huebert had no mill. Wieler had no job.

She continued to attend the services held among the Russians. Many of them ended with a call to repentance and conversion through a living faith in Christ. The Word of God worked like a hammer on stone, softening hard hearts. In the hushed quietness after the preacher had spoken, sounds of weeping were often heard. Many of these Russians took the Gospel back with them to their communities.

One day even Efrosinia's job was threatened. The local officials had heard of the revival among the Russians and were inquiring how these people had become infected with this new teaching.

"We told them of your joyous testimony of the saving power of Christ's love and about the preaching of Gerhard Wieler, who has brought us to a new understanding of the power of God's love," her Russian friends told her. Next, in January 1862, the governor of the Tavrichesk district sent to the minister of internal affairs a letter complaining of the subversion of the Orthodox members by the *Stundists*. Then one day as Efrosinia was preparing the evening meal at the Hueberts' the door rattled under a powerful fist. Mrs. Huebert answered, and a rough voice boomed out, "Efrosinia — where is the girl?"

She walked timidly to the front door where her uncle stood glowering. "What are the people saying about you? I'm ashamed of you — and you a Morozowa. Causing people to go astray—"

"But, Uncle—"

"You are coming with me. Get your things and let's go."

Neither she nor Mr. and Mrs. Huebert could convince him that she was not doing anything wrong or illegal.

Efrosinia packed her few belongings, said good-bye to the

Hueberts and left with her uncle by wagon for Ostrikow. At his home he demanded she give up the foolishness of joining the *Stundists*. When she refused, he beat her savagely and locked her up in the attic. When after two weeks she still had not given in to his commands, he drove her to the village of Gnadenheim, several miles south of Liebenau, to work in another home. He told her the Brethren had not penetrated this area with their teaching. He demanded she say no more about her faith to anyone. In this new place, without the encouragement of other *Stundists*, he was convinced her faith would die. Sadly she agreed to his demands.

Each evening before she retired, though she was tired and the light was poor, Efrosinia took out her little Russian New Testament* and read it, then knelt to pray. One evening after she was already in bed, she heard a brisk knock at the door. It was the man and woman for whom she was working.

"We heard you mention our names," said the woman. "Why do you talk out loud to yourself about us each evening?"

"But I wasn't — I was talking to God, praying you might come to know the peace I know." God had answered her prayers. The way had been opened for her to talk to them about Christ's love without breaking her promise to her uncle. She told them the story of how she had come to the Hueberts, the Bible verses she had learned with the children, and how Mr. Huebert had showed her the way of salvation. Within a matter of days the man and woman became Christians and wanted to start meetings in their home. When Efrosinia's brother, who operated the local tavern, asked her about what was happening, she was able to tell him also how Christ's indwelling presence took away all longing and desire for sinful habits. He was converted, and before long closed his business, for he saw he could not sell liquor because it led people into sin. Here and there in the community, when believers gathered, Efrosinia became known as one who had true life in Christ. She had many opportunities to witness more openly.

But within her grew the old longing to complete something which had been left undone when she had to leave the Hueberts. She wanted to be baptized. When she requested baptism, the Mennonite ministers all shrugged their shoulders. It was too dangerous for them to baptize a Russian because of the laws

---

* *First published in Russian in 1862.*

restricting proselytizing among the Orthodox Russians. To baptize a Russian meant severe persecution.

One evening after the service, the leaders of the Brethren told Efrosinia that a minister who was leaving for the Kuban, the new settlement of the Brethren, was willing to baptize her that very night. The next morning he would be gone before the government officials could find him.

With a happy heart Efrosinia rushed to get her new white blouse and skirt which she had prepared many months ago in anticipation of this very event. On May 26, 1864, in the late evening, a small group of Russian believers, a Brethren minister and Efrosinia walked to the river where she was baptized secretly "in the name of the Father and of the Son and of the Holy Ghost."

But the news of what had occurred that evening spread quickly, though the arm of the law worked more slowly. Though she was still working at Gnadenheim, Efrosinia heard one evening at the village store that her former employer and friend Heinrich Huebert, the leading minister of the Brethren and therefore its promoter, had been arrested and imprisoned because he had baptized her. First he had been held in a local jail, and then taken to the Russian village of Tokmak without a trial. The report also said that, because of Efrosinia's open testimony to the members of the Russian Orthodox Church, they had fallen prey to the strange heresy of abstaining from marital relations to become the chaste bride of Christ.

"Not true, not true." The words burst from her mouth when she heard the report.

But it was true Mr. Huebert was in jail. And because of her. He was suffering pain for her. Efrosinia knew she had to find some way to visit Mrs. Huebert in Liebenau. One Sunday afternoon, when she had some free time, she persuaded her brother to take her to Liebenau so she could talk with Mrs. Huebert.

She found Mrs. Huebert sickly as usual. The officials had taken her Heinrich though he had not been feeling well either. The Liebenau congregation had posted bond for his release from prison where he was being held for questioning, but the bond had been rejected because he refused to say who had baptized Efrosinia. He denied having done it himself. He had sent her word she should not divulge the name either. Mrs. Huebert did not seem angry with Efrosinia even though her husband was in prison because of the girl. Her former mistress added that the Brethren had deposed her husband from office because he had not suppressed the wave of emotionalism which had swept through the group.

Efrosinia returned to Gnadenheim perplexed and downcast. Would the Lord who had so often heard her prayers answer even now? She did not know what to pray. She had wanted to be baptized to obey God, yet now others were suffering because of her desire. Had she been selfish?

On August 4, 1865 the word arrived in the village that though Huebert was still in prison the Brethren had reinstated him as minister after casting lots. Mrs. Huebert was allowed to visit him and supply him with laundry and food, but the place of imprisonment was a damp hole and he was coughing a great deal. Efrosinia felt her own chest tighten to think of it.

Week after week no word came, then in November the news arrived in the community that Mr. Huebert had been released on bail provided by some estate owners of Liebenau who recognized him as a law-abiding, moral citizen. He had been confined for ten months. Thorough investigation of the charges against him had been ordered.

For nearly three years Efrosinia worked and waited for the outcome of the investigation, praying daily for the man who had showed her the way to peace. In the meantime the church grew and gained the recognition it wanted.

In 1867 the summons came to Efrosinia to appear in court. The evidence was ready to be presented. Efrosinia, now a young woman of nearly 20, entered the courtroom to see three men from the Kuban, several Russian converts from the Ostrikow area, Mr. Huebert, looking much older than his years, and several members of the Brethren present. The courtroom was nearly full.

After the preliminaries, the Russians who had attended meetings in Liebenau in the Hueberts' home were asked whether he had taught them the doctrine of celibacy within marriage.

"No." The answer was firm.

Huebert also denied the charge.

Then came the other charges. Some Russians not connected with the *Stundists* and Brethren witnessed that when these people gathered in their homes, they prayed to God, and they were not aware of any wrongdoing concerning them. It was impossible to say anything but good about them — there were no drunkards or thieves among them. On the contrary, there had been instances where a man, formerly a drunkard or thief, upon joining the sect became a good man and stopped drinking and stealing, got a job, and went to work.

Another witness said: "I received a new heart and became a new person when I became a Christian. Previously I had lived a licentious life, and used all manner of profanity. Then I realized that my life was sinful. I was baptized and became a changed person."

Another witness could not remember any unpleasantness between the Orthodox people and the *Stundists* or the Brethren. Another said they were good people, but they did not attend church, did not make the sign of the cross, but sang songs, prayed together, and read the Gospel. They named their newborn children themselves, and permitted them, when they had attained the age of accountability, the opportunity to accept or reject the ordinance of baptism.

Efrosinia wondered whether her turn might come soon. But there was more to come.

A town clerk accused Huebert and the leaders of the new group of misleading the Russians. They taught the Orthodox people that their priests were leading them to hell. He had overheard Huebert say to a Russian that only "their faith was the true faith; they did not bow down to icons and did not make the sign of the cross."

But Efrosinia breathed a sign of relief when some Russians testified the clerk had been under the influence of liquor when he had overheard the conversation between Huebert and the Russians. "We do not consider him a witness, not even a man, because he is never sober. He is a proud person, nothing more," they said.

Finally Huebert had a chance to speak up: "I have something to say concerning those who are received into our fellowship. They are not received unless they repent of their unrighteous conduct, feel convicted in their hearts and souls concerning their former sins, are born again and are convinced they should live righteously. Thus only he who becomes convinced from the Gospel that he must fulfill the Gospel in every detail to live as a holy servant of God can become one of us."

Surely that should be enough to convince the court officials that Mr. Huebert was a good person. The spokesman for the defense contended that in order to establish that the accused was guilty, it was necessary to show he was guilty of evil intent. The accusations against Huebert showed absence of evil intent. If anything was evident it was his good will.

Next came the question of who had baptized Efrosinia. The question was first addressed to the defendant. Again Huebert denied having done so.

"If you did not baptize her, who did?"

Efrosinia heard the man with the soft voice, the man who had led her gently into his home that day long ago and told her she could stay, tell the court he could not betray his brother.

The atmosphere was tense. The court official gazed around the crowded room. They had now come to the real issue. "If the person who baptized this young woman is present, let him stand up."

Efrosinia gasped for breath and clutched the arms of the chair. Now would another of the Brethren be imprisoned because of her?

Abram Dyck of the Kuban rose slowly and came forward.

"Did you baptize this woman?"

"I did."

"Did you instruct her to be baptized?"

"No."

The officer in charge turned to Efrosinia.

"Did this man instruct you to be baptized?"

Efrosinia hoped her words wouldn't dissolve in tears, but that she could speak as clearly as she did in the harness room when the believers gathered. She took a deep breath: "No. I learned to read the Bible, and God's Word showed me that I must be converted and baptized. I wanted to be baptized for many months but no one would do so. Finally, Abram Dyck agreed to baptize me one night before he left for the Kuban."

"Do you agree?" He looked at Dyck.

Dyck acknowledged the truth of her statements and how he finally had been compelled by the Spirit of Christ to baptize her. "As I stand before this tribunal, so I stand before God, and am not at all afraid in the face of the fact that you condemn me. I am not afraid of what I have done. I trust in God, and I stand firmly, as our forefathers did, for the faith in Christ. Am I breaking the law or harming religion because I read the Gospel and preach its message and baptize in the name of Christ? You can only accuse me of not doing anything contrary to God's will — this constitutes my crime. Now judge me as you see fit."

The officials deliberated for five minutes. Then they acquitted both Huebert and Dyck. The court was dismissed.

Into the sunshine of the day walked the Brethren, their sadness lifted, for they were one step closer to full freedom. A stork flew overhead headed in the same direction they were going — toward the sun.

"God with you, *Wirt* Huebert," Efrosinia called one last time to the greying man.

"And with you, Sister. Go spread the Word."

Bibliography

Bekker, Jacob P. *Origin of the Mennonite Brethren Church*, translated from the German by D. E. Pauls and A. E. Janzen. Hillsboro, Kan., The Mennonite Brethren Historical Society of the Midwest, 1973.

Friesen, P. M. *The Mennonite Brotherhood in Russia (1789-1910)* translated from the German *Die Alt-Evangelische Mennonitische Bruederschaft in Russland*. Fresno, Calif.: Board of Christian Literature of Mennonite Brethren Churches, 1978.

Karev, Alexander, General Secretary, Russian Evangelical Christian Baptist Convention. *The Russian Evangelical Baptist Movement*, or *Under His Cross in Soviet Russia*. Translated by Frederick P. Leman, D. D., Evansville, Ind., n.d. n.p.

Katharina Reimer Claassen, wife of Johann Claassen, spokesman for the Mennonite Brethren in Russia, watched the new group forming before her eyes. She accepted lengthy absences from her husband and all kinds of hardships as her contribution to the establishment of the church. Historian P. M. Friesen recorded much of the correspondence between her and her husband during their many separations on behalf of the Brethren. Six of her ten children died in infancy or early childhood. She died of malaria in the Kuban at age 42.

2

LIVING APART FOR THE LORD

Katharina Reimer Claassen (1827-69)

By Betty Suderman Klassen

"Johann, why have you worked the horses into such a sweat on Sunday afternoon?" Katharina asked her husband as she emerged from the kitchen, wiping her hands on her long, dark apron. It was March 27, 1860, and he had just returned by carriage from Halbstadt, the municipal center of the Molotschna Mennonite settlement in south Russia. He stepped from the entrance into the living room of their home.

"We'll talk about it after the children are in bed," he replied, placing his satchel on the desk in the corner.

"The unpredictable events of the past months frighten me a little," Katharina admitted to herself as she sat down in the rocker to read the bedtime Bible story to Jacob, David, and Johannes, aged seven, four, and two. She thought about their Bible study group. New joys and challenges faced them every time they searched the Word. Their attempts to apply the New Testament Scriptures had led them to a fork in the road, separating them from the *Kirchliche* Mennonite mother church. Johann had defended the persons who had observed communion in a Bible study without the sanction of an officiating elder. After all, no church officials were mentioned in Acts 2, where believers were breaking bread from house to house. Yet, being kicked out of a church business meeting at the suggestion of those who found their piety unpalatable, seemed unwarranted. This in turn, had led to the organization of their "Mennonite Brethren" group on January 6, 1860.

The new group now fellowshiped in their living room, but the tensions with Mennonites of different moral standards and religious piety had increased and moved into the civic arena. The municipal offices had ordered the "Brethren" to return to their former churches and threatened to imprison the leader. Johann would never call himself the leader, Katharina knew, but he was regarded as the spokesman, and functioned as the leader. Five of the seven Mennonite elders (or bishops) backed the civic leaders in opposing the Brethren. Johann had showed her their statement, dated March 15, the day baby Maria had been born, just two weeks ago.

After the story, bedtime prayers and good-night kisses, Katharina closed the door to the children's room and went to pick up the crying baby from the cradle in their bedroom. As she sat in the rocker, nursing tiny Maria, Johann pulled up a chair beside her.

"Katharina," he began in a subdued voice, "someone warned me that the Mennonite authorities are going to arrest me on charges of leading an illegal secret society. I must leave tomorrow night. If I don't, I may be in jail by Tuesday or Wednesday."

"But Johann," she protested, "where will you go?"

"Don't ask me where," he replied, laying his hand tenderly on hers. "You know I wouldn't be safe anywhere in the settlement. Do you remember where I went several years ago to get a permit for the Gnadenfeld high school?"

She nodded as a tear trickled down her cheek.

"I won't name the place, so that when they come to arrest me, you can say I didn't tell you where I was going."

Monday, March 28, was busier than a Saturday at the Claassen home. The maid, using tub and washboard, had to scrub the diapers and the regular laundry, as well as Johann's good shirts. The latter had to be starched, dried indoors because of the rain, then dampened slightly and pressed with a flat-iron heated on the metal cooking plate on top of the brick firebox. While the oven was warm, Katharina toasted all the leftover *Zwieback* to a crisp and put them into a little cloth bag. Little Johannes, whom they fondly called "Hannes," climbed onto Papa's knee and wanted to play. But David sensed that it wasn't right for Papa to be in the house on Monday.

Late that evening Johann talked for some time with Heinrich Huebert, a mill owner in Liebenau. Alone in bed, Katharina pulled up the goosedown comforter and tried to get some sleep. But Huebert left, and she heard Johann shuffling his papers and occasionally clearing his throat. The clock had just chimed one-thirty when she heard her brother Cornelius' voice. The two men tiptoed through the house and into the adjacent barn. She knew they were taking out the riding horse. The barn door rolled shut. Then she heard Johann's footsteps again.

"Katharina, are you asleep?" he asked softly.

"No," she whispered. "Do you have everything? Your visa?"

"Yes, it's in my pocket. I couldn't leave without it," he replied. "Shall we pray together?"

She slipped out from under the covers and they knelt together. They committed each other to God's care, though Katharina paused after every phrase to fight back the tears. They rose from their knees, Johann embraced her once more and said, "Cornelius and the other brethren will help you if you have a problem. In a few days I will write and tell you where I am." She watched him walk with resolute stride out the door.

She stood by the window, barely able to discern the two figures and the horse in the darkness. Then he was gone. Gone to do what was necessary to help their newly formed fellowship with its legal problems. But what could she do? She went back to bed. Was her only contribution the sacrifice of getting along without him? She didn't have much choice there. Should she keep on opening their home for worship even if he wasn't around? Yes. That was something she could and wanted to do. With that thought, she fell asleep.

The next forenoon she was startled by a loud knock at the door. She opened it, her heart pounding.

"We want Johann Claassen," demanded the officers from the municipal court.

"He's not here," she replied, trying to keep her voice steady. The men burst through the door and searched every room in the house. They even combed the cellar, the attic, and the servant's quarters in the barn. Finally they left.

The maid put the steaming bowl of *Borscht* on the table for the noon meal. Katharina asked the blessing, thankful not only for the soup, but also for a husband who was free, even though he would be traveling for three weeks before he reached the capital city of Petersburg (now Leningrad).

Spring came to the Molotschna settlement, and to the village of Liebenau. Katharina kept busy with the four children, housework, hosting the fellowship group, and gardening their plot along the bank of the Tokmak creek. And even before two months had passed, Johann was back.

But after the happy reunion on May 23, he spent little time with his family. His summons to appear at the municipal court gave Katharina some anxious moments, though he came home unscathed. Then he organized an election of preachers for the Mennonite Brethren, held on May 30. As with other church business meetings, Katharina only heard afterwards that Heinrich Huebert and Jacob Bekker, who had clerked in their store for several years, had been elected.

Johann explained that a legal paper he had signed on February 10 promising not to make any more ecclesiastical moves without the express permission of the Mennonite authorities made it impossible for him to accept an official position in the new group.

"But I still think you would make a better leader than Bekker or even Huebert," she responded wistfully.

This thought kept cropping up in her mind, even during the ordination service, when she observed Heinrich Huebert, thin and slightly hunchbacked, in front of the group. She glanced over to the men's side, at Johann, in his fine Sunday suit with the velvet collar. He looks like a leader, she thought, with his handsome features, dark hair, intense brown eyes, and regal bearing.

Summer passed uneventfully for the Mennonite Brethren. Despite the busy harvest season, they met for communion and worship on numerous occasions. On October 9, 1860, two evangelists reported on their itinerant ministry at a meeting in Katharina's tidy living room. The interjections of "Hallelujah! Glory! Victory!" by the one man seemed a little artificial to her. But on the other hand, the words reflected a beautiful new life, joy, and freedom that was lacking in most of the services of the old *Kirchliche* church. Everyone appeared reverent again when Johann spoke the closing prayer. Then two men asked for baptism and gave their testimonies. With joyous singing and shouting the group walked down to Tokmak Creek for the baptism by immersion. Katharina thought the noise was out of place so late at night, but she wasn't ready to say anything about it, except to Johann, later.

Some of the neighbors, however, complained about the noisy rites to the municipal officials. Consequently, Johann, the preachers, and several others had to appear in court. The inspector ordered them to return to their respective *Kirchliche* Mennonite congregations within two months, or be deprived of their Mennonite privileges and colonist status. When Johann arrived at home after that encounter, he announced, "Katharina, I'm buying Heinrich Huebert's covered wagon."

Knowing what that meant, she asked, "Do you have to go again?" He nodded. "Will it be long?"

"Longer than last time, no doubt."

On October 31, 1860, Katharina again assumed the hardships of separation as her contribution to the Mennonite Brethren Church. This time Johann left her a specific assignment: to get his visa renewal from the municipal office before it expired at the end of November. So several weeks after his departure, her brother Cornelius and Heinrich Huebert took her to Halbstadt. In the austere courtroom, the administrator rejected her request.

"What shall we do now?" she asked Cornelius as they descended the wooden stairs of the municipal office and walked to the carriage.

"Send Johann a telegram." So she did, hoping he would reply, indicating a possible next move. Little did she realize that this would be only the first of many problems she would share with him by letter, giving Johann her perspective on church affairs. When one of the teachers lost his job because he was a member of the Mennonite Brethren, she empathized with the plight of his family of ten. Then one day, trouble came closer to home. Six-year-old David burst into the front door, crying.

"What's the matter?" Katharina dried her hands on her apron and led him to the children's bedroom. She sat down in the rocker and took him on her lap. "Tell me what happened."

"He — he said I'm a d-devil!" That unleashed a new torrent of tears.

"Who said that?" she probed.

"Th-the mayor. He came walking down the path and said, 'Well, you pious little devil, where's your Papa?' Papa has been gone so long," he sobbed. She stroked his dark brown hair as she rocked back and forth. Finally an anxious little voice asked, "Am I a devil, Mama? Am I?"

"David," she stopped rocking and looked into his intent brown eyes. "You are not a devil. You are Jesus' little lamb, just like I told you." That satisfied David, and soon he went out to play, this time in the backyard sandbox, secluded from hostile traffic. Now Katharina struggled with her own feelings. She wanted Johann to get legal recognition for the Mennonite Brethren, but vicious barbs aimed at a defenseless child hurt her deeply.

The winter months dragged by without major crises. April 15 began as any other spring gardening day. The maid stayed home with the baby while Katharina, her apron pockets bulging with seeds gathered the previous autumn, walked out to their garden plot next to the bank of Tokmak Creek, in its high water stage. With her was the hired hand, carrying a bucket of seed potatoes, and her three sons, Jacob, David, and Johannes, shouldering hoe, rake, and spade. After an hour of preparing the soil, the younger two tired, so she let them play for a bit. Just as the hired hand began to spade holes for the seed potatoes, David screamed, "Hannes! Hannes!"

Katharina looked up. Where was Johannes? David pointed to the creek. She sprinted across the loose dirt to the bank. Some bubbles surfaced several yards from the edge. Panic clutched her heart. She couldn't swim, but she waded into the flood, groping for her child. The hired hand slipped off his boots and plunged in. The minutes slipped by. The current nearly swept her off her feet before she retreated to the edge.

Late that evening she and sister-in-law Gertrude dressed the little body and laid it in the wooden coffin that Cornelius had built.

After they left, Katharina sat down beside the bier. Nearly seven months ago, her Johann, for the sake of the Brethren, had seemingly stepped out of her life. Now she had lost her little Johannes. It was much harder to give up the responsive, loving 2½-year-old than to lose infant babies. Four times during their first four years of marriage Johann had comforted her when their babies had died. Now she sorrowed alone. She went to Johann's desk, folded down the top and pulled up a chair. Deliberately she recorded the traumatic events of the day in a letter to Johann. Then she cried herself to sleep.

Several weeks later she received a letter from Johann. He had enclosed correspondence from Baron von Mirbach regarding the possibility of a land grant that would enable the Mennonite Brethren to move out of the Molotschna and Chortitza settlements, where they were suffering economic boycott and other persecution. But in essence, Mirbach only expressed regret that he couldn't help. Johann's handwriting at the bottom of the page caught her eye. "This letter is confidential. Keep it in a safe place so no one can misuse it. Your Claassen." Then she unfolded the short letter Johann had written.

"Dear Katharina, Here is a brief overview which shows you with what sort of dignitaries I have associated and still do. And just think, in spite of it, still no prospects." He listed 16 persons with assorted titles, whom he had contacted, and concluded, "Those who want to help can't, and those who can don't want to. Your Claassen."

Katharina bit her lip as she folded the letter. Quickly she went into their bedroom, knelt beside the double bed and poured out her frustrations. How much longer would she have to be alone? After a while, the words Heinrich Huebert had read at little Johannes' funeral filtered through her troubled thoughts, "Ye know that your labor is not in vain in the Lord." Johann's labor? Her solitary labor? Maybe hers wasn't so solitary after all. Her labor of hospitality for the worship services was not in vain, she told herself.

But that Sunday, their living room was unusually crowded. The minister harped on the need for baptism by immersion, and the dedication of the Penner and Voth children precipitated a new struggle with tears. Only three short years ago they had dedicated little Johannes, and now he was with the Lord. A bittersweet comfort. Sister-in-law Wilhelmine noticed how weary Katharina looked and said, "Next Sunday we'll meet in our big machine shed. It's too crowded here and it's too hard for you during this time." Katharina didn't object.

The rows of beets and carrots in the garden were ready for thinning when she received copies of Johann's latest petitions for land, which, he assured her, implied recognition for their church group. "I'm sending them so that you may know that our Lord and Savior is in charge of the matter . . . and not Claassen of Liebenau," he wrote. Those words helped her focus on the Lord rather than indulge in self-pity. By the time he wrote that he had received the news of Johannes' death, her feelings had settled and she was able to answer, "I'm so glad that you have found peace about the way God has led." But reflecting on their separation, she confessed her frustration, "I don't like the fact that you are staying still longer. The Lord will have to give me patience." She also wrote him that baptism by immersion had become a big issue in their group.

On May 28, 1861, her brother Cornelius and his wife Gertrude took her and the children along to the meeting at her brother Jacob Reimer's place in Gnadenfeld. Again, immersion was the sermon topic. This time the minister gave an altar call for anyone whose baptism had not symbolized dying to the old life and resurrection to the new. Katharina went with the group, down to the river, to witness the baptism. As they returned along the back hedge of the Reimer farm and approached the machine shed, Katharina heard some strange thudding sounds. As they entered, she saw one of the men beating his drum while others sang and clapped their hands. The rest were leaping, dancing, and praising the Lord.

Her brother's usually placid face turned red. "Stop it!" he shouted. "I will not tolerate such bedlam on my property!" By this time Katharina noticed that not the whole group had participated in the dancing and shouting. Gertrude, the children, and a number of adults, had taken refuge in the quietness of Grandfather Strauss' cottage on Jacob's yard.

Among the Russian Mennonites, Christmas, Easter, and Pentecost called for three-day celebrations. On Pentecost Monday, June 15, Jacob and Wilhelmine took Katharina along to visit a group of believers in the village of Kakbas, outside the Molotschna settlement. It wasn't long before Katharina wished she hadn't come. The tambourines and drum nearly drowned out the singing. The empty space of the large building (formerly a mosque) seemed to invite leaping and dancing, and the shouts of "Hallelujah! Victory!" echoed and reverberated from the hard walls. Jacob raised his voice, saying, "Let us pray." But the leaping and shouting continued, so that Katharina, sitting not far from him, couldn't understand what he was saying.

In the quietness of their home that evening, she vented her frustration by describing the meeting in a letter to Johann, ending with, "It seems sinful to me!" How would Johann react? They agreed that the Christian life should be joyful, but would he understand that this exaggerated emphasis on joy had become quite ridiculous? To add to her consternation, one of the men informed her that the *Kirchliche* Mennonites were sending a delegation to Petersburg to complain about the rowdiness of the Brethren. And Bekker seemed pleased about such "persecution."

As the summer progressed, Katharina became more relaxed about the problems as some of the men urged for moderation in the services. At a Sunday service, minister Heinrich Huebert read a letter from Johann. As Katharina noticed how Johann reasoned, first with the "happy" Brethren, and then with the "serious," she felt gratified in having helped him get a balanced perspective on the situation, even at a distance of over a thousand miles. Surely his advice would be accepted. She determined to keep him posted on further developments. But she wasn't prepared for the reaction to Johann's P.S., requesting reimbursement of 30 silver rubles for legal expenditures. Several of the Brethren objected to his "extravagance!" Others doubted whether he had actually contacted the dignitaries to whom he said he had submitted petitions. Some asked whether he was making promises with which they could not concur. Katharina's heart pounded as the integrity of her beloved was questioned. She felt like getting out his letter and revealing the list of dignitaries. But she couldn't. A confidence had to be honored.

She thought about it the next day while she and the maid scrubbed the clothes. She understood that the Brethren objected to unexpected requests for money because many of them were being boycotted by the *Kirchliche* Mennonites. Heinrich Huebert had been forced to sell his mill. Cornelius had told her that some Liebenau villagers were driving to Schoensee, or even all the way to Halbstadt to do their shopping. Though he claimed that business at the Liebenau store was stable, she knew that Johann hadn't sold any grain in Berdiansk for over eight months. That usually accounted for more than half the business. When Johann was a wholesaler, he always had plenty of money and gave liberally. Now the tables were turned. The Brethren had promised to support him financially. Nevertheless, it hurt to hear him criticized. She felt relieved when Heinrich Huebert came over and assured her that Johann should continue to negotiate for the Brethren, and that the money would be sent after all.

On July 23, 1861, the Brethren met in the Claassen home for worship. When Heinrich Huebert arrived, he informed Katharina that several ministers from the *Kirchliche* in Ohrloff were coming to see for themselves whether the emotionalism of the Brethren was as outrageous as they had heard. Katharina noticed that Benjamin Bekker fidgeted with his watch chain while he preached. And one of the visitors took notes throughout the service. A few murmured "Praise God" during the prayer session, but she felt comfortable with the atmosphere. It didn't even resemble the meeting at Kakbas. At the conclusion of the service the leader of the visiting delegation said, "I hope we can be united once more." She sensed that he had agreed wholeheartedly with the preaching of the Word and had not been offended by a bit of audience participation.

On October 4, 1861, Katharina again found herself in an unusual position: she, a Russian Mennonite woman was initiating legal negotiations on her husband's behalf, for another visa renewal. Though her brother Jacob did the talking, she found it embarrassing and frustrating to be turned down. She didn't worry about it unduly, however, since Johann had already obtained one renewal through the Petersburg police department. Their eight-year-old son's attitude toward school was her greater, more immediate concern. The Liebenau teacher, Gerhard Wieler, had been released because he had joined the Brethren. The teacher who had replaced Wieler couldn't capture young Jacob's interest and had curtailed the curriculum, cutting out instruction in the Russian language entirely.

With bedlam in the classroom, the teacher taught very little.

"Should we consider hiring a private tutor, like we had when we were children?" she asked her brother Cornelius one day.

''Are you thinking of giving Gerhard Wieler a job?''

''He and his wife could easily live in the summer cottage on our yard.'' A petition to the municipal authorities to engage Wieler as private tutor for several families was turned down. Even a second request wouldn't change Administrator Friesen's mind. Katharina felt angry. What could she do? Were Johann at home, he would surely get some action. But he was gone. Gone for over a year for the sake of the Brethren.

Gerhard Wieler, meanwhile, moved to the Chortitza settlement. How surprised Katharina was when he showed up at their meeting in Liebenau on March 2, 1862. He reported that the Chortitza Brethren had experienced severe persecution, and that he was on his way to Petersburg to join Johann in negotiating for them. He suggested that footwashing and communion would constitute an appropriate send-off. Asking for a bucket of water, he proceeded to wash the feet of Katharina, then Gertrude, Sister Huebert, several single girls, and then a number of the men. When he called for a time of prayer and praise, Katharina noticed that her brother Jacob refused to participate.

''What's the matter?'' Katharina asked him after the meeting. ''The praises didn't get out of hand.''

''That's not it,'' he answered. ''Why did you let Wieler wash your feet?''

''It seemed a bit strange,'' she admitted. ''But it happened so quickly that I didn't think through the implications.''

''I don't ever want to see you or anyone else in our group involved in mixed footwashing again,'' he admonished. Katharina sensed that Jacob had not understood that she had been caught off guard. That hurt.

Certain Brethren, however, disagreed with Jacob. They picked up Wieler's style and called it ''the doctrine of freedom.'' Saying that in Christ there is neither male nor female, they promoted a free exchange between sexes that was repulsive to Katharina. Before long, one of the ''free'' Brethren, as well as a single girl, was excommunicated for immorality. Jacob Reimer pointed out that the problem had originated with mixed footwashing, so the Brethren agreed to segregated footwashing in the future.

Springtime came to the Molotschna, and Katharina again found herself working in the garden, where a year ago, little

Johannes had drowned. Her big Johann had been gone for a year and a half now. Finally, on June 30, 1862, Johann alighted from the mail carriage in front of the Liebenau store. Jacob and David bounded right across the front flowerbed in their excitement. Tears of joy rolled down Katharina's cheeks as he embraced her. But she felt the pain as deeply as he did when two-year-old Maria refused to greet her own Papa.

That evening Johann showed Katharina the papers in his briefcase. The Tsar had granted his petition for protection for the new group and guaranteed their Mennonite privileges at a proposed new settlement in the Kuban River area. During their evening devotions, they reaffirmed their commitment to the Lord, to the Mennonite Brethren, and to each other.

On July 2, the Brethren met for worship in the Claassen home. Katharina listened intently as Johann reported on his lengthy mission in the capital. When he pleaded for reconciliation between the "happy" and the "serious," she knew she had contributed to the welfare of the Mennonite Brethren by keeping him up to date on what had transpired during his absence.

Katharina experienced no particular difficulties with Johann's five-week trip that summer to inspect their prospective land in the Kuban area, in spite of her morning sickness. On April 1, 1863, she gave birth to a baby girl whom they named Aganetha, after Johann's mother. By the time Katharina was on her feet, Johann was getting ready for another trip to the Kuban to get the land grant. Because the grant had not yet been cleared when he arrived in Stavropol, he had to make another journey several weeks later. Katharina kept busy with the four children, the garden, drying fruit, attending Bible studies, and keeping aware of what was happening in the fellowship. Then she had to get along without him for two months again, so he could obtain the occupancy permit for several families who had been severely hit by the Molotschna drought and wanted to move at once.

It was good to have him home that winter, though he spent much of his time recruiting settlers for the Kuban. Many of the Brethren who had prodded him to complete the negotiations in Petersburg now seemed reluctant to sign up for the move. In spring Johann and Katharina made a decision that spelled more separation. Johann and their eldest son, Jacob, would go to the Kuban with a group of settlers and establish a home there. Johann would complete the legal negotiations that would guarantee the Mennonite privileges for the settlement, and then, probably the following spring, Katharina and the rest of the family would move also.

During the month of May, 1864, Katharina sewed, baked, and packed food for her men. On May 27 Johann and son Jacob, who was nearly as tall as she, left. A week later, her brother Jacob Reimer left also. Now it was Katharina's turn to support her sister-in-law, Wilhelmine, who had often helped her through discouragement.

The first letter Katharina received from Johann sounded dismal. She could hardly imagine living in a covered wagon, felling trees to frame a house, cutting the sod, bundling the thatch, and getting along without the convenience of a wood floor, a decent oven, or a productive garden. She knew he would be helping and advising everyone else as well as trying to get a roof over his own head.

But what he wrote on August 16 bothered her much more. "It seems to me that the spiritual life is on a higher level in the Molotschna than here at the Kuban, for here everyone is in need. Thus covetousness is really put to the test. . . . Here at the Kuban I have experienced only little joy." Now Katharina prayed even more earnestly for Johann. In November she helped Gertrude bake and pack so that Cornelius and their nephew Johann could leave for the Kuban. But again, the traffic moved in both directions; Gerhard Wieler returned from the new settlement to Liebenau.

Meanwhile, tension built up among the Mennonite Brethren at the Molotschna. The hyper-emotionalism at the services led to bitter disagreements and rash excommunications of various members, including her brother.

On December 7 Johann wrote that the Kuban settlers had observed footwashing and a love feast in the thatched Claassen cottage. Was the atmosphere in the Molotschna improving? Had the dissension been bridged? She hoped, but couldn't be sure. Tears welled up in her eyes as she read, "Jacob and I have become quite ragged during the summer. What we really need very much is to have Mother with us for a while. Well, the loving Savior knows what is best for our souls." If they needed Mother, she surely also needed a husband and father. She could handle the little girls, keeping them happy with Bible stories and Gospel songs. But David needed a father. He grumbled about being bored in school and was continually begging for books. She had little money, and could think of no easy way to keep his inquisitive mind occupied.

Further, the Molotschna Mennonite Brethren needed Johann to bring about reconciliation. Heinrich Huebert had told her one of the Brethren was going to write him demanding he return. So on January 11, 1865, she wrote, "Now I beg you, please be obedient to the brethren and come back. For God cannot be with you because of the way you are confronting one another."

He agreed to come as soon as the road permitted. On March 12, however, he was still at the Kuban and explained why:

> I have no money. We want to see if we can sell a wagon to obtain some cash for traveling. We had a buyer for the wagon, but he offered us 20 rubles less than we had originally paid for it at the Molotschna. Both Cornelius and I thought that was too great a loss, since a little money has to go a long way here, mainly for bread. Yet, we believe that somehow a door will open so that I can fulfill what the church has required of me. I don't know just how that will happen. God has a solution for all problems.

As Katharina read the letter, she let her mind wander back over the years. Once they had been well-to-do, in a position to give to anyone in need. Often they had supported evangelists. Though she was still living in a comfortable house, she had no money. Her Johann had been gone intermittently for five years. He was living far away, in a sod hut, without money also. What would become of them and their children? Why had they done it? Was it worth the effort? the deprivation? She reached for the Bible and turned to a passage in Matthew 10 that she and Johann had read together many times. It ended, "He that loses his life for my sake shall find it."

Then, on May 4, 1865, Johann and their son Jacob arrived in Liebenau. After a brief family reunion, Johann set out to do what both he and Katharina knew he had come for: to reconcile the Brethren. First he walked to the Chortitza settlement, accompanied by one of the Brethren. When he returned after ten days, Katharina could tell by the smile on his face that he had accomplished his purpose, though he was tired and muddy from the 70-mile walk.

Next he visited both the "happy" and the "serious" Brethren in the Molotschna settlement, trying to restore the sense of brotherhood and curbing the unilateral dictatorship of the "apostles." Katharina didn't see much of him. When self-pity tried to rear its head, she prayed for the people he was to visit and asked the Lord to give him wisdom, understanding and love for each situation. The new notice posted by the municipal court in Halbstadt caught her off guard. The officials issued a warrant for Johann's arrest on charges of organizing an illegal sect. Consequently, he had to travel under cover of darkness and remain in hiding. "Why must I bear the added burden of wondering whether he will get home safely from each trip?" she asked herself. She never found an answer, though prayer brought a measure of peace.

During the nine short days Johann spent at home between May 4 and July 20, he and Katharina forged plans for another year. Johann still had to negotiate the Mennonite privileges with the Caucasian government in Tiflis. He had spent so much time helping new settlers that his dwelling was nothing more than a sod hut. Further, it would be better to have the new baby delivered by an experienced midwife in the comfortable Liebenau home than at the Kuban. The fact that Gertrude and her family were going to join Cornelius at the new settlement made the prospective winter look even more lonely to Katharina. After praying about the situation, she told Johann she would try to endure another separation for the sake of the church. On July 20, 1865, it began again.

Baby Katharina was born in January, 1866, when Johann had spent three months in Tiflis, and Katharina had not seen him for over six months. A letter he had written after nine months' separation finally arrived in Liebenau almost a month later. He expressed his accumulated feelings to Katharina:

> Often I wonder why this lot has fallen to me. Why does the Lord not distribute the load? Why must I be the one who is always far away from his family? I talk about the situation to the Lord himself, and remind him that I am dust and ashes. I tell my Lord that I am human and have a heart filled with longing. You have given me a wife and I may not embrace her. You have given me children and I cannot instruct them, and I wouldn't even recognize my baby. My wife has a husband,

> and yet she must bear the burden alone. The children have a father, and the little ones know him not.

Tears trickled down her cheeks as she read it. He had said it for both of them.

On May 30, 1866, Johann finally received the last legal document necessary for the settlement at the Kuban. When he arrived in Liebenau in June, Katharina didn't even mind the mess of packing and moving. One of the last things she did was to take a hoe and rake and visit the Liebenau cemetery. She chopped the weeds around the lilac bushes she had planted as markers, and raked the little mounds on the graves of their four infants and little Johannes. It was her last deed of love to their memory. On August 1, the entire family, this time including David, Maria, Aganetha, and baby Katharina, rumbled off to the Kuban in a covered wagon.

The dusty dirt floor of the sod hut was only one of the primitive pioneering problems Katharina had to contend with. They put their good furniture into the house, and she added such feminine touches as embroidered linen curtains and Scripture mottos, making the place feel like home. Johann assured her that they would build a house like the one at Liebenau as soon as it was financially possible.

Overwork and illness, however, took their toll in the pioneer community. A little over a year after the Claassen family arrived at Kuban, a new grave was dug in the cemetery behind the schoolhouse in the village of Wohldemfuerst. Baby Katharina was no more.

Swamp fever was a common illness that the Kuban pioneers dreaded. Some guessed that it was contracted from the damp night air of the river. Others thought it was caught when working newly plowed soil. No one suspected that the mosquito was the carrier, and that prevention and cure were only a few decades away. When Katharina fell prey to the intermittent chills (later known as malaria), she knew the prognosis. It would sap her strength. She might recover for a while, only to suffer a relapse and eventually succumb. On July 25, 1869, at the age of 42, Katharina Reimer Claassen breathed her last. She, too, was buried on the grassy knoll behind the Kuban schoolhouse.

Like any mother, she had hoped to see her children reach maturity and find a place of service in church and community. But she didn't live to see their son Jacob take over the Wohldemfuerst store and tree nursery. She would have been gratified that her intelligent "problem" child, David, became the principal of the local school, and later spearheaded the Mennonite forestry, an alternative to military service, because he believed the teachings of Jesus regarding peace. She never saw the brush barriers replaced by wooden fences, and she never moved their furniture out of the thatched sod hut into a brick house with a tile roof. Many tears had marked the prolonged separations from her Johann. Yet, she accepted the deprivations, hardship, and loneliness as her contribution to the establishment of the Mennonite Brethren Church.

Bibliography

Classen, Dietrich J. *History of the Classen Family.* Bakersfield, Calif., 1946.

Friesen, P. M. *The Mennonite Brotherhood in Russia (1789-1910)* translated from the German *Die Alt-Evangelische Mennonitische Bruederschaft in Russland.* Fresno, Calif.: Board of Christian Literature, 1978. A biography of Johann Claassen by Elizabeth Suderman Klassen, entitled *Trailblazer for the Brethren,* was published by Herald Press in 1978.

Anna Wiens Braun was a reader and thinker, a wife, mother, and midwife, and a widow three times over. Life never daunted her. After raising eight children to adulthood, she said good-bye to them one by one as they left for the new world. Her son Jacob became the leading elder of the Krimmer Mennonite Brethren Church in America.

3

SHE PASSED ON THE FAITH

Anna Wiens Groening Wiebe Peters Braun (1810-76)

By Connie Wiebe Isaac

Baby Anna (pronounced Ahnna), the eighth child in the Wiens family, was born on a cold March 9, 1810. The three older girls, Katherina, 12, Margaretha, ten, and Helena, eight, were excited about the new baby. The four younger ones were not too surprised; new babies arrived with regularity in those days. Franz Wiens was a proud father that day, but he was also very worried about those turbulent times. The baby had been born during the unstable days of the Napoleonic Wars.

Prussia had been the Wiens family's home for many generations, possibly as early as 1568. Anna was born in the beautiful community of Marienburg where her father had been born 37 years before. Franz and his wife had been well-to-do dairy farmers on the Vistula River, producing and selling butter and cheese. Anna would have inherited a happy-ever-after type of life had it not been for Napoleon and his French soldiers quartered around their peaceful Mennonite home. The soldiers came and made off with everything they owned — cows, calves, chickens, eggs, and wood for fires. The entire country was destroyed. Her father was ruined financially.

Many times after that Father Wiens would suggest to his wife that it was useless for them to stay in Marienburg, and remind her that many Mennonites were migrating to Russia. They both knew of the new land available and the religious freedom there. But the whole family, including Anna, dreaded leaving the beautiful community of their fathers and making the long journey to Russia where the unknown waited for them.

During those years in Marienburg Anna knew they were poor, but she was too busy going to school and playing around the windmills and canals with her younger brother and sisters to be unhappy.

One spring day when Anna was six and Maria was nine they went out to the fields to gather flowers by the canal. Perhaps they went to the bank of the canal to look for tadpoles and Maria leaned too far. Perhaps they tried to go wading and Maria, older and braver, went in too deep. That day Maria drowned and Anna watched helplessly. She cried for many days thereafter.

Finally, when Anna was 15 years old, the family decided to leave what home they had for Russia. It had taken years to make this decision. Anna knew that going to Russia would mean never seeing her sister and family again. She wished that her sister had listened to her parents when they had warned her against the young Prussian she thought was so handsome. Well, now she had what she wanted! But Anna could tell her sister's heart was breaking; good-bye was forever.

Since they owned little, all the Wienses had could be packed onto the *twe roda* (small cart). They had one small horse that Mother Wiens was to ride; the rest walked. On the road the children played games or made up wild stories about what lay ahead. Soon, however, they got tired, and many times they stopped in villages where Anna, and all the others who could, had to work hard to earn money to buy food. She didn't enjoy having to work for strangers, but she learned many new ways that would help her later in life.

The travelers couldn't follow a highway with restaurants and rest areas. They didn't even have a road to follow; every time they came to a stream or river they had to swallow their fears, hold each other's hands tightly and wade across. The little children rode across on bigger people's shoulders, but Anna felt the mud or sharp rocks on her bare feet and the cold water drenching her clothes.

After walking and working for 95 days, the Wiens family finally arrived in the Mennonite colony where they were to stay for the winter. It was November 27, 1825. They were destitute, but Father left no doubt in their minds that they should be thankful. Many times on the journey Anna had felt they were forsaken; and, as the wind blew colder and colder, she feared they might not make it to the Mennonite colonies before they froze to death. Once she had mentioned it to Father, and he had said sternly, in Low German, "God has brought us so far. We cannot doubt his guidance." And, of course, he was right.

A month later, at Christmas, the Wiens family had little time or money to celebrate because they were hard at work for other people. Even Anna was a servant girl and had to do anything her employers asked to make their Christmas festive, but she could not enter into the fun.

In the evenings Anna filled her spare time with reading the few books in the village. She liked to study, and since she empathized with people, she found herself learning to be a nurse.

In the next few years Anna matured and became interested in a young man named Abraham Groening. His parents had come to Halbstadt, the head village of the Molotschna Colony, in 1804, and they were good farmers. Abraham impressed Anna by telling her about the time when, at the age of nine, he had seen Tsar Alexander. She told him about the good times she had known in Marienburg. They were married on October 24, 1831; she was 21 and he, 22. They made their first home in Halbstadt where their first child, Abraham II, was born ten months later. In another year and a half, another son, Franz, was born to the young parents. Less than two months later, however, Abraham became ill. Anna nursed him as best she could, dividing her time between her husband, the tiny baby and the toddler. At first she was sure that he would get well in a few days, but weeks passed, and he became increasingly ill and weak. After five weeks, on April 27, 1834, Abraham died at the age of 25, leaving Anna alone with the two little ones.

Anna was exhausted and sobered by the experience. People stood by her, for she had a good reputation. Within a few months a

29-year-old man from Neukirch who thought much of her was glad to take on the responsibility of the children if she would marry him. So only six months after her first young husband had died, Anna Wiens Groening married Jacob Wiebe. Anna and Jacob looked on their marriage as a new start in life together.

Anna was happy with Jacob and they soon bought a small farm (*Wirtshaft*) in the village of Margenau. Anna's two children loved their stepfather as their own; he was a strong, loving husband and father. Anna kept busy with her duties as wife and mother, and doing the hard work of housekeeping. She and Jacob became the parents of eight children, bringing her family to ten.

Anna liked to tell her family about what life was like when she was a child in Marienburg. She could share talk about Prussia with Jacob because he had also been born there, in *Elbinger Gebiet,* and had also made the long trek to Russia with his parents and 214 other families when he was 13.

When Anna married Jacob, the oldest of a large family, he was illiterate. Her patient tutoring and love paid off, and soon she had taught him the unbounded joy of reading. In fact, he became a fluent reader, carrying a New Testament with him constantly, traveling or working, reading while the horses were being fed. Anna felt much pride in Jacob and she was glad for the way God had led in her life.

In those days, very little reading material was available except for the works of Menno Simons, Dirk Phillips, and *The Martyrs Mirror*. Since Anna was an avid reader, she spent her spare moments reading what books and pamphlets were available. The words of her Anabaptist forefathers, as well as influential men of her day, like Wuest and Bernhard Harder, made inroads in her thinking.

Her son, Jacob A. Wiebe, was indelibly influenced by her life. Sensing he could be a spiritual leader someday, she taught him diligently, including the necessity and practice of prayer. She warned and admonished him about terrible punishment that awaited those who were evil. Anna influenced the rest of her children similarly, and later on, as she nursed the sick, her views were expressed to her patients as well.

One day when Anna had been married to Jacob for 19 years, he came in from the field in the middle of the afternoon. Anna went to greet him immediately because this was unusual. She noticed his flushed complexion and clammy hands and realized that he had a disease she had always dreaded — typhoid fever. She quickly decided the children must be kept away from him no matter how trying such separation would prove to be. Even the littlest ones knew something was wrong. Anna nursed Jacob with her heart in her hands and prayers on her lips for 17 days before he died.

That night after her ten children had gone to bed, Anna cried her heart out to God. She thought of how much responsibility now would fall to Abraham, her oldest son, and was thankful that he was already 21. She also thought of what would become of the others, especially the unborn one even now moving in her womb and reminding her that life goes on. The funeral was well attended and many people tried to console Anna. She knew others had suffered, too, and surely God's ear was not deaf. But life was so uncertain!

After Jacob's death, Anna's world exploded in war — the Crimean War (1853-56) between Russia and Turkey, England and France. Mennonites were forced to help in much hard and noncombative work. Because the war was being fought near her home, Anna was expected to help freight supplies and to nurse and lodge wounded soldiers. Her extra duties were a great burden on the fatherless family. Out of desperation she offered to give her farm to anyone who was willing to relieve her of her duties. But not one Mennonite accepted her offer. So Anna not only cared for her family and nursed the wounded and dying, but also continued as a capable midwife in Margenau. Thus her busy days were balanced between the horrors of war and the joys of the births of the next generation.

After the war ended, Anna and her family were barely surviving. Word of her situation somehow reached a well-to-do farmer from Kleefeld named Herman Peters, and he proposed marriage in 1856. For Anna the proposal was a "godsend" even though Mr. Peters was much older than her 46 years. For him it was a marriage of convenience because he was a sick man and needed the care Anna could give him. He brought money to the household that Anna promised him would stay with the farm. He lived less than four years.

In the colonies, death remained a very present factor, especially to Anna. In the six years following her third husband's death, she experienced the grief of seeing two of her young married children die painful deaths. Abraham became ill at the age of 29. On his deathbed he remembered his mother's training, cried to God for mercy, and found forgiveness. He then admonished his brothers and sisters to do the same and find Jesus as personal Savior. Anna brought the four children still at home to his bedside to hear his warnings also.

Daughter Helena died as a young mother of 25, leaving three small children. Anna had been pleased that Helena had married Cornelius Wedel, the village schoolteacher, six years before. Helena also gave an influential witness of her faith which was instrumental in at least one brother's conversion. One of Helena's children, Cornelius H., later became a noted historian and the first president of Bethel College. Anna did not know that the other boy, Peter, would grow up to be educated in Rochester, New York, become an effective evangelist, and finally a pioneer missionary to the Cameroons, Africa.

Anna's family, along with all the Mennonites, had a period of relief in Russia after the Crimean War. The government gave them their freedom and everyone prospered. Grandmother Anna, like many others, felt that the church had gotten *too* comfortable, and she made her influence felt where she could. When Anna's seventh son, Heinrich, was to be married, weddings in some villages lasted until midnight and were celebrated with dancing and drinking. Anna definitely ruled this out, although it caused quite a stir.

In January, 1863, at the age of 53, Anna married a partner who stayed with her the rest of her life. Abraham Braun helped her raise her last four children to adulthood.

In the early 1870s the new Russian military service law shocked many of the Mennonites who had gone through spiritual revival, including Anna's family. Anna's children were all married or of marriageable age, and they chafed under these new restrictions. Compromises were offered by the government, but her children felt the government was taking away more freedom of conscience than they were willing to give up. Anna had taught them to be spiritually earnest and now they no longer felt secure in Russia.

Anna's family began to emigrate to America. Jacob A., her third son, was the first child Anna sent off to America. On May 9,

1874, he came to say farewell in the Molotschna Colony and to make final arrangements for emigration. He led the first church group of 35 families on a new wave of migration that would have great importance. Later he became Elder Jacob A. Wiebe, leader of the Krimmer Mennonite Brethren in America. The other seven surviving children and their families followed shortly, some on the *Teutonia* and some on the *S.S. Kenilworth*. Anna bade farewell to all her children and grandchildren within the period from May 30, 1874, to July 17, 1876. She never saw them again.

Anna's biggest responsibility in the insecure and uncertain world of birth and death, war and emigrations, had been to raise her ten children — to help them survive, both physically and spiritually — to pass on the belief that the God of their martyred forefathers would lead them, too. Her job done, her children and grandchildren destined to become spiritual leaders in the new world, she could rest at last.

She died in Margenau where she had moved with Jacob, and was buried in the cemetery there in September, 1876, almost two months to the day after the last child arrived in New York City. She had taught her children to follow their conscience and dare to adventure through life's difficulties for the Lord. She taught and they learned well.

Bibliography

Wiebe, David V. *My Parents*, Hillsboro, Kan.: Mennonite Brethren Publishing House, 1955.

Wiebe, Jacob Z. *Genealogy Record of the Groening and Wiebe Families*. Garden City, Kan.: Garden City Telegram Publishers, 1945.

Wiebe, Joel A., Vernon R. Wiebe and Raymond F. Wiebe. *The Groening-Wiebe Family, 1768-1974*. Hillsboro, Kan.: Mennonite Brethren Publishing House, 1974.

Wiebe, Peter A. *Kurtze Biographie des Bruders Jacob A. Wiebe, Seine Jugend, Seine Bekehrung, und wie die Krimmer Mennoniten Bruedergemeinde Gegruendet Wurde*, translated by Connie Wiebe Isaac and Joel A. Wiebe. Hillsboro, Kan.: 1924.

In early days husbands risked, women supported. Many, like Justina Friesen Wiebe, found an additional ministry in hospitality and homemaking. Her heart was big enough for 12 children (seven of them foster children) as well as anyone who needed her love. Seven children died in infancy. Born in 1833 in South Russia, she died in 1916 in Hillsboro, Kansas, after 59 years of marriage to Elder Jacob A. Wiebe, first leader of the Krimmer Mennonite Brethren Church, and son of Anna Wiens Groening Wiebe Peters Braun.

4

LOVE IN DEED

Justina Friesen Wiebe (1833-1916)

By Esther Jost

"Why do you stop here?" asked Justina, searching Jacob's face as he eased the horses to a standstill.

"We have arrived at our home!" Jacob announced.

"What! We are going to live here in this deep grass?" exclaimed Justina. Her tears overflowed.

Justina was not one to weep readily, for she had weathered poverty, hardship, sickness, deadly spider plagues, and had been acquainted intimately with death. But had she come to America for this empty prairie? Had she said good-bye to her comfortable home surrounded by beautifully blooming acacia trees for these acres of dry prairie weeds and long-stemmed grass? Had she left the green fields of Annenfeld (Anna's Field) near Simferopol in the Crimea to feel this searing hot wind blowing across her face? Her tears continued to flow.

This morning, long before sunrise, while Justina had rested in the train car parked on a side track of the Santa Fe at Peabody, Kansas, joy had surged through her five-months-pregnant body as she had awakened to the sound of her husband's loud, clear voice asking, "All asleep?" Instantly the whole family had opened their eyes, scrambled to their feet, and rushed out the door of the train. As soon as possible they had climbed onto a wagon to drive 14 miles to their new home. Again and again Jacob had urged the horses to move in a northwesterly direction as they meandered from one drinking hole to another in the little creeks along the way. After ascending and then descending the last hill, Jacob had turned left and then right again, though there was hardly a trace of road in the heavy grass. Justina had noticed he was looking for landmarks. Then the horses had stopped in the middle of the prairie. Only weeks before, vast ocean waves had engulfed their ship; now sunburned prairie grass blown by the August wind closed around their wagon. Justina's eyes blurred with tears.

Jacob wiped his sweat-covered face and stepped from the wagon. He had done his weeping a month ago before his family had arrived from Elkhart, Indiana, where they and other members of the Crimean Mennonite Brethren Church had waited while he and Franz R. Janzen looked for land in Kansas. While alone in Peabody, awaiting the arrival of the 35 families, Jacob had felt overwhelmed by the responsibility of deciding where his people should live. He had sat down on the stone steps of a store and thought of the families who would soon be arriving by train. They were poor, without provision, and had no friends in this new world. Winter was approaching, and the people would need warm homes, agricultural implements, seed and other necessities — all of which carried a high price tag. Only ten days before, on August 6, 1874 (Jacob's 38th birthday), grasshoppers had devastated everything green in Kansas except the grass, which, true to their name, they had hopped over and spared. Even then, as he had sat on the warm steps, the sun had shone fiercely. There was no prospect of rain, only a hot, searing wind, dust and uncomfortable heat. What would his friends say to his selection of land? Suddenly his tears had flowed freely. Mrs. August Seabold, a Lutheran citizen of Peabody, who had seen him weeping, had admonished him, "Mr. Wiebe, what ails you?" She pointed to the street. "Do you see those stones? They are sometimes entirely under water. It can rain very hard here and it soon will rain. Cheer up, Mr. Wiebe. People such as you will make their living."

Her words had encouraged him. Now he must encourage Justina.

Tall prairie grass enveloped the wheels of the wagon which had carried Justina, Jacob, and their children, Johann, two, Jacob, four, and Katharina, 15, the 14 miles from Peabody. In anticipation of his family's coming, Jacob had purchased a team of horses, a wagon, and a scythe. With the scythe he now cleared a spot of ground; with a spade he dug a hole and laid stones around it. Looking at Justina, he said gently, "Mother, hand me the kettle."

Soon Justina was no longer weeping, for the family must be fed. She had learned from her experiences in Russia to live in the present. This was not a time for tears. Together she and Jacob thanked God for his protection and care on their long journey and sought his guidance for their new life in this strange country where Jacob would be leader of the Krimmer Mennonite Brethren.

* * *

On Tuesday, December 5, 1833, Justina Friesen was born to Johann and Katharina Jantzen Friesen. (Johann was the oldest of 11 children. His father was Daniel von Riesen, later changed to Daniel Friesen.) Three sisters: Aganetha, four, Maria, three, and Katharina, two, had joined the family before Justina. Then came Sara, Anna, and Helena. However, when Sara was six and Anna four, both died on the same day, February 15, 1842. Another Anna and Sara were born, and after that three brothers, Jacob, Johann, and Peter. On February 27, 1850, eight hours after Peter's birth, Justina's mother died. About a year and a half later, the Friesen children acquired a new mother when Father married Katharina Wallen on September 11, 1851.

Coming from a large family did not interfere with Justina's education. At the early age of eight, she had mastered the Gothic script and was accomplished in the art of *Fraktur* (typical German text) writing. She encircled the beautiful script with flowers painted in a rainbow of colors. The message on one read:

If one builds and it again breaks to pieces,
what has he then by that excepting work?
If one prays, and again curses,
how then shall the Lord grant?

Thus it is with the person
who fasts for his sins again and again.
Who will grant that prayer,
and of what value to him is fasting?

To leave off sinning is a divine service
which pleases the Lord, and to cease wrongdoing—
that is a genuine expiatory sacrifice.

Sirach—du Prediger Salomos—Ecc. 34 u. 35*
Halbstadt, November 10, 1841
Justina Friesen

Justina used the same script to make a New Year's greeting, which she presented to her family on January 1, 1844. Her proficiency in the arts did not include voice, for she could not sing. However, she married an excellent soloist.

Her father, the *Oberschulze* (mayor) of Halbstadt and the highest authority in the village, ** was in need of a coachman. With this on his mind, as well as concerns for his community, he was on his way to the customary "wolf chase," for packs of predatory animals were depleting the farmers' stock. While attending the event, Mayor Friesen noted a strong, mature young man on a fast steed singlehandedly kill a large wolf with a club before others arrived on the scene. Mayor Friesen, impressed by this young man's bravery, hired him and gave him charge of all his vehicles.

Justina was much attracted to this sensitive young man, Jacob A. Wiebe, who trained his horses — not with whip and hard words — but with patience, foresight, and gentle commands. She became his wife at the age of 24. Justina and Jacob were married April 11, 1857, in Halbstadt, South Russia. The wedding was officiated by Elder Diedrich Warkentin, who also had baptized them, Justina at age 17 and Jacob at 20. After baptism, they had both become members of the Petershagen Mennonite Church. The wedding took place in Halbstadt, at the home of the bride, and probably with much food, drinking, and folk dancing, the customary way to celebrate such occasions. Couples wishing to be married had to meet three requirements: first, be of age, which

---

* From Apocryphal writings. Ecclesiasticus 34:28, 29, 31; 35:5.

** Some records disagree that he was the mayor.

was about 21; second, have the ceremony performed by a minister; and third, the applicants were expected to join the church before the wedding took place, if they were not church members. Justina and Jacob fulfilled all three.

After the wedding, the young couple moved several miles from Justina's parental home to Ohrloff, where they had purchased a *kleine Wirtschaft* (small farm). Here they experienced both joy and sorrow. Their first child, Anna, was born March 26, 1858, but died on March 14, 1859, shortly before her first birthday. Six months later on September 20, 1859, their second daughter, Katharina, was born.

Justina was near enough to her family so they could visit each other often, but this arrangement soon ended. Jacob and Justina and other Mennonites discussed the possibility of relocating to the Crimean Peninsula. England, France, and Turkey had come to a peace agreement with Russia in 1856, after fighting a war, mostly on the Crimean Peninsula in South Russia. The Mohammedans, who had occupied this area, were ordered to leave; the Wiebes, with other Mennonites, bought the village and settled at Annenfeld.

Operating a horse-operated flour treadmill and owning some acreage, the materialistic-minded Jacob, Justina, and the others who moved to this area hoped to become rich quickly. Instead, they experienced great poverty. Their lack of farming knowledge, the scorching winds, extreme droughts, deadly spider plagues, and severe livestock epidemics added to their problems. Although Justina's husband was a trained horseman, they lost 18 horses during the first year. One of the Mennonite group despaired of the situation and committed suicide.

These experiences caused Justina and Jacob to spend much time reading God's Word, praying, and searching for meaning for their lives. Justina was sensitive to her husband's turmoil as he agonized in prayer. She rejoiced with him when his battle ended and he experienced peace and joy as he claimed the Lord as Savior and friend. "I am happy you have found rest for your soul," she told him.

However, faith is a personal matter and Justina did not automatically experience the same peace that Jacob had because she was his wife. She often felt such great fear for not belonging to Christ she did not know which way to turn. She wanted to commit herself completely to the Lord and, as a result, was often on her knees praying. She asked her husband to help her pray.

In the fall of 1865 she became ill while visiting Jacob's mother. After being confined to her bed for eight days, at eleven o'clock on the eighth night, a great fear overcame her. She found breathing difficult, so she awakened Jacob to say, "I'm dying," then screamed, "Oh! what will happen? I'm dying, I'm not ready. I am lost forever and must burn in hell!"

Jacob replied, "You are not dead yet. We are going to pray fervently. There is still time."

But Justina answered, "It's much too late. There isn't any time." She fainted, and it seemed to her someone was pulling her into hell, for she cried out, "It hurts! It hurts!" When she regained consciousness she said, "It seemed as if lightning hit me. I was unconscious and the words I screamed left my lips without my saying them." Again she screamed, "Hell, hell, hell!" Her eyes turned heavenward; everything was radiantly white and soft. She sang a song and lifted her hands. Then it seemed as if someone took her arms and pulled her into a white place, but she could see no one. She asked out loud, "Who is pulling me?"

Jacob, standing by her bed, answered, "The Lord is pulling you. Taste and see that the Lord is good." At that Justina regained consciousness to find her family surrounding her bed. "Did I sing a song?" she asked.

"Yes," they answered.

"How could I have sung? I can't sing!"

She asked Jacob to read Scripture after Scripture to her. Her mother-in-law had prepared some coffee and wanted her to eat and drink, but Justina was not hungry for food — only for God's Word. She read until the morning dawned. Then the Bible fell from her hands and she slept for several hours. Justina, like Jacob, had won the battle and claimed the Lord as her Savior.

Justina described her experiences in a letter to her father and family, datelined Margenau, Russia, April 11, 1866. "Examine your own relationship to Christ," she wrote. "I have examined my life and I try to change things that are not right. I have always tried to be loving in my relationship with people and have never consciously hurt someone's feelings or betrayed a confidence. But I am sorry that I exhibited much pride in the past, especially in my dress. Lately, I have disposed of a ruffled cap which I feel I should not wear anymore. I don't want you to change just because of my letter, for each must be accountable for himself."

A year earlier, in 1864, Justina and Jacob had joined the *Kleine Gemeinde* (Little Congregation). In 1814 this group, led by Klaas Reimer, had been the first ones to separate themselves from the original Mennonite Church. They were conservative in their views in regard to doctrine, education, and dress.

After Justina and Jacob had searched the Scriptures and read *Martyrs Mirror*, they wanted to be rebaptized by immersion on their new-found faith. However, the rules of the *Kleine Gemeinde* forbade rebaptism. Jacob and Justina had both recognized that "selfish and worldly interests and pleasures must die and be buried, and a new man with spiritual desires and joys in his heart must be born." The *Kleine Gemeinde* did not insist on a lifestyle in keeping with these views.

Though Jacob had been elected as minister of the *Kleine Gemeinde* in 1867 and ordained as an elder in 1869, because of these differences, the Wiebes and several others severed their membership with the *Kleine Gemeinde*, and on September 21, 1869, the Krimmer Mennonite Brethren had its beginning. Seventeen were rebaptized.* Kornelius Enns, a layman, baptized Jacob; then Jacob baptized the other candidates. The first baptism took place in the Karuza River ("wonderful water"). Justina and the other candidates were baptized according to the form they believed was taught by the Word of God and practiced by the Apostolic Churches as recorded in *Martyrs Mirror*. Candidates for baptism knelt in the water and were dipped forward. The complete immersion symbolized the burial of Christ, and the rising out of the water, as out of the grave, the new life in Jesus Christ.

The new members subscribed to the following principles of faith: the Bible as God's Holy Word; an emphasis on brotherly love; the ordinances of baptism, Lord's supper, and foot washing; and the practice of missions, evangelism, and church discipline. A Sunday school was established, which before had been unknown. Other innovations were audible prayers by both men and women and free delivery of sermons.

The members of the new Krimmer Mennonite Brethren Church practiced simplicity and nonconformity to the world in

---

* Some sources say 19

lifestyle. They felt that formerly there had been too few differences between people of the church and those of the world and too much rivalry in the display of fine clothes and jewelry.

Justina rejoiced in her new-found faith and in the fellowship of their growing church, but also suffered many sorrows. Five times she prepared a cradle for an expected infant and then, within weeks or months, a coffin for the child's burial. On March 8, 1862, her first son Johann was born and on February 22, 1863, he died. On June 12, 1864, Jacob came to bless the home and died when he was four months old. Little Justina was born July 25, 1865, and died the next day. On May 4, 1867, Abraham arrived but died before he was a year old. Another Justina was born September 7, 1868, and died July 18, 1869. Then another Jacob was born on July 4, 1870, and another Johann on February 28, 1872. God be praised! Both remained alive and well. Anna arrived on November 17, 1873, and lived until January 16, 1874.

Materially, Justina and Jacob prospered. They learned to till the soil and their land produced bountiful crops. However, this material gain was short-lived.

The announcement in 1870 that Tsar Alexander II had ended military exemption for the Mennonites came as a surprise not only to Justina and Jacob but also to the Mennonites as a whole. Because they believed in biblical nonresistance, the Krimmer Mennonite Brethren Church decided to emigrate as a group. Justina had to leave Annenfeld where she had experienced the great joy of a new walk with Jesus, where she had faithfully stood by Jacob's side in the founding of a new church, and where she had given birth to sons and daughters and buried five children. Justina was leaving because following the teachings of Jesus and practicing "brotherly love in peace" was important to her and Jacob.

On May 29, 1874, Justina and Jacob were among the 35 families from the Krimmer Mennonite Brethren Church who viewed through misty eyes their cherished homes surrounded by beautiful acacia trees, now in full bloom. Claiming Romans 5:5 as their comfort, they said, "Good-bye, good-bye, Annenfeld."

In ill-fitting, dark homespun garments, the men wearing baggy pants, long vests and *Schildmuetze* (flat cloth caps), the women in full-skirted dark dresses almost reaching to the ground and covered by ample aprons and with a *Tuch* (kerchief) on each woman's head (and the children looking like minatures of their parents), the Crimean group boarded Tartar vehicles for the Black Sea. With baskets of toasted *Zwieback* (rolls), the Crimean church began its journey to the land of freedom.

Justina and Jacob and the 35 families crossed a calm Black Sea and arrived in Odessa, where they waited in a large tin shed until train time. After boarding the train, the Crimean group rumbled through a bleak forest to Pidwollosk, where their passports were checked and new tickets purchased to travel through Austria. They arrived in Krakau on June 6, with one extra passenger — a newborn baby girl! Justina wondered what the new life stirring in her womb would be and where her baby would be born. They spent the night in Oswiecim, a border town between Austria and Prussia, leaving June 7 for Breslau where they had a major time change. (Old time was by Julian calendar and new time by the Gregorian calendar — a difference of ten days.)

Instead of 35 individual families, the group was more like one large family as they lived and traveled together on land and sea. They crossed by land to England, and then on July 2, they finally embarked for America on the *City of Brooklyn*. En route a strong wind beat against the ship so that the whole group became seasick and remained in bed. The ocean thundered and roared and their *Kiste* (Russian chests) slid from one end of their berths to the other. Justina prayed to God and trusted him to help. Morning dawned on tranquil waters. But this was not for long, and a new storm furiously pelted the bow of the ship. Eventually the passengers got used to the storms. Toward the end of the week, the weather turned bitterly cold so they donned jackets and *Pelzen* (fur coats) while on deck. Justina was glad for what warm clothing she had brought.

The journey lasted 12 days. A coast pilot boarded the ship on July 14 to guide it up the Hudson River and into the New York harbor. Here a doctor examined all passengers and another official gave them directions for debarkation.

On July 16 the Crimean group began their travels by train through lush grass, green forests, over small streams and rivers and around blue lakes to Elkhart, Indiana, where John F. Funk, editor of *Herold der Wahrheit* (Herald of Truth) was to receive them. But his daughter, Grace Ann, had died during the night.

Funk, exhausted and overcome with grief, was asleep when the group arrived on July 19 and had to be awakened. He took the tired and hungry immigrants to a vacant house, and called a grocer to open his store so that newcomers could purchase provisions. How good it felt to wash, clean up, and cook their own food. By two o'clock, Justina and her children, as well as the other immigrants, were ready for the first church services in the new country, after which Franz Janzen and Jacob left for Kansas to find a place for them to live permanently. Justina and her children said good-bye to Jacob not knowing when they would see him again.

Almost a month later word came that the men had found land. The families from Crimea boarded a train on August 14 at Elkhart and traveled via Chicago, Atchison, and Topeka, arriving in Peabody, Kansas, early Sunday morning, August 16, 1874.

Justina's journey had encompassed trials, disappointments, poverty, disease, and death. She had also encountered prosperity, and peace, love, and joy as she had journeyed from Halbstadt, Ohrloff, Margenau, Annenfeld, Odessa, Hamburg, Liverpool, New York, Elkhart, and Peabody to Gnadenau. Soon she would celebrate her 41st birthday! God had been good to her and to the entire Krimmer Mennonite Brethren Church. They had arrived!

That same evening a "love feast" and "thanksgiving service" were held in the new barn on the Peter Funk farm, about three miles northeast of the place Jacob and Justina would call home. The Peter Funks, immigrants from Prussia living in the Bruderthal community, had completed a barn before Funk died on June 23, 1874. His widow invited 14 families to live in it until their homes were finished. Others lived in temporary shelters on the meadow with the tree-lined Cottonwood River in the distance.

The next day, Monday, August 17, the men staked out the village of Gnadenau (Grace Meadow), a name which expressed their spiritual and physicial needs and ideals. Not wanting to become American citizens immediately, Jacob A. Wiebe and Franz Janzen had bought 12 sections of Santa Fe Railroad land for three to seven dollars an acre, for they feared that homesteading (which entitled them to free land) might jeopardize their religious freedom. Following the plans of a Russian village, the men laid out the new village on a road running east and west in the middle of Section 11. Each farmer had some acreage close by and more farther out. The huts, all built on the north side of the road, were spaced at regular intervals with the sod church in the center. It served temporarily as a school. Later a small cemetery with irises bordering every grave was located near the church.

Justina's first home was a canvas hut. After their barn was finished, it served as a home for her family and 13 other people for a time. The immigrants also built thatched-roof, A-frame structures which started from the ground in the high prairie grass. A constant fire hazard was the adobe chimney projecting about 12 inches above the grass roof and the knee-deep grass next to it on the ground. John Risley, a friend of the people of Gnadenau (the Wiebe family shared his home for a short time), informed the settlers of the danger of fire. With five pairs of oxen, he plowed six furrows around the village. Then he burned the grass between the furrows, and the charred strip served as a fireline around the village. Justina felt more secure after that. A joint well was dug in the center of the village, from which Justina and the village women carried water.

In time, adobe homes replaced the A-frame dwellings, followed by frame structures. Brick wall ovens of Russian design in the adobe homes were heated with straw. The walls retained the heat, keeping the house warm for hours. Since *Zwieback* and dark rye bread were essential items on their menu, the settlers erected a grist mill operated by a Dutch windmill to grind the flour, which was needed in large quantities.

By the summer of 1875, Justina and Jacob lived in a red frame house built on the Russian model, a maze of small rooms and passages with stables and granary. Livestock lived under the same roof as the family, and wheat stacks were located at the back door. Their home had the standard household items for village homes of that era — a large Russian *Kiste* (chest) filled with bedding and household articles, and an old-fashioned German timepiece, reaching from ceiling to floor, with a large dial, and weights and pendulum of polished brass.

The settlers soon built a schoolhouse, to which Jacob and Justina sent their children. At first, teaching was conducted in the German language, but later the teachers taught in English also. Part of this schoolhouse served as a home for the teacher.

Justina practiced both faith and works, or "love in deed," as commanded in the Book of James. Scarcely a day passed without her entertaining guests, often for days or weeks at a time. After

Sunday morning services, as well as at other times, as many as 16 to 20 people seated themselves around Justina's dinner table. After the adults had finished eating, the children ate. Justina could not run to the store to pick up food for unexpected company, for Peabody was 14 miles away and Marion Center about ten; so she maintained her own larder with vegetables from her garden and home-cured hams from hogs which the family raised and butchered. A typical dinner consisted of fried slices of ham, fried potatoes, a large bowl of *Plooma Moos* (fruit soup), dark bread and butter, *Zwieback* and coffee. Usually her guests stayed for *Fesper* (a light lunch of *Zwieback* and coffee) as well.

Justina's long, full skirt did not hamper her from getting up again and again to refill her guests' coffee cups. She wore the customary long dresses made of blue or black calico with tiny white flowers or figures sprinkled generously over the material. An ample apron made from calico also, covered the dress from the waist down. Its deep pocket usually contained sugar cubes which Justina, in her quiet way, helped into some small child's hand. Trimming was not allowed, but the cloth used for Justina's clothes was of the finest material available. Her head was usually covered by a small ruffled cap.

Justina also practiced her faith by giving a home to the homeless. She cared for another child soon after her infant son Peter died in early 1875, the first winter in the new country. She and Jacob adopted Maria Flaming, who was born June 13, 1875, and died two months later. Then they adopted seven-year-old Maria Hart on April 14, 1876. Her father had drowned during a flood, and her mother was unable to care for her family. All together, Justina and Jacob accepted into their home seven foster children, whom they treated like their own children, giving them dowries at the time of their marriages like the ones Justina and Jacob's own children received. On March 4, 1877, Justina gave birth to her 12th and last child, another Peter.

Justina was a quiet person and expressed her love in deeds while Jacob did the public speaking. He liked his home to be quiet and orderly. It disturbed him when Justina banged pots, pans, and stove lids in the kitchen. (Was she really being that noisy on purpose or was it getting more and more difficult for her to discern between soft and loud noises? Was something happening to her hearing?)

Although short and stout, her excess weight did not keep her from working hard at cooking, baking, sewing, and other homemaking tasks, and with helping her husband in his "medical work" as well. In addition to his church work and farming occupation, Jacob was a "bonesetter" and children and adults came to him for help. When Jacob called, *"Yustina, kum halp me"* (Justina, come help me), she not only assisted him with his work, but later also treated the patients to coffee and cookies or kept them for a meal. Whiffs of the smell of liniment lingered in the Wiebe home at all times. Justina and Jacob refused payment for their services, but when pressed accepted money for liniment and splints. They believed in a literal translation of Christ's words, "Heal the sick, cleanse the lepers, raise the dead, cast out devils: freely ye have received, freely give" (Matt. 10:8). While living in the Crimea, they had chosen love as their goal and tried to show it always. Though they believed in divine healing, they never carried it to the extreme. They did not hesitate to apply home remedies or to call Dr. Fillipin, a black physician.

The Gnadenau Church was zealous in spreading the Gospel. Though transportation was limited and traveling difficult, Jacob and other ministers visited neighboring hamlets, counties, and states. They preached the Gospel, baptized, and organized churches. This meant that Justina had full responsibility for the family and farm while Jacob was absent. Yet she never complained about the hard work. She supported Jacob in his church travels of a month or longer and in his preaching and spiritual counseling at home. He served the Lord by preaching; she served the Lord by giving him for church work.

In 1898 Justina returned to Russia to visit her two sisters and three brothers still living there. Father Friesen had died January 6, 1875, and Jacob's mother in 1876.

On April 11, 1907, friends of Jacob and Justina — more than two thousand of them — traveled from near and far to the Gnadenau Church, now no longer the little adobe structure in the village, but a white frame building two miles south of Hillsboro. The reason for the traffic was Justina's and Jacob's golden wedding celebration. The day was doubly important, for their granddaughter, Justina Block, was being married to Jacob R. Klassen.

As children and relatives spoke, read greetings, and sang

songs, Justina's face beamed. She thanked each one individually and put their written messages into a packet beside her. However, she could not hear a single word! She had become deaf. Since she had not learned the English language, the only way to communicate with her was to write messages to her in the Gothic script. One verse of a poem written by her oldest son for the celebration read:

> Mother long heard less and less
> But was not void of joyfulness.
> For her heart could hear joy's tone
> Flowing down from God's own throne.

Instead of gifts for the couple, an offering was taken which Justina and Jacob designated for the poor in Russia.

In their old age Justina and Jacob moved to Lehigh, where Jacob and Susanna, the Wiebes' oldest son and his wife lived. Here their home soon became known as a place both old and young could go for help. One day one of the schoolboys sprained his thumb, and without hesitation he dashed to the Wiebe home nearby to have it fixed.

In 1914, after Jacob suffered a slight stroke, they entered the Salem Home and Hospital for older people and invalids located near their former home in Gnadenau.

Love through deed had been Justina's practice all her life, but now her activities were limited. Daily she read a chapter of the Bible to Jacob. On the afternoon of November 27, 1916, as Justina read, "Yea, he loved the people" (Deut. 33:3), her Bible dropped from her hands and her eyes and mouth closed. She died two days later at the age of 82.

Justina loved people and people loved her. Since the Gnadenau church was not large enough to hold all her friends, a temporary addition was built for the funeral. Seven ministers and one college professor spoke. In the obituary Jacob had written: "She was always an industrious wife, having concern for my well-being and standing by my side in the work of the church as well as offering hospitality to the many people who came to our home. She undergirded me in all of my undertakings including my many travels that my work required of me." Then the congregation walked to the nearby cemetery where K. D. Willems concluded with a message based on Psalm 116: "Precious in the sight of the Lord is the death of his saints."

Justina was buried in the Gnadenau cemetery where villagers had planted evergreens which spoke of eternal life.

Bibliography

Barkman, J. G. "Der Fuenfundsiebzigste Jahrestag." *Hillsboro Journal*. Hillsboro, Kansas: September 8, 1949.

________. "Das Erste Schulhaus in Gnadenau." *Hillsboro Journal.* Hillsboro, Kansas: September 15, 1949.

Barkman, Peter M. Unpublished dairy.

Ebel, B. E. *Brother Jakob*. Hillsboro, Kansas: Mennonite Brethren Publishing House.

Friesen, Jacob J. *Survey Presented to Funk-Friesen Generations.* Compiled by Jacob J. Friesen Family. Unpublished. December, 1952.

Harms, W. W. *History of the Springfield Krimmer Mennonite Brethren Church and the Community's Culture*. Hillsboro, Kansas.

Klassen, Esther and Justina. Scrapbook (Golden Wedding Clippings).

Wiebe, David V. *Grace Meadow*. Hillsboro, Kansas: Mennonite Brethren Publishing House, 1967.

________. *They Seek a Country.* Hillsboro, Kansas: Mennonite Brethren Publishing House, 1959.

Wiebe, Jacob Z. *Genealogy Record of the Groening and Wiebe Families.*

Wiebe, Jakob A. "Mutter J. A. Wiebe Tot." *Der Wahreitsfreund.* Chicago: December 13, 1916.

Wiebe, Joel A., Vernon R. Wiebe, and Raymond F. Wiebe. *The Groening-Wiebe Family, 1768-1974*. Hillsboro, Kansas: 1974.

Wiebe, Justina. Unpublished diary.

________. Letter to her father and family. *Mennonitische Rundschau* and *Herald der Wahrheit*. February 26, 1908 and March 4, 1908.

Wiebe, P. A. *Kurze Biographie des Bruders Jakob A. Wiebe.* 1924.

* * *

Interviews with Henry, John and Kathryn Barkman, Anna Block Hodel, Mrs. A. R. Jost, Esther and Justina Klassen, Mrs. J. E. Klassen

Few modern Mennonite women will travel as far and experience as much as Elizabeth Unruh Schultz. Born near the Poland border, she moved with her family to South Russia, then to Asia, and from Asia to Nebraska and South Dakota in the United States. She finally settled in Saskatchewan, Canada. Her life reveals a curiosity about nature, a love for people, and a desire to be God's person. At the age of 38, her husband died and left her with ten children to raise in difficult times. Yet when Elizabeth looked back, it was with praise for God's goodness. When she looked forward, it was with courage and faith.

5

IN JOURNEYINGS OFTEN

Elizabeth Unruh Schultz (1866-1943)

By Katie Funk Wiebe

Clicketty, clacketty, clicketty — CLANG!

From her corner 14-year-old Elizabeth listened to the mixture of noises as the horse-drawn wagon lurched eastward. Kettles and pans rattled in the trunk-like box at the back. A similar box in front held feed for the horses. Under the wagon hung a lantern, the old iron pot, a folding table, and chairs fastened to the back axle with a chain.

Her parents, Cornelius and Eva Unruh, had lived in Gnadenheim in the Molotschna for about five years when suddenly a strong migration fever gripped many Mennonites in the area. A few years earlier, in 1874, the same fever had taken many to America. Now the movement was eastward to Asia to escape the threat of military conscription and Russianization. Services and meetings were called, with much preaching, praying, and singing. A few men were elected to ask the government for permission to migrate and for freedom of speech and religion.

The delegates returned several weeks later with the message that the way was open to Asiatic Turkestan, recently conquered by Russia, but not under military laws. The officals warned, however, of the dangers and hardships of living among uncivilized people. The Mennonites were undaunted. Elizabeth had sensed the excitement of the new challenge as land and house were offered for sale and furnishings and equipment sold at auction. The women prepared roasted bread and buns, dried fruit, pot barley, beans, and smoked meat for the long journey. They sewed. As the departure date neared, farewells were held in several localities, with up to two thousand people present at one. Brothers, sisters, parents, and children were separating, perhaps never to see each other again. Elizabeth was glad her grandmother and grandfather were going with them.

Then one day a caravan of 125 wagons for the 80 migrating families began the long journey to Turkestan under the leadership of Abraham Peters. Elizabeth and her family crawled into wagon No. 44, which was to be their home for the next 18 weeks. At night her mother and the three youngest children slept in the wagon and her father and the two older girls in a tent.

One evening, after only two weeks traveling, the children were sent to a relative's wagon for the night. Elizabeth's grandmother said her mother had a headache. In the morning Elizabeth saw her family's wagon standing strangely apart from the others, and ran to it. Her grandmother greeted her with the words, "We nearly lost your mother last night." From the wagon Elizabeth heard the soft snuffling of a newborn baby and her father's low voice. For a moment she didn't know whether she liked the new little brother who had nearly killed her mother, but then she clambered into the wagon to welcome the newcomer.

Because the wagon had no springs, travel was delayed for two days so her mother could regain her strength. Then the caravan picked up the trail again. On it went across rivers, through desolate, uncultivated plains, passing whole tent towns and gypsy camps. From her seat in the wagon Elizabeth watched with wonderment the shiny mosques of Orenberg, on the Ural River between Europe and Asiatic Russia, as they glittered in the sun.

The trail wound upwards into the Ural mountains where the trekkers could look down on the clouds. Through rain and snowstorms, over long stretches of desert and the occasional water-filled gullies and rushing streams, where the Cossacks, Turks, and Jews lived, they traveled. Sometimes the wagon train never met another person all day long. People died, babies were born, young people were married. If no wood was available for a coffin, the body was carried in the wagon for a day or more to the nearest town.

Finally the trek stopped in the town of Taschkent, where negotiations for land were to begin. Each morning when Elizabeth got up she looked for a cloud. Each evening she went to bed not having seen even a little one. Even the stars and the moon beamed hot rays down on her at night instead of coolness. All the land was irrigated. In this environment, the trekkers battled skin diseases, typhus, and smallpox.

After nine months of debating what to do next, the trek leaders decided that part of the group, including Elizabeth's family, would go to Bukhara, and the others to Auliata. One hot morning the new group of 45 families started forth again. As Elizabeth clutched the sides of the wagon or held the smaller children, she feared for her life. The wagon shook and swayed from side to side over the rough, seldom-used roads. Her mother, who had broken her arm, found the horses' stumbling over the camel or donkey trail too painful, so she frequently got out and walked. From time to time wagons broke down and the people in them got sick, delaying the journey.

One evening the group camped near the shallow Saraftan River about half a mile from Syrabulak. Once again discussion moved back and forth whether to stay in the area or move on. Elizabeth listened to her elders try to decide whether to settle in the green valley where they were camped. She watched the large flocks of sheep and goats grazing on the mountainside. Life might be pleasant here.

At one evening service Elizabeth heard a young man from their group ask forgiveness of a local Sarten boy whom he had wronged. She felt stirred by his testimony. Her little brother born on the trail had recently died. The memory of her father taking seat-boards from the wagon to build a small coffin was still fresh in her mind. Where was her brother now? She pondered how good it must feel to have one's sins forgiven and become a child of God. Although she often prayed, and the Lord had even answered her prayers, especially when she had been forced to work harder than her young body had strength, God had helped.

Elizabeth had thought about becoming a Christian a number of years ago back in Gnadenheim, when Abraham Schellenberg, preacher of the Mennonite Brethren, had held services in homes. She had been 13 and had gone along with some of the neighbor girls to the service. But her father, though he was an honest, upright man, was opposed to the Brethren and their strange ideas, and her father's word was law in their home. So she could not discuss what she had heard at home, for if she did, she knew she would be forbidden to go again. Instead, she went quietly to the meetings, where she learned many new songs and Bible verses, and kept everything to herself.

Now the old yearning to know more about God grew strong. As soon as the family to whom her parents had hired her out were asleep, she went outside behind a building to pray until she received peace of mind. The night air was damp and she stayed outside longer than she had planned. By morning she too had typhus. For 18 long weeks her temperature would not drop. She thought she would die. But instead the Lord showed her he had much work for her to do in her lifetime — which would be a long one.

While the group was at Syrabulak, a caravan of 15 families arrived from the Trakt Mennonite colony on the Volga River accompanied by the well-known preacher Klaas Epp. The group had been forcibly evicted by government officials because they did not want the group to settle there. Elizabeth had heard how these families had gone to the mountain country, taking with them the superior attitude that they alone were the righteous, the elect, out of the whole original group which had left the Ukraine. Because Jesus had said all his children were priests and preachers, each one of them had become a preacher. They had also made a few new rules. One was forbidding marriage. Another was that communion was to be observed every day.

When the two groups came together, Bible studies were conducted afternoons and prayer meetings in the evening. Klaas Epp explained the books of Daniel and Revelation. Revival broke out among the people as they waited for the weather to change, for sick people to get well, and for some clear indication where they should settle permanently. During this time many individuals were reconciled to each other. Others were converted. Elizabeth and 20 of her friends were baptized and joined the church.

Full of renewed faith and joy, the trek began once again. Through Samarkand, Bukhara, and on to Khiva through sandy deserts and swift-flowing rivers. At night, as the caravan settled down, Elizabeth listened to the cries of tigers, hyenas, leopards, wild pigs, and small jackals in the forest nearby. The latter sounded just like little children crying, she decided, and shivered beneath her covers.

Finally at Khiva, close to South Siberia, outside Russian territory, near two large dams, the caravan stopped to build a permanent home. They erected mud huts with thatched roofs, a church and school. Elizabeth helped to make bricks, sewed for the family, helped with the gardening. But as fast as the settlers built, all kinds of molesters tore down. Wild pigs, peacocks, and insects ate the young garden plants. Swarms of grasshoppers devoured the foliage. Roving bandits robbed the settlers of horses, attempted to steal women, and even killed some of the people. For two years, in an unfamiliar climate and terrain, faced by wild animals and barbaric human foes, the settlers doggedly worked to establish themselves. Then one day Elizabeth overheard her parents talking about looking for another home. Perhaps America, where some Mennonites had gone in 1874, would be better than this. Another murder one evening by the bandits convinced her parents it was time to move again.

But some of the Mennonites didn't want to pull up their shallow roots so soon. They taunted the ones who wanted to move by calling them ungodly. "You are heading for the devil's wrath," they said. One woman told Elizabeth, "Your ship will sink on the ocean." Elizabeth heard the hateful words as she and her friends huddled silently together in the gathering darkness. At last one of the girls had the boldness to say to the woman, "How can you say such things? We have done you no harm. Some day you may move to America too." Two years later, the woman and her family were living in Kansas.

Once the word was out to move, Elizabeth busied herself once again with sewing and food preparation. The wagon was overhauled and prepared for the tedious journey back to Russia.

One day the wagon train found the trail again, only this time over a different route, but one which was no easier, for it led over impassable roads over the desert and dangerous river crossings. At one place, a dam had to be built across a wide stream. About a hundred men worked for three days. Some laid brush, others rolled logs down the mountainside and bound them together. Others mixed wet loam, spread it on the dam and covered it with a layer of dry earth. By the fourth day, the dam was barely passable. All who were mobile walked across. Then the men led the skittery horses and the wagons slowly but surely across the flimsy footing. Elizabeth watched from the far side, holding her breath when it appeared as if a wagon might tip into the water.

The trek moved westward up the Ustjurt Mountains, then down toward the Ural Sea, where the nature-loving Elizabeth recorded in her journal that she had seen turtles as big as washtubs, grazing like cattle. The weather became hotter and drinking water harder to find. Each day the caravan pushed in the new direction into the Cossack settlements in Russian Asia and finally to Orenburg. This trip lasted only nine weeks. In Orenburg the group received passes to migrate to America via Germany. The next part of the westward journey was made by train and then from Germany by ship to the new country.

In 1884 Elizabeth, now 18 years old, and her family sailed past the Statue of Liberty, glistening in the sun, and arrived in New York City. Their American destination was Nebraska. Perhaps when they arrived there, their traveling days would be over, she thought as she contemplated her life thus far. She had been born in South Russia between Poland and Odessa. At the age of nine she had been hired out to work for other people. As a young girl she had accompanied her mother to visit in Poland. Then the family had moved to the Molotschna, in the Ukraine. From there they had gone to Asia, and now from Asia to America. Surely that was enough travel for one person! She had traveled on wagons, on camels, on boats, and on foot — now for three days and nights the group rode by train to Beatrice, Nebraska, on the Santa Fe line, to the home of Mr. and Mrs. Cornelius Jansen, whom her father had known in Russia.

In Nebraska her parents immediately began building a house and started farming. Elizabeth was hired out as a maid at two dollars per week to Senator Peter Jansen and Mrs. Jansen in

Beatrice. But her days at such work ended when her family moved to South Dakota, closer to their relatives. Here, on June 17, 1887, Elizabeth was married to Abram H. Schultz. He was 19, she 20. The day was a happy one, yet marred by several events, one large one small. The sister of her maid of honor died in childbirth the day of the wedding and was buried the same afternoon. A bad omen. When the new couple sat down after the wedding ceremony, Abram sat down a trifle sooner than Elizabeth did. A few guests commented he would die before she would.

After the wedding Elizabeth and her young husband moved in with his mother. One month later the harvest on the plains began and she and one of Abram's brothers stooked sheaves in the hot July sun. Elizabeth collapsed with sunstroke. She had begun the rigors of a pioneer housewife.

Son Henry and daughters Anna, Helena, Elizabeth and Aganetha were born during the first six years of Abram and Elizabeth's marriage. The second winter the young couple experienced a terrible blizzard in which many people lost their lives, including a school teacher and 13 children. The teacher had tied the children together and intended to follow the fence to the nearest farmer's house because she had no fuel in school. All died in the storm. Many cattle also perished. Elizabeth, as she looked after her own children, also worried about marauding Indians who passed nearby.

In South Dakota a great revival broke out. Her parents said it was similar to the one they had experienced in Asia, after Klaas Epp and his group joined the caravan. Elizabeth and Abram attended the Krimmer Mennonite Brethren Church, or Peters Church, but belonged to the Prussian Mennonite Church in Beatrice, Nebraska.

Before long the couple decided to return to Nebraska, where Abram was appointed foreman on a large sheep ranch. Here he first complained of stomach cramps, which plagued him until the day he died.

In the fall of 1894 Elizabeth, in her sixth pregnancy, felt lonesome for her parents, though she had many friends and visitors in her own area. She had not seen her parents for two years, so Abram's employer, Senator Jansen, gave them a month's vacation to go to South Dakota. After a week's journey and one week's rest, on November 8, 1894, daughter Albertina was born. "We really had been taking a chance," Elizabeth told her mother, for the birth had not been expected for another three weeks. When Abram returned to Nebraska to complete his contract with the Jansens, she experienced her first long separation from him. She and the six children stayed in South Dakota; he planned to return in two months to take up farming there again. The Nebraska interlude had been only a temporary move.

What a happy day when he finally arrived in South Dakota to join the family. "I had so much to tell him about my and the children's doings. We both were still young and interested in each other's experiences." she wrote in her diary. "I enjoyed the songs in the service so much that day. How thankful we were that God had kept and protected us all."

South Dakota was to be home, then, not Nebraska. They wanted to stay close to parents, relatives, and friends. They found a house to live in, but even closeness to parents, relatives, and friends could not protect them from the series of difficulties which befell them in the next few years. Elizabeth broke her arm. But the housework had to continue. Her young son had surgery in the home for a growth on his arm.

One day a tornado struck the community. Elizabeth looked out at the daylight which had turned to night's blackness and prayed, "Please, God, protect everyone!" The house shook but did not fall. She stood at the window stunned, too frightened to move. The tornado whipped its tail over their farm and moved on. First her husband appeared from behind the barn, looking terror-stricken. Two children showed up from the field, safe and sound, faces black with dirt. They had fallen to their bellies and clung to fence posts. When the tornado was gone, they and the horses were turned in the opposite direction. The neighbor's buildings were destroyed; only the foundation of the big barn was left standing. The orchards were ruined, the bark peeled off the tree trunks revealing their naked whiteness. Shortly thereafter the heavy sows ate hedge mustard seed and died.

"Why, Lord, why?" asked Elizabeth. What was to blame? She examined her life. She and Abram took their turn having the church services at their house. Otherwise they stood on the sidelines of the church community, watching the others. Abram was a church member, but not a believer. She had been converted in Asia but had not been baptized by immersion. Yet to be immersed was to deny her first baptism. She knew, however, she had become lukewarm in her love for Christ. So she cried to God to revive her. For a few days the battle raged within her. Was she a Christian? The devil told her she had never been one and that she had denied the Lord. While praying one day, suddenly the light of God's love opened to her again and she thanked God for being his child. She believed what she could not see. She told her family, and all rejoiced with her.

Their neighbor invited Abram and her to some special meetings held in the neighborhood by two preachers from the Church of God. First the meetings were held in homes, later in tents. But the visiting ministers created a big uproar, for they taught that a second experience of the filling of the Holy Spirit was necessary for salvation. After being saved, a Christian would never sin again. Although many wrongs were made right and sinners were saved, nearly everyone was confused by the new teaching. Some thought they had received the filling of the Spirit but later found out they were still sinning. Abram felt drawn to these preachers, but resisted, for he sensed something in their teaching was not right.

In the late summer of 1897 their sixth daughter, Mathilda, was born, and Elizabeth and Abram were full of hope for the future. Before Mathilda was two years old, a seventh daughter, Mary, joined the family. Elizabeth had her hands full cooking, sewing, and mending for the large family. Son Henry and the three older girls attended school and the four younger girls stayed home with Elizabeth. Despite the stresses of the large family, Abram and Elizabeth enjoyed their children. There were many tears, but also much laughter around the table where the family gathered each evening. Elizabeth never found any child a burden. She loved each one dearly. One year each child wanted to recite a little verse at Christmas, so Elizabeth taught them. She could hardly restrain her pride as one after another said his or her verse clearly and distinctly before the congregation.

But life was not destined to move along smoothly. In 1900 her parents left for Saskatchewan to take up a homestead or to buy land. Another son, Alexander, joined the family group about the same time as Abram's stomach troubles returned. And in the midst of these testings the awareness came to her that Abram wanted to go north also. One evening he broached the subject.

"But I don't want to move to Saskatchewan, even though my parents are living there." Elizabeth had finally said the words which had burdened her heart ever since she had known what Abram was thinking. For some time now she had tried to go about her daily work with her usual buoyancy. But deep down, every time she thought of moving to Saskatchewan, a deep feeling of dread overcame her. Some tragedy lay ahead in that cold country so far to the north. She didn't want to face it.

"Listen to me, Elizabeth." Abram looked directly at her as they sat in the kitchen. "I think we would do best if we moved to Saskatchewan, closer to your parents. Then we would be close together. If suddenly something should happen to one or the other of us. . . ."

Elizabeth felt her skin grow clammy. Abram had sensed something too. What was this strange thing they both felt and neither could speak about freely? Finally she admitted her fears.

"Why worry? It seems to me you should be only too glad to move where your parents are living, for they have helped us so much already."

"That's true, but I'm scared of Saskatchewan." Elizabeth's voice trembled and tears clouded her eyes, so that she could hardly see Abram — his drawn face, his shoulders and thighs thinned out where there should be strong, sinewy muscles. Abram looked at her, perplexed. He patted her gently with his hand, but her tears flowed. He turned and walked to the barn.

Soon he came back into the kitchen to tell Elizabeth to get ready to go to Minnesota for Pentecost to visit his brothers. While they visited there, Abram told his brothers openly that next spring the Schultz family was moving from South Dakota to Saskatchewan. Silently Elizabeth accepted the news with her usual fortitude. The Lord would give grace for what lay ahead.

The family returned to their farm to prepare for the coming move and to earn as much money as possible before they left. But even this did not turn out as planned. One day a tornado cut a ten-mile swath through the area, destroying everything in its path. Hail, rain, wind and shredded grass made the air look green. At the Schultz farm the double corncrib and all the wheat stacks were gone. But the house and children were all safe. Elizabeth had been at the store during the storm; and when she came home, her frightened children surrounded her, standing knee deep in water and crying. Through the broken windows she could see the limp bodies of turkeys and hens floating in the water. Across the yard a new full-bodied stream flowed. Abram and Elizabeth counted their blessings as they cleaned up. The storm had not hit where Abram had been threshing. The corn was still good — over three thousand bushels, large kernels — but the price was low, so that by the time expenses had been paid, there was little money left over. The pigs were selling very cheaply, so Abram determined to take them along to Saskatchewan.

Word came from up north that Elizabeth's father and brother-in-law had picked a homestead for them. They were satisfied with the climate and believed that Abram, who was often sick with stomach cramps, would improve physically.

Slowly they prepared for the trip — 100 sacks of seed wheat, 200 sacks of shelled corn, 40 sacks of flour. They butchered nine large pigs, cured and smoked all the hams, and prepared 100 gallons of lard, 80 gallons of canned meat, cracklings, and many jars of canned fruit and dried fruit. In February the auctioneer sold the rest of the pigs, except for three farrowing sows. Into the freight car for the journey went three good cows, 12 horses, and all their machinery, household goods, paint, and other necessities, filling one and a half freight cars. The family was allowed to travel on two and a half tickets. Abram, son Henry, and Abram's brother Jake traveled free on the freight wagon. Five families from Turner County and several single persons joined them in the move to Saskatchewan. All together their belongings filled five freight cars, so the train was long.

After a night and a day, all the immigrants were transferred to an immigration train car, where they could spread out their bedding and rest. But there the comfort ended. The heater did not work, so they could not make themselves hot food. The children had to stay in bed and the grownups never got out of their overcoats and overshoes. Elizabeth thought the trip was much worse than the long Asian trek over mountain and desert.

North of the Canadian border the snow blew fiercely. Progress came to a complete standstill when the train got stuck in a snowdrift. Their only food was cold meat and milk. Little

Alexander had an earache and cried day and night. Elizabeth, who felt the faint stirrings of another child within her, found herself growing weaker from loss of sleep and food. Finally a woman from another immigrant train brought her a spoonful of *Alpenkraeuter* to give the baby, and Elizabeth slept for several hours. After a day and a night in the snowdrift, the train forged across the snow-covered plains. On March 18, 1901, at eight o'clock in the evening, the American immigrants arrived in Rosthern, Saskatchewan, where father, brother, and brother-in-law greeted them with big smiles, warm hearts, and open arms.

Fifteen loaded sleighs were required to move their belongings to Elizabeth's parents' home. The first homestead site did not appeal to the Schultzes, so they picked a second one, and for a time Elizabeth and Abram and family lived with her parents. In spring Abram and his brother Jacob broke 18 acres and seeded it to oats. The next task was to build a house, but before it was finished, on September 16, 1901, son Arthur made his appearance. By the end of October the new house was finished sufficiently to move into, although the outside only had a layer of siding and the inside still needed to be logged and plastered. The downstairs was divided into two rooms. Otherwise the partitions were curtains.

The next spring after seeding, the men felled trees to build a large barn for the cattle, pigs, and chickens. The summer was a busy one breaking more land, making hay, harvesting, and building a horse barn.

That year was also memorable, for on September 16, 1902, Abram and Elizabeth were baptized and joined the Krimmer Mennonite Brethren Church. The leading minister gave Elizabeth two verses: "The Lord bless thee and keep thee," and "My grace is sufficient for thee, for my strength is made perfect in weakness." As Elizabeth heard him quote the words, she wondered at his choice. What lay ahead? God had promised her a great work to do and a long life.

Once again Abram and Elizabeth looked ahead with hope. Abram moved into custom threshing. She canned wild fruit, and, with the children, tended a large vegetable garden. With the second harvest, on October 3, 1903, son Phillip was born. Elizabeth watched the debts mount as the threshing machine broke down repeatedly and new parts had to be purchased. And time and again Abram staggered into the house, gasping with pain because of his stomach. When he could not work, he worried about the mounting bills. Finally one day in discouragement, he said to Elizabeth, "I will soon ditch everything, for to serve God does not seem to help. Everything is against me and goes differently than it should. Nothing helps."

Elizabeth could not see it that way. "What has God to do with it, if the men break your machine?" She advised him to oversee the threshing operation even if he could not work himself. At bedtime they knelt and told the Lord their troubles, asking for his forgiveness for doubting him and for being discouraged. They prayed for strength, wisdom, and love. Abram, encouraged, praised God for a wife who was so unwavering in her faith. But Elizabeth felt unworthy. She knew the doubts which assailed her whenever she looked at her husband's strained face. Yet she was thankful the Lord had drawn near.

Abram felt stronger and remained with the threshing outfit more often. Harvest took until Christmas. They plowed the foot-deep snow from the machine in 25-below-zero weather so they could move it from place to place. The house was not yet finished, for they were waiting for the income from threshing operations to buy the needed materials.

A third winter passed and a third spring and a third summer. Her husband bought more land, and a stallion in the hope that the stud fees would bring much-needed cash income for the family of 13. Each day Elizabeth woke to the multitudinous tasks of baking, cooking, sewing, knitting, mending, washing, and canning for her large brood.

In late summer the congregation voted Abram as Sunday school teacher, a task for which he felt unprepared. Elizabeth was sure he could handle the task, for he had often helped in the teaching. But he felt unsure, and as they drove to church, their ten-month-old baby on her lap, Abram asked Elizabeth to teach him the song, "I will trust the Lamb alone to lead me." She sang it slowly, many times, until he could sing along with her. Later she cherished the memory of the intimacy of that ride. The next Sunday he opened his class with the song she had taught him, but during the period he felt his stomach pulling together in pain. The pains grew more intense for several days. One day, as he was lying in bed, weak and pale, he told Elizabeth he had seen himself in a white robe, lying in a coffin, in a yard full of people. He had heard a voice saying, ''You wanted to know what would happen to you. You will know in one week.'' ''What does it mean?'' he asked her.

Elizabeth stood up aghast. Her husband was to die? ''My God,'' she cried out. ''What will happen then?'' Her tears flowed freely. The two sat close together, as he stroked her face and hands.

''Maybe I should not have told you this, for our dear Lord can change things and make me well and strong again,'' he said. But she could see from his expression he knew he would die.

On August 12 the family celebrated Abram's 37th birthday. The following Sunday several people were baptized. Abram prayed after the service and communion for the newly baptized members, for the whole congregation, for his wife, children, parents, brothers, and sisters. Some people wondered at his long prayer, for he was usually a man of few words.

Each day that week his strength slowly faded. One day when he was feeling a little better than usual, he asked Elizabeth to tell her father to drive to Hague to get a stomach plaster for him. He also asked her to bring back a piece of ice from Rosthern, for he was hungry for ice cream. She left soon, and after completing her errands, while at the store, she suddenly remembered he had said he would love to have a black sateen shirt to wear Sundays. So she purchased a few yards of material. But the journey back was agony, for the 22 miles were much too long. She knew her husband too well. She feared Abram might have attempted some work and been stricken with stomach cramps again. When she turned the horses into the yard, she hardly dared get off the wagon and walk into the house. But as she had feared, there he was, sitting on a bench, hunched over. He reached for her. As she rushed to his side, she knew what he would say before he spoke. The boys had come home with a broken sickle. Unable to see the work stop, he had welded it for them and soon thereafter severe cramps had started again. He felt very ill. He looked at her with sadness, misery, and longing.

They clung to one another. ''We had so much to say to each other, and I could not grasp that I was to lose him soon. I did not know what I should do or wanted to do or could do without my husband. I had always relied on him, and now I felt as inexperienced and helpless as a child,'' she wrote in her journal. ''We loved each other dearly, even if sometimes we had misunderstandings. He had a quiet friendly character and a giving attitude. He loved to help and do good wherever he could. He was well loved all over, and that was why he got credit readily.''

They talked a long time that night — about their many debts, the stallion, the threshing machine, the mortgage, about what she should do if he died. She found she could not let him go. He comforted her as she had often strengthened him. ''God knows best, and he will be with you and provide for you better than I could. You have so often comforted me when I was discouraged and pointed me to God. Now do you find it hard to have faith in his help?''

But she could not give in. He sighed and groaned as the pain controlled him. She wept.

Suddenly she sat erect. ''My God, why did we have to come to Canada?''

''So you could be close to your parents, so they can help you.''

But his strength was getting less by the moment. His once strong hand took hold of her wrist. His head sank onto her shoulder. He asked her to let him go, for he had to die. He gave her a last kiss. He prayed and several others who had gathered by the bedside prayed also. Then he said, ''Jesus, Jesus—'' and was gone. They had been in Saskatchewan barely three years.

The wheat harvest was nearly ready for the sickle when Abram succumbed to the Grim Reaper. The night before the funeral the grain froze. Elizabeth woke the next morning to see a whole field of promise wiped out. Her oldest son, Henry, was 17 and the youngest child, Phillip, a little over ten months. In between were nine other children. Elizabeth was 38. She faced the management of a farm burdened with debts at a time when strong men found farming difficult.

After the funeral, at which Abram was dressed in the new black sateen shirt, when she attempted to pull together her financial resources, the bank officers would not accept her signature alone on a note. She faced the winter inexperienced and unprepared in every way. ''We were all beginners in this new land,'' she wrote later, ''and everyone was afraid to be guaranty for another, for all were struggling to get ahead.'' Finally five brethren in the church backed her note for three months. She faced the future assured that the grace of God the minister had promised her at her baptism would be sufficient. She sold what livestock, machinery, tools, and land she could, paying a little to each creditor each year. With the children, she worked and saved. The girls worked alongside the hired man, even pitching bundles during threshing. One of the younger boys drove the horses from stook to stook. One daughter was on the binder for two summers. Each year the girls ploughed, disced, harrowed, made hay, and stooked. The family stayed together and, in general, enjoyed themselves.

One by one the children grew up, married, and established their own homes. In her old age, Elizabeth praised God. As a family, they had never gone hungry. They had always had a home, enough clothes, enough fuel for the stove, and did not have to move from place to place. Her journeyings had finally ended, except for the last one to glory. And they had had God's Word as a daily source of strength and comfort. Though poor, they had been rich. God, true to the promise he had given her many years ago when she had been sick in Asia, had given her a long life and a great work to do in bringing up her family to his honor. She died in 1943 in Saskatchewan at the age of 76.

Bibliography

Unruh, Elizabeth Schultz. *What a Heritage.* Journal translated by Annie Schultz Keyes. n.d., unpublished manuscript.

Even in the latter decades of the nineteenth century women were combining home duties with an active career outside the home. Though largely unschooled, Sara Block Eitzen found wide acceptance of her medical skills in the Hillsboro, Kansas, area, and left a legacy of medicine as a profession to her family. She and Dr. Katharina Schellenberg were close friends.

6

HORSE AND BUGGY MIDWIFE

Sara Block Eitzen (1840-1917)

By Esther Loewen Vogt

Sara Block started toward the house, her shapely brown head bowed. She walked slowly, her slight figure swaying like a reed in the wind. She was scarcely aware of the pink hollyhocks nodding over the white picket fence, the deep green shade of the stately elms. It was incredible. Get married — at her age? The thought stabbed her again. Why, she was 28. Most girls her age already rocked cradles and cooked and baked and sewed for a husband and a houseful of youngsters.

She had been born to David and Sara Block at Rudnerweide, South Russia, on February 2, 1840, the oldest of seven girls and two boys. The paramount experience of her life occurred when she had surrendered her life to Jesus Christ as revivals swept across the Ukraine. She was baptized upon the confession of her faith and joined the Mennonite Brethren Church. Her second highlight happened shortly after. Serving the Lord in helping others was her highest aim, and so she chose a career in medicine. For some time now she had been apprenticed to a physician and accompanied him as he made his rounds from village to village. She assisted him with delivering babies; and, as her gentle hands cared for the newborn infants, she never ceased to marvel at the miracle of birth.

She boarded in the home of Mennonite Christian friends in the village where the doctor practiced, and it was to this comfortable shaded house she now paced her way pensively.

There it was again — that stark fact: Abraham Eitzen, a widower with four children, had asked her to marry him, and she hadn't said yes, nor no. But she had promised to think about it. The tall, dark-bearded, brown-eyed young man had been sincere in his proposal.

"I need a wife, and my children must have a mother," he begged earnestly. He had observed her, and saw she was gentle, he told her, and her faith in the Lord deep and abiding. And that was important to him.

She knew she couldn't take this matter lightly. She had to commit it to the Lord. Mentally she reviewed all she knew about Abraham Eitzen — this man who had asked her to share his life.

Born in the village of Lindenau on August 18, 1830, he was ten years her senior. His father, Cornelius Eitzen, was born in East Prussia and had migrated with his parents to South Russia around 1800. Here, families lived in villages and owned, as a rule, a strip of land for orchard or garden beyond the house and outbuildings, commonly connected into one unit. This practice continued.

Somehow the young men of Blumstein didn't take kindly to "foreign" suitors who came to court Blumstein girls, and were prone to play pranks. When young Abraham Eitzen rode into the village to court Susanna Isaac, the beautiful and only daughter in the family, her father consented to look after Abraham's horse and saddle. As an outcrop of Abraham's persistent courtship he and Susanna were married on August 30, 1856, and established their home in Blumstein.

In the early years of their marriage, they, with several others, grew deeply aware of the superficial religious life of the Mennonite church as it was then. Attending Sunday morning church service seemed to fulfill the entire Christian obligation. How one lived during the week was beside the point.

Abraham and Susanna, together with the other group of seekers, met for Bible study and prayer, and through the help of an evangelist they accepted Jesus Christ as Savior and Lord. But Father Isaac was very angry.

"I'll give you the best farm in the village," he vowed to his son-in-law, "if you promise to keep away from those fanatic 'brethren'!"

Abraham's heart sank. He knew if they continued to worship with the Mennonite "brethren" as the believers called themselves, their ties with Susanna's father must be severed. The young couple didn't hesitate long. Their Christian convictions couldn't be traded for a farm. In 1861 they were baptized by immersion and became members of the newly organized Mennonite Brethren Church.

Late in the summer of 1864, Susanna succumbed to an illness — possibly typhoid fever — and after lingering for 16 days, she passed away quietly on September 9. Young Abraham was left with his brood of four children under the age of seven. In 1866 he moved with his children to the Kuban area. Here he became acquainted with Sara Block, the young medical apprentice, and asked her to marry him.

Sara agonized over the proposal, and prayed long and hard for the Lord's leading. There were many perplexing questions: Would she be a good wife to the tall, handsome widower? Would she be a fit mother to his four children? Should she give up her promising medical career and settle down to be a homemaker?

"I just don't know the answer," she told the people with whom she lived.

Upon their suggestion, she consented to the drawing of a lot, and she received the assurance of God's guidance. There was no turning back. God had spoken. So she married Abraham Eitzen on November 20, 1866. While in Russia, two children were born to them — David and Sara — David, however, passed away in infancy. Abraham had already served his term in the government forestry, so they settled into the typical Mennonite village life with their five children.

During those early years the Russian government abrogated some cherished privileges originally granted to the Mennonites. The Imperial Decree of 1870 contained provisions which implied radical changes: the anomalous supervisory commission in Odessa was to be abolished; Russian was to be the official language in the local colony administrative office as well as a subject of study in all schools; and worst of all for a Mennonite, military exemption was to be terminated. Many Mennonites chose to leave for America, and to settle on the vast prairies of Kansas and other midwestern states and Canada.

The Abraham Eitzens joined the great Mennonite migration to America. Arriving in Peabody, Kansas, in mid-July, 1876, they stepped wearily from the grimy railway coach with hot winds, dust, and cinders blowing into their faces. The Mennonites had brought with them as much equipment as possible: cylindrical threshing stones, copper tea kettles, clocks with heavy brass weights, leather-bound hymnals and Bibles, strong wooden chests, and even large wagons with flaring boxes called "ladder wagons." Since Sara's parents, the David Blocks, had migrated with the Crimean group in 1874, and lived in Gnadenau village, the Eitzens moved in with them temporarily.

Five lively children and several adults bustling in and out of the tiny sod house forced Abraham to look for a place for his family. He found a partly-improved 160-acre farm two miles east and 2½ miles southwest of present-day Hillsboro. The farm, belonging to a Civil War veteran Charlie Woodward, lay along the lush Cottonwood River bottom on the northeast quarter of the section. Part of the land was already in cultivation but some acres still waved with high prairie grass. Beyond the hill at the end of a long driveway stood a small three-room house.

In the loft of the house the Eitzens stored the precious Turkey Red hard-winter wheat for seed which they had brought with them from Russia. Here Abraham and Sara Eitzen settled into the new land with their family. In time two more daughters, Anna and Mary, were born to them.

Pioneering on the vast raw prairies of Kansas was quite different from living in comfortable middle-class homes which many had enjoyed in Russia. But the joys of religious and political freedom tempered the rigors of frontier life. Aside from rugged field work and the battle with winter's snows and summer's heat, almost no medical help was available. Death stalked relentlessly like a grim specter across the prairie as dreaded epidemics and complications of childbirth took their toll of people.

One day a sad-faced young woman clattered up the long lane of the Eitzen farm and stepped ponderously from her buggy. Sara scooped up a fresh apron and tied it around her slender waist and patted her black lace cap. Then she drew her visitor into the kitchen with a kiss.

"Do sit down, Sister Fast," she said. "You look worn out. Here, have a chair."

Mrs. Fast sighed and shook her head. "I need your help, Sara. I'm afraid to have my baby without anyone to attend me. You helped the good doctor in Russia. Surely you can help me!" she begged.

"Oh, yes, I helped him with birthings," she demurred, "but I would rather not undertake the delivery alone."

Mrs. Fast pleaded tearfully, and finally Sara yielded. She dug out her medical books and studied birth procedures to refresh her memory.

When the time came, a messenger drove her in the top buggy to the Fast farm home. All went well with the delivery and a healthy baby was born. This event marked the beginning of a long career which was to interrupt many of Sara's days and nights in all kinds of weather. In fact, Abraham sometimes grew anxious for his wife's delicate physique when husbands and relatives rushed her away in buggies and wagons in summer, or in sleighs in cold, snowy weather. He would wrap a great Russian fur coat tenderly around her before she left to make sure she kept warm.

The tremendous medical need prompted her to study and practice homeopathy and midwifery, using Dr. Puscheck's kit of drugs. According to records, she delivered more than 1,800 babies during those years. When complications threatened, she remained with the new mother until all was well.

The Eitzen daughters — first Katherine, then Sara — learned early to manage the household during their mother's frequent absences. But as time wore on, the older children married and left home. In the meantime, Abraham and Sara built a three-story house into the side of the hill just east of the three-room frame house. It was built with a "roof" or double set of rafters *between* the first and second stories. In case of a tornado the first level would remain as a shelter. The first floor housed a large kitchen and dining room, a huge pantry and storage room; the second and third floors contained the "parlor" and five bedrooms. A large verandah ran the full length of the east side of the house, and opened from the second story. It was an ideal place to spend the quiet summer evenings in family devotions and Bible reading. The house was big and comfortable, set in an old-fashioned garden in a riot of phlox, bachelor's buttons, zinnias, and aromatic herbs. Along the driveway Abraham had industriously planted mulberry trees and mulberry hedges, for a "silkworm industry" at Peabody clamored for mulberry leaves to feed the silkworms. To the south he planted a huge orchard, adjoining the orchard of neighbors Cornelius Hieberts to the south. The farm was appropriately called Pleasant Hill.

During those early years, droughts and depression, boom-or-bust periods hit the Kansas settlement; however, Abraham and Sara never shirked their work for the Lord. Since church services were held in the nearby schoolhouse for those first seven years, it was easy to become a part of the growing congregation. Soon Abraham was elected deacon, in which office he served for nearly 30 years. He also served as church treasurer, and kept his books meticulously. Later, when the church was built 1½ miles south of Pleasant Hill farm, it became the focal point for their lives.

After the three-story house was built and dedicated, visiting preachers and missionaries found their "Elisha's room" tucked away in a quiet upstairs corner. Two foster sons, Peter K. Hiebert and Thomas Fischer, were reared to adolescence in the Eitzen home.

Sara was also active and interested in women's work of the church, especially in the "sewing circles" which were first held in homes. Her slight, spare figure bent over many a wooden frame as she knotted pieced comforts.

But church life wasn't without ups and downs. Peter Gaede's advent into the community splintered the congregation and lured some of its members into the Seventh Day Adventist teaching, daughter Katherine and her husband Jacob Friesen among them. Abraham and Sara Eitzen were stunned. Their oldest — forsaking the faith of her childhood to follow another teaching? It was unbelievable! Where had they gone wrong? What was more — Katherine and Jacob sold the farm Abraham had given them as her inheritance from her natural mother and moved to Battle Creek, Michigan, a Seventh Day Adventist stronghold. Abraham especially was crushed. But Sara's strong faith and gentle compassion tempered the hurt and carried them through this difficult period.

Sons Abraham, Jr., and Daniel married and settled on their farms nearby and become industrious, God-fearing farmers. But John, the oldest son, was born with an innate sense of adventure and soon made friends outside the Mennonite community. He was no longer satisfied with the "outlandish" Mennonite ways and wanted to be a full-fledged American and learn to speak the English language. He decided there was more to life than the narrow confines of community culture. He decided to go out into "the world" where there were things to see and money to be made. Later, after marriage he settled at Tucumcari, New Mexico. His spiritual life sagged to a low ebb. Again Abraham and Sara were driven into an agony of despair. But Sara loved Abraham's children as much as her own, and she committed them all to the Lord. She knew he would not fail any of them.

"Some day John will return to God," she often said with confidence.

She continued to visit the sick and deliver babies, her shiny black top buggy with its gentle brown mare skimming down the country roads in a cloud of dust. (She is remembered for having a "fast horse"!) She dispensed medicines, and practiced physiotherapy, homeopathy, and obstetrics. Her delivery fee was usually a modest $2.50 per baby.

One warm summer day Helena Bekker was bitten by the dread scourge of the prairies, a rattlesnake, and death was certain unless something was done quickly. Sara was summoned to the Jacob Bekker farm where she asked immediately for a live chicken. When it was brought to her, she tore off its head and laid the still-warm, pulsating chicken's body on Helena's badly-swelling leg. The poison seeped into the chicken, and after some tense hours, Helena recovered. Later, Helena married Daniel Eitzen, Abraham's youngest son by Susanna. Helena, too, showed a propensity for the homeopathic arts and often accompanied her mother-in-law on her visits to the sick and for many years delivered many babies.

South of the orchard gate a path meandered to the Cornelius Hiebert farm an eighth of a mile away. This was very convenient for "borrowing purposes," for the early pioneers practiced the pioneer philosophy "to be neighborly is to borrow." The path through the two rows of apple trees soon became hard-packed as the Eitzen and Hiebert youngsters scrambled back and forth. Young John K. Hiebert set his eyes on comely daughter Sara Eitzen with the laughing gray eyes and sparkling wit. In 1890, when the couple decided to marry, Father Abraham Eitzen suggested: "Why don't you move in with us? Our house is roomy, and I can use John's help on the farm since my sons are gone."

This seemed a practical solution for all concerned. Sara continued to manage the household during Mother Sara Eitzen's absences while John worked as hired man for the first eight years, and later became a joint farmer. When their babies arrived, Grandmother Sara delivered them all. The Eitzen-Hiebert household grew, as five sons and one daughter were born to daughter Sara and husband John K. Hiebert. One son died in infancy. Breakfast was preceded by singing a hymn, after which Father Eitzen read a generous Scripture portion and prayed. The framed verse on the wall in ornamental lettering served as a reminder of the family motto: "As for me and my house, we will serve the Lord" (Josh. 1:9). John felt the call to preach and served the Ebenfeld Mennonite Brethren church as minister and pastor for many years.

As the years passed, Father Abraham Eitzen began to ail. He had always been a handsome man, erect as a soldier. From his spotlessly shined shoes to his bald head, he carried himself with dignity. He was opinionated and didn't brook much opposition. He had definite convictions of right and wrong, and there were no gray areas. He believed in honest labor, and to him his word was as good as a bond. His well-groomed horses hitched to his shiny top-buggy were his pride. He tried to suppress an innate sense of humor, for to him it was unbecoming as a "pillar in the church" to show wit. His grandsons who carried the name of Abraham (and there were several) felt special. Now as he became more and more unwell, his shoulders sagged and tired lines criss-crossed his face. Sara grew anxious for her husband. Even though she lamented the fact that she was unable to help him from her store of medical knowledge, she nursed him faithfully during those long months. His illness culminated in pneumonia and on December 1, 1906, Abraham Eitzen died and was buried in the Ebenfeld Mennonite Brethren cemetery.

"It's been a good marriage," Sara remarked tearfully, her

narrow, stalwart shoulders erect, "and I've never been sorry for the result of the lot-casting. God knew what he was doing!"

Her medical practice in the community dwindled as more trained medical help was available. She still went wherever needed, and nursed her own family through their illnesses. It grieved her when two of John's daughters died of diphtheria in 1912.

She continued to make her home with John K. and Sara Hiebert. Always tidy and precise, for as long as she lived she wore a black lace cap of alternating fluted lace and seven yards of black satin ribbon. She is remembered for her standard "uniform" of black shirt and striped waist, with its perky white lace collar and black tie, and her slender fingers encased in neatly tailored gloves while driving her buggy. She was conscious of her appearance, and sometimes patted a tiny sifting of white powder on her smooth face, but all without a grain of vanity. It was her granddaughter Esther Hiebert's job on Sunday mornings to pick a few flowers from the garden and fix a tiny nosegay of mint, thyme, and perhaps a rosebud or bachelor button, with a damp cloth rolled snugly around the stems, for Sara to carry elegantly to church. Her custom was to sit in a pew near the front where she often prayed publicly.

She loved her grandchildren's visits to her in her upstairs bedroom at home. She shared her devotions with them, but when she wrote letters they knew they must be very quiet! Grandson Abe E. Hiebert remembers her encouragement in his schooling. One morning early he went down to the basement to practice an oration while the big house was dim and quiet. Suddenly he felt a gentle tap on his shoulder. It was Grandmother.

"Come back to bed," she said softly. "You'll make it!" He followed her meekly upstairs. As usual, she was right. His oration won!

One piece of equipment fascinated the grandchildren. A homemade clothes mangle stood in the granary. As their mothers came over to smooth out coarse-grained towels and voluminous bedlinen on the tight wooden rollers, the youngsters liked sliding back and forth with the rollers!

Christmas was always a happy occasion. Sara prepared simple gifts for her grandchildren — usually a bit of candy, some nuts and cookies, a pair of knitted socks, and always a shiny new dime. That precious dime was savored to be spent only on special occasions.

In December of 1912, son John surprised Sara and the Hieberts with a visit. He was dejected and lonely, and it was obvious he was ill.

"Oh, I won't stay long," he said brokenly. "As soon as I'm rested and my strength returns I'll go back to New Mexico."

Sara greeted her oldest stepson with her usual kiss. "Stay as long as you wish, John. The door is always open!"

He loved his stepmother, and he knew she loved him in spite of his waywardness. His stay lengthened into spring, and as the mulberry trees began to leaf along the long driveway and the wheatfields thrust out new green shoots, he lay gravely ill. She spent hours reading to him and praying. She nursed him in his painful hours. While he was ill, John found his way back to God and Sara was comforted.

During her last years she no longer practiced medicine. She had developed an arthritic condition in her shoulder and grew slightly humped. She read the Bible or wrote letters to missionaries, especially to Dr. Katharina Schellenberg, Mennonite Brethren medical missionary to India. She took a keen interest in the development of Tabor College, and faithfully attended the Bible conferences, which were conducted in the German language in earlier days.

Traveling to church conferences in Kansas, Nebraska, and Oklahoma, she was welcomed with interest for she was known in many Mennonite circles for her midwifery, which created a common bond with women everywhere. After an extended trip to California to visit her sister in 1910, Sara's appetite whetted for travel and she, together with her children, the John K. and C. A. Hieberts, went to the exciting San Francisco World's Fair in 1915.

She continued to be deeply concerned for the health of her family, and handed down to them a heritage of helping and healing others. It would have pleased her to know that 13 grandsons and great-grandsons later entered the medical profession.

During World War 1, 1917, when military conscription became evident, Sara Block Eitzen grew distressed. She prayed she would never live to see the day when Mennonite young men would be drafted into the army and kill people. One day while visiting her daughter in McPherson, Kansas, shortly before school began, she arose early, about five o'clock, and started down the stairs. Her feet slipped and she hurtled down the steps, fracturing a collar bone and several ribs. She also sustained internal injuries.

"Lord," she prayed, "don't let me be a burden to anyone. Take me home soon!"

Her prayers were answered promptly, for she passed away in her sleep on September 5, 1917. She never knew that the first Mennonite young man was inducted into the army that day.

After a large memorial service at the Ebenfeld Mennonite Brethren Church, she was buried beside her husband. She shares a tall, slender grave marker with him. Very simply, and without fanfare the inscription reads: SARA EITZEN, WIFE OF ABRAHAM EITZEN – BORN FEBRUARY 2, 1840; DIED SEPTEMBER 5, 1917.

Sara Block Eitzen is remembered today not only for her generous medical help in the days when it was much needed and appreciated, but also for her cheerfulness, her contented nature, and her interest and concern for people of all ages. She always went when suffering humanity called. Wherever she visited, she "walked in with a smile and left with a smile." Her devotion to her Lord and her family was unstinting. Her medical services to the community were memorialized by furnishing the obstetric department of Salem Hospital, which was built in Hillsboro in 1918.

Katharina began her medical career late, but it stretched over many years — 1907 to 1945 — as one of the first medical missionaries of the Mennonite Brethren Church to India and its first woman doctor. She never had children of her own but found a family wherever she worked. Most of her adult life was spent among people she loved in India. She remained single so she could be free to serve.

7

FREE TO SERVE

Katharina Schellenberg (1870-1945)

By Esther Jost

The last day of school was over! Katharina had finished four years of medical training at a homeopathic school of medicine in Kansas City, Kansas. Now at age 34 she was Doctor Katharina Schellenberg, the first woman doctor of the Mennonite Brethren Church. She seemed almost too small in stature and slight in weight to be a doctor! The year was 1904 and women at that time seldom chose to devote themselves to a profession or to a life of being single. They were mothers of large families, or, if unmarried, children's maids, housekeepers, or nurses — but almost never doctors! To become a doctor had been no easy task for Katharina. Her mother had died when Katharina was young, leaving a large family for the girl to care for; so a formal education had been out of the question. However, Katharina's commitment to God's will, her dedication to a task, and her intelligence contributed to her completion of the requirements for the medical degree.

Katharina was born November 28, 1870, in the village of Tiegerweide, South Russia. She was the first daughter and the second child of Abraham and Katharina Lohrenz Schellenberg. In 1874, soon after Tsar Alexander II denied military exemption to the Mennonites, Katharina's grandparents, Mr. and Mrs. Peter Lohrenz, emigrated to America and settled near Halstead, Kansas. The move was difficult for them and for their children who remained in Russia. They missed each other very much.

Soon after Katharina's grandparents left, her mother was very ill for almost two weeks after the birth of Maria. Because she was in a coma she was unaware that Baby Maria died after nine days. Katharina and her brothers Abraham and Peter grieved the death of their baby sister.

Although Katharina experienced sickness and death at an early age, she also knew music, beauty, and joy. She loved to sing. Her father wrote to her grandparents in America: "*Tinchen* (Katharina) does not go to school yet but she has learned to sing very well. She knows almost all the melodies and the songs that we sing. When we came home from church Sunday evening, she said, 'I am so happy when we all sing.' " Katharina also loved the beauty of nature, and after a long winter of being cooped inside, she and her young brothers welcomed the spring and the opportunity to play outdoors. She was interested in learning and could spell many words before she was old enough to go to school. She knew about work and responsibility at an early age. In time another Maria and Elizabeth joined the family, and Katharina helped her mother with the children and housework. When her mother wrote a letter to her parents in America, Katharina stood by the table to watch her mother write: "Katharina is eagerly waiting for some pictures which we have already paid for. She thinks the pictures will be very pretty and wants us to send you a picture of each of the children for a Christmas present."

Conditions became more threatening in Russia; so in 1879 the family emigrated to America and settled near the Peter Lohrenzes, her mother's parents, in the Halstead, Kansas, vicinity.

In 1884, when Katharina was 14 years old, her mother died. Although Katharina had been a big help to her mother, now she had to shoulder the responsibility of caring for her three brothers and three sisters. One day they trudged the quarter of a mile from their farm home across the prairie to spend a few moments at their mother's graveside. Katharina was strangely moved as she stood there, and she told the little brood of children. "If we want to get to the place where Mother is," she said, "we must pray." Then they all knelt and she prayed with them. Often the family sang together, to the accompaniment of Katharina's autoharp, for they all loved to sing. Her favorite songs were: "*Ziehe deine Kreise um den Meister her*" ("Make a Circle Around the Master") and "Haven of Rest." Her father, Elder Abraham Schellenberg, a pastor, conference moderator, and one of the first Mennonite Brethren leaders to encourage missions, often read missionary stories to his children.

After several years Katharina's father married Susanna Flaming, and the family was increased by another 13 children. Because Katharina was needed at home, she didn't join the others when they left for school each day. Despite her busy schedule, she still got together occasionally with a group of cousins in the neighborhood. At these gatherings Katharina was always the leader.

At the age of 19, Katharina accepted Jesus as her Savior when Rev. P. H. Wedel, missionary from Africa, was conducting evangelistic meetings in her home church. One of her sisters remarked later, "Her daily Bible reading gave us the impression that conversion and reading the Bible belonged together."

A respectable young man, a farmer in the community, became her suitor but she refused to marry him. He proposed to her again a number of years later, before she left for the mission field, but her answer was still "No." Later, before leaving for India, she remarked to a friend, "A woman who goes to the foreign field by herself should be very sure." She was.

As a young woman of 24, Katharina left home to work in the Sprunger Orphanage in Berne, Indiana. The school had a class for the boys, the girls, and the small children, with a worker in charge of each class and a strict regimen of study, work and play throughout the day. After supper, during evening devotions, the workers taught the children songs, Bible verses, and how to pray, for many of them had no homes. Katharina loved the children and earned their confidence.

Next, Katharina and a friend, Anna G. Suderman, moved to Chicago to study the Bible as well as nursing. After training at the Deaconess Hospital in Cleveland, Ohio, Katharina served as supervisor of the Goessel Hospital, Goessel, Kansas.

During sessions of the General Conference of the Mennonite Brethren Churches which convened in the Ebenezer Church, Buhler, Kansas, Katharina indicated she wanted to become a missionary. Dr. Peter Richert, a homeopathic physician of Goessel encouraged her, however, to get more medical training first. Katharina's schooling had been very limited, so she agreed to this difficult assignment. She entered the Medical Institute of Homeopathic Medicine at Kansas City, Kansas, in 1900 and graduated in 1904. Since she was unable to leave for missionary service immediately, Katharina established a private practice in her hometown of Buhler, Kansas, until arrangements for her passage to India were finalized. She was proficient in her work. One day as her two brothers were chopping bark from a tree with a corn knife, her youngest brother, Dan, chopped his finger. It was left dangling by a bit of skin. His parents took him by horse and buggy the seven miles to his sister's office. Without anesthesia, Katharina sewed his finger back together. It healed quickly and never bothered him again.

Finally, in the fall of 1906, Katharina's desire to serve as a medical missionary was realized. The place was India, the only Mennonite Brethren mission field at that time outside North America. At first the Mennonite Brethren had thought of beginning a mission in Africa, but the first missionaries sent there met with such tragic experiences that the idea of starting a mission field in Africa was given up. The conference turned instead to India as a possibility, for the Abram Friesen family from Russia were already ministering there, and the American Baptist mission field had been blessed by a large Telugu revival. The N. N. Hieberts, together with Elizabeth Neufeld, arrived in India in October, 1899. The Hieberts served one and one-half years before they returned to the United States because of ill health. They were followed by Rev. and Mrs. J. H. Pankratz in 1902. In 1903 Anna G. Suderman began the first medical missionary work under the Mennonite Brethren Conference. After years of service, she returned to the United States for a furlough.

In the fall of 1906 Katharina and Anna G. left for India and, after a long and tedious journey, arrived there in March, 1907. Katharina immediately plunged into language study. Because of her musical background and her knowledge of several languages,

Telugu was easy for her to learn. After language study came medical work at the Mulkapet Station from 1907 to 1909. When Katharina first began her service, she had no examination room or hospital, so all patients were examined and treated on the floors of missionary homes or in some room on the compound. On tours of the villages, the work was carried out in front of the missionary tent or trailer house. A Hindu woman after having been cured of a serious disease said, "Your God must be a very good God to send a doctor to us women; our gods have never yet sent us a woman."

The Mennonite Brethren mission area stretched from Hyderabad City on the north and eventually reached the Tungabadra River on the south, an area of 10,500 square miles. In 1909, Katharina left this area for Nagarkurnool, about 75 miles south. Here she went to the bazaar on Bazaar Day at the villages of Nagarkurnool and Bhijnapally, with her chest of medicine, dispensing it to those who asked for it, people who would not have come near her otherwise. Disease spreads rapidly in this tropical land with its congested, unsanitary living conditions. Skin diseases, sore eyes, scorpion stings, snake bites, malaria, bubonic plague, pneumonia, hookworm, smallpox, dysentery, cholera, tuberculosis, and many other ailments were common, as well as diseases resulting from poor nutrition. Katharina encountered many children with weak resistance to disease.

Life was difficult for the national Christians in India. Often their homes were destroyed while they were erecting them and they were driven from the village. As a medical missionary, Katharina was able to remove many barriers of fear, prejudice, and superstition in the mission field. Because more and more nationals came to her for treatment, especially for malaria, she asked the conference in America for a hospital to carry on her work. In 1912 the first hospital on the Mennonite Brethren mission field in India was completed at Nagarkurnool. The 38- by 15-foot building had three rooms with 16-foot ceilings, and two verandahs. The south verandah was closed ten feet from each end to provide the luxury of a bathroom and a small private room for patients. The medical work grew as people from long distances away, from various castes, and with various diseases gained confidence in Katharina. The hospital served 7,673 out-patients and 45 in-patients in the first year. In 1915 Katharina moved to the Hughestown station, a one and one-half-acre plot enclosed by a compound wall and with many factories in the immediate area. A cigarette factory was located directly across from the bungalow in which Katharina lived. As usual Katharina took a special interest in all her patients. Once she was brought a mental patient whom other doctors had given up. About six months later the patient left the compound fully restored to health. Malaria and a number of other illnesses were prevalent in this area, forcing Katharina and the other missionaries to leave this field. Years later, after conditions improved, Hughestown was served again by Mennonite Brethren missionaries.

As early as 1915 Katharina worked in Shamshabad, 12 miles south of Hughestown, but no enlarged plans for her work could be made since the government had not sanctioned it as a mission center. Mr. Ratnam, a native worker, had been stationed there since 1904, however, and Rev. H. H. Pankratz had served this area while residing in Mulkapet. One day a native preacher said the village headman of Shamshabad was willing to sell the missionaries his place, consisting of 34 acres located a mile from Shamshabad and 12 miles southwest of the city of Hyderabad. Early in 1914 the Hyderabad government had stipulated that mission stations should not be located near a mosque or Hindu temple because several Mohammedans who had heard the gospel at the Mulkapet Mission (which was near a Mohammedan community and mosque) had renounced the prophet Allah and accepted Christ as Savior. The government wanted to avoid this happening in the future. Pankratz made sure there was no Mohammedan prayer wall within one-half mile of this land. In 1920 the government granted permission for a mission station near Shamshabad, so Katharina and Anna Hanneman, coworkers in Hughestown, moved medical and educational work into temporary buildings erected for that purpose on the new station. At once Katharina established a dispensary at the new station as she had done in each of the other fields where she had worked. Her ministry opened the door of many a national's heart to the gospel.

Katharina's patients received loving care and the necessary medicines, and heard of the Great Physician who is able to heal the soul as well as the body. Through her patient teaching and practical demonstration, the health standard of the entire district was raised. Many superstitions concerning diets, medicine, and so forth were dispelled and many evil practices were abolished. The people came to realize the importance of having a clean water supply and an adequate sewage system.

Katharina took only two furloughs from her work in India. The first one was in 1914 and the second in 1923. When she left for her second furlough, her health was poor and became worse on her journey home. After prayer, she became somewhat better while in America. Katharina visited all her brothers and sisters, traveling throughout Canada and the United States. In Canada, illness overtook her again, and for 11 days relatives and friends gave up hope for her recovery. However, her work was not yet finished, and she recovered again. She keenly felt the need for a hospital at Shamshabad and made it a matter of special prayer. While Katharina resided in Hillsboro during her furlough, the women's mission class she was teaching accepted her vision for the hospital. They contacted interested sewing circles in and around Hillsboro and raised money for the building project.

Three years elapsed before Katharina returned to India for her third term. Friends questioned her whether she would not rather stay home. With tears in her eyes she answered, "My heart is in India and that is where I want to be in service for my Master." Katharina returned to India in 1926, and on December 14, 1927, she had the joy of moving into a newly built hospital consisting of six rooms and two anterooms. At its dedication on January 1, 1928, after she opened the doors, she said, "We have waited, hoped, and prayed for this occasion for a long time and the Lord has given this hospital to us. The Lord be praised for his provision and help." Then everyone knelt for prayer and thanked the Lord. That year, 1928, the first year the hospital was in operation, 8,519 patients were treated.

Dr. Schellenberg trained her own nurses and also made an attempt to train a national doctor, but he died of influenza before he finished his education. Then she started training another national worker, but he left her before he finished the course. The hospital work had its trying times. To train and keep her staff was difficult. Her compounder (a man trained to mix medicines) was faithful, but kept asking for higher wages to meet the demands of higher living costs. One nurse had to be dismissed because of bad behavior and another nurse was lazy and did as little as possible. Another left to get married soon after she was trained. One woman who was hired to do the cleaning didn't stay because she considered the work disgraceful. The matter of workers was no small thing, for higher wages were being offered in the city. The India caste system was also an obstacle to Katharina's work, for it did not allow persons to eat food prepared by a member of another caste; so one or more persons accompanied a patient to cook food over fires kindled among a few stones in the hospital compound. It was easier to care for the poor outcastes than for the high caste people, since the high caste rules often interfered with the orders for the patients. Many a prayer was made concerning such problems.

Katharina was the first on duty in the hospital in the morning and last to leave at night. Sometimes when her staff went on leave, she did their work also. Before retiring, she made the rounds to see that every patient was taken care of. Her staff could call her at any hour of the night if someone needed her help. At once she got into her car to pick up a patient or attend a confinement case. Often she worked seven long days each week, frequently doing the most menial tasks for the sick. She witnessed the deaths of many patients to whom she had shown the Way of Life. Several times when a malaria epidemic raged, she worked day and night to relieve the suffering. On another occasion a serious plague broke out in the villages. In spite of the dangers, Katharina went into the villages daily, vaccinating the people and helping wherever possible. When friends and fellow missionaries spoke to her about her indefatigable spirit and seemingly unlimited resources of physical strength, she answered humbly, her eyes filled with tears, "I have besought the Lord for this." She said she was conscious always of the presence in her body of an extra reserve of strength that carried her through times of special strain, and of a replenishing of this strength when it was depleted.

Missionaries and national coworkers were always refreshed by her fellowship and her humor. When she was around, she was the life of the party. Her comment about any portion of the Word and the frequency and freshness of her prayers revealed that communion with God was a living reality to her and the secret of her fruitful career. It was a practice in the hospital to begin each day with a devotional and prayer service. To help her with the spiritual work, Katharina engaged a full-time Bible woman, whose duty it was to speak to all patients about their salvation. Often on Sunday afternoons, Katharina refreshed her patients by singing for them and playing the autoharp. Although she had much work, she still found time to pray for and with her patients. She also taught a Bible class and did personal work.

She was endowed with a strong personality and in her character were blended firmness and tenderness. She bore a deep inner conviction of right and justice; all wrong and falsehood were an abomination to her. She expressed herself decisively when occasion required it. Once a national who was ill and weak came to the hospital, where he was given medicine and food. He was poor and seemed to have no friends or relatives, so he stayed a long time. He listened to the gospel but did not seem interested. As his health improved, he left the hospital for a half day or so to walk in the nearby jungle, he said. Though he smelled as if he had been drinking palm wine, when questioned he denied this. Since he had recovered physically, Katharina asked him to leave the hospital. He cried hard and did not want to go, but she remained firm. After he left, she continued to pray for him.

Katharina continued to work as hard in her later years as she had in her youth. Besides the medical work, she maintained her own household, supervised the girls boarding hostel of the school for five years, kept a fruit and flower garden, managed some farming, and raised turkeys, chickens, buffalos, and cows. Many of the patients who entered the hospital were malnourished, so Katharina denied herself the milk her cows produced and gave it and other produce she raised on her farm to them. Fellow missionaries frequently enjoyed Katharina's hospitality, for she had a way of making others feel at home with her. Her home and the work on her little farm gave her all the relaxation she needed. She took little time off. In May of 1936 she did permit herself the luxury of going to the hills during the hot season. The Mennonite Brethren Conference had bought a home in 1906 where missionaries could go for physical and spiritual refreshment. However, Katharina did not stay there. With Anna Hanneman and Katharine Reimer, she rented a cheaper place. They did their own housekeeping so they could eat and drink whatever they liked from the selection of meat, fruits, and vegetables in the area. She even went horseback riding into the mountains. Though she was 66, she missed few of the adventures there.

Though Katharina never married, she had the privilege of adopting a foster child, an eight-month-old infant named

Sunderraj, meaning "beautiful king." His mother had died when he was a small baby. An Indian doctor who took pity on the child asked Katharina to take him. Although her medical work kept her busy, she accepted the boy gladly into her home for a number of years. At age eight he could speak three languages: Telugu, Urdu, and English. Katharina continued to supply him with clothes and so forth even after he moved to the boarding school. He loved his doctor *Ama* and visited her often. Also, under God's providence, a number of the children of the missionaries proudly proclaimed Katharina's home as their birthplace. These children, too, visited her from time to time.

Because of Katharina's loving care many patients received relief, including those afflicted with eye diseases. Many blind people always stood begging by the wayside or wandering from village to village. The cause for so much eye trouble was rooted in lack of sanitation, carelessness, smoke in unventilated houses, dust, glare of the sun, and the many eyeflies which carried the infection from one to another. In addition, folk remedies caused much blindness. Once an oxcart with a number of people came to the hospital from a village a long way off. Among the people were four cases of sore eyes: two women, one little baby, and a girl. Someone had told them an eye doctor who had good medicine for sore eyes lived in their own village. Off they went to him. He put medicine into their eyes which made them burn and pain even more. In their agony they came to Katharina. She had to tell them their eyesight was gone.

On her 70th birthday, November 28, 1940, Katharina enjoyed a surprise celebration attended by many of the missionaries. The occasion refreshed her, for often she felt lonely after Anna Hanneman left, and sometimes a bit tired, too. She had been in India almost 15 years without a furlough. At this occasion, Katharina testified, "By the grace of God I am what I am" (1 Cor. 15:10).

Katharina wanted to continue in the work in India as long as she could be useful. Although advanced in years, she worked like a much younger person. During World War 2, she and Helen Warkentin served alone on the mission station for two years because of the unrest in the world.

During the Christmas season of 1944, Katharina attended the programs on the Shamshabad Station as well as at Hughestown.

On Christmas morning, she distributed gifts to her Indian coworkers and servants of the household, worshiped at the services in the church and brought a special Christmas offering at the close of the service. Then she invited her cousin and his wife, Rev. and Mrs. J. H. Lohrenz, to dinner that evening. After eating they walked to the village of Shamshabad to take part in the Christmas service held there. On December 27, Katharina accompanied other missionaries to a conference held at Mahbubnagar, about 45 miles south of Shamshabad, and took an active part in all the meetings. During the last years she had been hard of hearing so when she gave her testimony at the end of the conference she said that she hadn't understood all that had been said, but was thankful for what she had been able to hear. Then Katharina related the story of her conversion and how it had been evident to her at that time she should be a missionary. She told of her struggle to get medical training as a woman. On the way home the missionaries stopped at Jadcherla, near the center of the mission stations. This spot had been suggested as a suitable place for a central mission hospital. Katharina walked around the plot, deeply absorbed, as she planned for the expansion of the work so dear to her heart and pointed out to the others where each building would be situated.

During the conference, Katharina had expressed her readiness to accompany the Lohrenzes to America within a few months. However, she dreaded "closing off" and making preparations for leaving, and she said, "You see, things have accumulated, there is this and that to dispose of and I cannot see how I can ever get ready to go."

She was spared the trouble, for on December 31, 1944, after looking after a patient, she became ill but did not think it was serious. Mr. and Mrs. Lohrenz prayed for her and gave her some medicine which she had prescribed for herself. The next morning during the devotional period Katharina offered a short prayer. Her pain increased, and at eleven o'clock on January 1, 1945, she died.

Many people gathered for the funeral, January 2, 1945, in the church on the Shamshabad station and at the graveside service at the large cemetery in Hyderabad. At both places, her Indian brethren and fellow missionaries spoke highly of her years of service. She was buried in a teakwood coffin in the St. George Cemetery at Hyderabad. Her years of service from the fall of 1906 when she left for India to January 1, 1945, are best described by the inscription on her tombstone:

She lived for Christ
She served others
She sacrificed herself.

A fellow missionary, Anna Suderman, who had worked with her from 1938 to 1945 paid Katharina a fitting tribute: "Truly a Mother of Israel has passed from our midst."

Bibliography

Articles

"A Life Dedicated to God," *Mennonite Observer*, August 12, 1960.

Wiebe, John A. "Forever with the Lord — Doctor Katharina L. Schellenberg," *Harvest Field*, Nov.-Dec., 1944.

Berg, Nettie. "37 Years of Missionary Service in India," *Mennonite Observer*, August, 1960.

Pankratz, J. H., Ed. *Report of M.B. Missions for 1913*.

Schellenberg, D. L. "Schwester Katharina Lohrenz Schellenberg," *Zionsbote*, January 24, 1945.

Schellenberg, K. L. "Aus Indien," *Zionsbote*, January 3, 1945; "Diseases of India: Eyes and Their Diseases in India," *Harvest Field*, Jan.-Feb. 1940; Report, *Licht und Hoffnung*, VI Jahrgang, 1898.

Suderman, A. Report written January 1, 1945 but published in *Harvest Field* dated Nov.-Dec., 1944; "Sunderraj" (children's story), *Harvest Field*, Jan.-Feb., 1940.

Wiebe, Katie Funk. "The Life and Work of Dr. K. L. Schellenberg" (Missionary Program), *Youth Worker*, VI, 1959.

Books

Esau, Mrs. H. *First Sixty Years of M.B. Missions.* Hillsboro, Kan.: Mennonite Brethren Publishing House, 1954.

Foreign Missions, *India: The American Mennonite Brethren Mission in India 1898-1948.* Hillsboro, Kan.: Board of Foreign Missions of the Mennonite Brethren Church.

Peters, Gerhard Wilhelm. *The Growth of Foreign Missions in the M.B. Church.* Hillsboro, Kan.: Board of Foreign Missions of Mennonite Brethren Churches, 1947.

Wiebe, David V. *Grace Meadow.* Hillsboro, Kan.: Mennonite Brethren Publishing House, 1967.

Letters

Lohrenz, Mrs. J. H., to Sewing Circle, January 24, 1941.

Lohrenz, J. H. and Mrs., on "Homegoing of Katharina L. Schellenberg."

Schellenberg, Abraham and Katharina, in Tiegerweide, South Russia, to Mr. and Mrs. Peter Lohrenz, Halstead, Kan.

Schellenberg, Katharina, to Mrs. P. P. Regier

Schellenberg, Katharina, and Anna Hanneman to Sewing Circles

Suderman, Anna, to Katie Funk Wiebe, 1979

Interviews with Regina Suderman, Dan Schellenberg, J. B. Toews and Maria Regier (the latter by Katie Funk Wiebe)

Wirsche, Dora Schellenberg. Biography of Dr. K. L. Schellenberg with notes attached by George Franz regarding Katharina's suitor. Unpublished manuscript.

Ebel, Esther (Mrs. A. R.). "Life Story of Dr. Katharina Schellenberg." Unpublished manuscript.

Magdalena Hergert Becker, the "kind white mother," spent 37 years as a pioneer missionary to the Comanche Indians in Oklahoma. For 28 of those years, she also served as United States Field Matron. Her enriched service won her the love and respect of Indians and white people. When she died, many people sorrowed, including her six children and husband, for "mother" was gone.

8

MOTHER TO THE COMANCHES

Magdalena Hergert Becker (1878-1938)

By Luetta Reimer

Through the dark cold night two figures scurried towards the house. The man carried a lantern slightly ahead of the woman, who clutched a dark bundle to her bosom. Inside, he hurriedly put wood in the stove while she whispered, "She's alive, she's still alive!"

The little Indian girl, left for dead by her grieving family, was indeed alive, but after three days of patient and loving care, she died, in the arms of the reservation's white mother, Magdalena Becker.

Almost immediately, preparations began for the child's funeral. Mr. Becker went out to his small shop and built a tiny wooden casket. His wife took the child to a small room attached to the church, where she prepared the body for burial. Then she helped her husband pad the coffin, lining it with soft white cloth. She worked late into the night, beautifying the little box with a border of fringe. Even while she worked the Indians' mourning could be heard — a haunting wail that seemed to express the depth of their loss.

Magdalena rose early the next morning to meet the relatives and friends of the little girl and to comfort them with assurances of God's love and eternal life. Some of the Indians believed in Jesus, and shared their confidence with the others. But many found it hard to give up their old customs and fears. When the Beckers first came to serve the Comanches at Post Oak Mission in Oklahoma, they saw rows of scars on the arms of some of the older men. They soon learned that these men had served as chief mourners in an earlier day when the custom was to slash one's arms with knives in a ritualistic identification with the dead.

But the Indians who brought their dead to Post Oak had given up such practices. They sat weeping while Becker reassured them of God's love, and wept again as they viewed the body. Finally the time for tears was past. As was their custom, members of the immediate family dried each other's tears. Each became instantly silent, and the mourners moved to the cemetery. As the coffin was lowered into the grave, several of the Indian women took off their beautiful shawls and draped them over the box. This custom, handed down for generations, was a token of love and respect for the dead.

The Indian women were willing to give sacrificially to honor the dead, but Magdalena Becker gave sacrificially to help the living. She found that ministering to the Indians during their times of deepest suffering and need was the most effective means of showing them her love. During her 37 years of service to the Indians, she participated in more than six hundred funerals or burials. Usually her role was multiple: she helped prepare the coffin, she washed and prepared the body for burial, and most importantly, she consoled the bereaved.

Magdalena Becker was a woman of seemingly boundless energy. She was a large woman, and strong. And every bit of her strength was needed, for pioneering in Indian territory was no easy life. In 1901 when Abraham J. and Magdalena Becker answered the call of the Mennonite Brethren Mission Board to the Post Oak Mission near Indiahoma, Oklahoma, Magdalena had little idea of the task ahead of her. With her husband and two small sons, she set out in a covered wagon for a lifetime of adventure and challenge. But there were plenty causes for discouragement.

Establishing a home out in the wild southwest meant that her children would miss out on much of the community life she had known as a child in Ebenfeld, Kansas. She and her husband would miss the fellowship of friends and family. However, Magdalena had felt God's call to be a missionary early in her life; and if he wanted her to go to the Comanches, she would go — with enthusiasm.

It must have been this hopeful confidence which helped the Beckers through the first discouraging years at Post Oak. "Discouraging" is hardly an adequate word for describing those early years, for, from the establishment of the mission in 1894 until 1906, not one of the Indians had found the grace to fully and openly live a Christian life. There had been no baptisms and no spiritual leadership developing from among the Indians. The Henry Kohfelds with whom the Beckers worked were leaving the mission. The Beckers had every reason to be disheartened and to question whether in fact God wanted them at Post Oak.

A major barrier to reaching the Indians was language. The Beckers knew little Comanche, and the Comanches knew little English. Few interpreters were available, and all were unwilling. A young man named Herman Asenap worked as an interpreter for the government in dealings with the Indians, but he stubbornly refused to interpret for Becker, even when offered good wages for his work.

Magdalena and Abraham prayed and fasted about this need for a trustworthy interpreter. With their coworkers, they had tried a variety of methods to reach the Indians, but now they were alone on the field. Between themselves, they decided that if they could not secure an Indian to work in this capacity, they would have to give up the work at Post Oak.

Sunday morning arrived and there was no interpreter, despite weeks of earnest prayer and inquiring.

"Do you really think God would have brought us here, just to have us give up in frustration?"

"I don't know, Magdalena, I just don't know."

"But we've given five years of our lives to these people. We can't give up now. Surely someone will come."

"But when? Perhaps this field is not ripe for the harvest. Perhaps the Lord plans to send us to China or India."

A knock at the door interrupted their conversation, and

Becker opened it to see a haggard Herman Asenap, government interpreter.

"I could not sleep last night. I know you need an interpreter so I have come. I will do it for you whenever you need me, and without pay."

Another affirmation of God's work at Post Oak occurred soon after during one of the annual stays of Indians at the Government Indian Payment Camp. Every year Comanches from all over the territory camped at "Pe-se-nad-ama" to receive government allotments for the use of their land. The name of the camp, translated "Rotten Village," aptly describes the drunkenness and frivolous spending which characterized this month-long payday.

Since the camp was located only about eight miles from Post Oak, the Beckers packed up supplies and followed the Indians, setting up a tent for evening gospel meetings. But interest was low, and there was no response to the call of Christ.

Magdalena had left three small boys at home at Post Oak. She had to cook on open fires and sleep on the ground in a tent. Camping at Pesenadama was physically and emotionally exhausting. Finally, one day she quit trying to restrain her emotions, and went into the woods near the camp to cry.

"Why are you crying?" asked the curious Indian woman who had quietly followed her.

Surprised by the question, Magdalena spoke from her heart.

"I'm crying because you Indians do not care to accept Jesus. He would save you and you could go to heaven, but you just don't care."

The Psalmist says that "he that goeth forth and weepeth, bearing precious seed, shall doubtless come again with rejoicing bringing his sheaves with him." Magdalena Becker surely knew the verse — she and her husband had often encouraged each other with biblical promises — but she certainly did not expect the dramatic fulfillment of the promise which occurred that very night at the tent service.

It had been a simple meeting, with Becker sharing the story of Christ so clearly that a child could understand. Herman Asenap interpreted almost routinely, the message being the same one he had heard and translated each night. Magdalena sat near the front silently praying for evidence of God's power. But when the missionary invited the Indians to come forward for prayer,

Magdalena was overcome with praise and rejoicing, for there by the altar knelt a large group of Indians!

One or two persons accepted Christ and were baptized each day from that evening on until the end of camp. God's promise had been fulfilled. The church at Post Oak had been born!

The Comanches had little reason to trust the white man, whom they saw as trying to take over their lands and destroy their ancestral way of life. Why should this white man and woman be any different? The Beckers soon learned to expect threats of violence and general hostility from the Indians. Gradually, some individuals and family groups began to trust them, but it took many deeds of love and kindness to convince them of their good will. If the mission at Post Oak was to grow, the Beckers would need a more effective way of communicating their concern to the Indians.

So when Magdalena Becker heard that the United States Government was looking for a woman to serve as field matron to the Comanches, she recognized the opportunity as God's provision. Not only would the work give her a chance to meet and serve the Indians, but the small salary would also help her save for her children's education — always a high priority with Magdalena.

After passing the Civil Service exam, Magdalena was officially assigned field matron of the area. The mission board was not opposed because the job was only a half-time assignment and, of course, they realized the financial need of the family. Had they foreseen how beautifully Magdalena would be able to dovetail her two jobs, they might have even suggested it.

As field matron, Magdalena had a host of responsibilities. Much of the work involved keeping records. Land ownership, rental contracts with white farmers, government allotments, Department of the Interior transactions with the Indians — all had to be carefully and accurately recorded. It was not a simple task to document land ownership. Often an Indian had married more than one wife, or divorced and remarried, with no legal filing of the proceedings. Then which son would inherit the land upon the father's death? It was a challenge for Magdalena to sort through family histories and create a kind of order.

Each month when checks were ready to be delivered to the Indians, Magdalena hitched up the buggy and horses the government provided, and made the rounds of the area. Usually she took one of her young sons along to hop down and open gates along the way or water the horses while she went inside homes to do business.

At first the Indians were indifferent and even suspicious towards Magdalena, but they soon welcomed her visits almost as much as their checks. They found that she had a wealth of wisdom on many subjects, and they often asked her for advice. In later years, she was well known as a peacemaker. Families were united and scandals avoided because of her unusual ability to mediate between persons with disagreements. More than once she found runaway children, and helped them make peace with their families. She knew that caring for the Indians' physical and social needs was the best way to get them to listen to the answer to their spiritual needs.

Magdalena became especially concerned about sickness among the Indians. Their ignorance and lack of medicine were largely responsible for the tribe's dwindling to less than two thousand persons by the time the Beckers came to the territory. At first Magdalena taught them simple first aid and hygiene. Then she persuaded officials at the Indian Hospital at Fort Sill to give her a small supply of medicines to keep at the mission for emergencies. The Comanches recognized their helplessness against illness, and before long they brought their sick to the mission, to the white mother, Magdalena Becker.

One night the Beckers were awakened by a pounding on the door. Mr. Becker peered out into the night to see a small boy, maybe six or seven years old, frightened and shivering.

"Come, please, Mrs. Becker. My mama is sick bad! Please come now!"

Magdalena recognized the boy. But his family lived a good three miles away.

"How did you get here?" she asked.

"I run, I run very fast. Please come!"

So while Mr. Becker hitched up the horses, Magdalena dressed and gathered up a few basic supplies and set out with the boy, quiet now but wide-eyed.

The Becker children, unaware of the night's events, awakened the next morning to see their mother approaching in the wagon, accompanied by five small children and their very sick mother wrapped in blankets. For occasions such as these,

Abraham had built a small "hospital" at the mission. Here Magdalena deposited the family and rushed to prepare breakfast for her own family and her "guests."

When a mother was too ill to be left alone, Magdalena brought the entire family to the mission. That way she could see that the woman received regular attention and medication, and that the children would not be left to fend for themselves. She was always concerned about the family unit, and often worked hard to keep that unit intact. During these periods of illness, it meant feeding and dressing the children for school, and watching the younger children during the day.

Because of Magdalena's faithful nursing, the Indian people eventually trusted white doctors and hospitals too. Although the medicine men were outraged, many Comanches recognized the superiority of medication over dances, incantations, and wild herbs.

Magdalena's role often took her away from her family, but her children loved her deeply, and never seemed to feel the resentment some missionary children experience. She wisely planned times just for the immediate family. There was virtually no social life or recreational facilities for the Beckers' six children, so the family had to meet their own needs in those areas. Often the whole gang piled into the wagon with a picnic lunch and rode to the nearby Wichita Mountains to climb or simply be together away from the mission and its demands.

At home, togetherness was built by shared responsibility. The boys loved to help their father, an expert builder, with work outside. But since there were five sons and only one daughter, the Beckers decided that each week one son should be assigned to help his mother in the house. As the sons rotated through the household assignment, they learned domestic skills like cooking and cleaning, but more importantly, they grew to appreciate their mother.

How could one woman do so much and never complain? She never screamed at her children in frustration or anger, yet they respected her word and hated to disappoint her. Her calm disposition reflected her inner strength and reliance on God. The children were inspired by her great expectations for them. Magdalena's chief concern for each of her children was that he or she should trust God and serve him. But she wanted them to be well-equipped for such service, so education was important. All her children eventually went to college, and when the older children graduated and began working, they helped support the younger ones still in school. While they were little children, they learned the joy of sharing whatever they had with others, and this became a pattern for a lifetime.

On Sundays at Post Oak, sharing took on special significance. The Indians came for services on horseback or in wagons, and later by truck or school bus. Each family brought enough food for themselves plus a little extra for guests. Then, after the morning preaching, they gathered under an arbor to share their lunch and fellowship. Mr. Becker custom-made a table and benches for each family, big enough for that family and a few guests. In the afternoon the family attended Sunday school classes and enjoyed the singing services, especially after Magdalena helped translate some of the favorite hymns into Comanche.

Almost every Sunday brought white visitors from Mennonite Brethren churches in Corn or Fairview, or Baptist friends from Lawton. These people, often unexpected, ate with the Beckers in their home. Occasionally Magdalena was asked how she always managed to have enough food for the guests on Sunday.

"Oh, we have a family code system," she answered with a twinkle in her eye. "If there's barely enough food I say 'F.H.B.' which means 'Family Hold Back!' And if there's plenty to spare I say 'M.I.K.' and they know there's 'More in the Kitchen!' "

While the family often heard her tell this story, none can remember her ever actually using the code. The children were just as amazed as everyone else that there was always enough food.

A sense of humor was one means of releasing tension for Magdalena. Another was music. She often sang while she worked. In times of stress, she sat down at the piano and played and sang. The children learned to interpret her moods and her concerns by the songs she chose. One of her favorites was "Does Jesus Care?" The affirmation at the end of the song expresses her lifelong attitude of hopeful confidence — "Oh yes, he cares, I know he cares!"

As a mother in her home, and as field matron to the Comanches, Magdalena Becker was an embodiment of Christ's care. Her love for people was genuine, and the Indians never sensed any condescension in her attitude towards them. She organized sewing, cooking, and flower clubs for the Indian women, and personally enjoyed their fellowship. The women were pleased to learn how to quilt and how to preserve fruits and vegetables for the long winters. Their favorite was the flower club, where they learned to make flowers from tissue paper to beautify their homes, but especially to decorate the graves in the Post Oak cemetery.

During her later years at the mission, Magdalena developed a tremendous burden for the many Mexican-Americans living in the area. Some of them had been attending services at Post Oak, but it soon became evident that they would need their own church. One intelligent young man named Salvador Rivera, accepted Christ at the mission and began to share Magdalena's concern for his people. Through the years Salvador became like a son to the Beckers, and he, in turn, called them his parents. After living in the Becker home and receiving much spiritual nurture from this Christian family, he went to Mexican Baptist Theological Seminary in San Antonio for more training. One of Magdalena's greatest joys was seeing a Mexican mission established in nearby Lawton with Salvador as missionary assistant.

Magdalena always gave God the credit for whatever was accomplished through her life. Yet she was eager to do her part to make her faith become reality. In Lawton, for instance, the Mexican Christians were ready to begin a church if only there were land on which to build. The Beckers circulated a petition to gain approval, and then Magdalena herself appeared before the city council to request a parcel of city land on which to build a nondenominational mission. Her presentation was obviously persuasive, for her wish was granted in spite of heavy opposition from local Catholic groups.

Magdalena simply did what needed to be done and what came naturally to her. She was freed to serve God because she recognized and accepted the gifts he had given her. She was courageous in circumstances that would have made many a man cower, and she was optimistic in situations that would have left many dejected.

Magdalena Becker served at Post Oak with her husband for 37 years, and as a U.S. field matron for 28 of those years. During that time hundreds of lives were touched by her love and by the love of God through her. One Lawton minister remarked that the love of God "radiated from her face — from her life" as completely and beautifully as he had ever observed.

It was that love which motivated a small band of Indians to meet quietly outside the Chickasha Hospital to pray. Inside, their white mother Magdalena Becker was very ill. Sensing she might not recover, groups of devoted Indians came every day to express their love with a brief visit or a gift. Magdalena Becker died on July 7, 1938, surrounded by her husband, her six children, her sister, and a brother. Her last thoughts were not of herself, but of her children. Like the Apostle John in his second epistle, she had no greater joy than to hear that her children "walked in truth."

Her "children" included not only her biological offspring, but also all those who had come to love her as "mother" at Post Oak. The Indians had always placed a high value on funeral ceremonies, but none had ever witnessed a funeral like Magdalena Becker's. Indians came, some with tents, from miles around. Mexican Christians came from three churches birthed by Post Oak. And white people came from many churches throughout Kansas and Oklahoma. Local newspapers recorded that over twelve hundred persons attended the funeral, which began in the morning with an Indian testimony service.

Herman Asenap, who had interpreted for the Beckers for 24 years before accepting Christ himself, reflected on the early years at Post Oak: "Us Indians didn't know nothing about Christ. We didn't care to hear nothing about Christ. We didn't care nothing about it. You see today what Mrs. Becker has done. I want to say more but my heart feels so heavy. We Indians, we loved her. She was just like a mother to us. She not only tried to build our character — she tried to build up our spiritual life too. We Indians, dear friends, we feel like Mrs. Becker is one of our Indian people. We love her sincerely."

An Indian blanket was draped over Magdalena Becker's coffin as it was carried to Post Oak Mission cemetery for burial. But in the hearts and minds of hundreds, her spirit continued to live and work. Many Indian families have told the story of this kind white mother from one generation to the next.

The inscription on her gravestone is a beautifully accurate description of Magdalena Becker's life:

> Who at all times and every place gave her strength to the weak, her sympathy to the suffering, her substance to the poor, and her heart to God.

Elizabeth Pauls Wiebe was another of those women whose heart was large enough to love each child who came to her, regardless of race, in addition to her own family. She and her husband were the first Mennonite missionaries to the black people in the South. A number of black Mennonite Brethren churches in North Carolina are the fruit of this early ministry there.

9

AFAR, IN THE BLUE RIDGE MOUNTAINS

Elizabeth (Lizzie) Pauls Wiebe (1876-1957)

By Connie Wiebe Isaac

"Going afar, upon the mountain, bringing the wanderer back again. . . ." The old familiar gospel hymn echoed through the wooden farmhouse, but was lost on the Kansas wind outside.

"Into the fold, of my Redeemer, Jesus the Lamb for sinners slain." The song paused temporarily.

Elizabeth was thinking about Elk Park again, to the time when she and Henry had gone "afar" to North Carolina to their "mountain" in the tree-covered Blue Ridge Mountains for almost eight years. They had brought "into the fold" some black children and young people who later became Mennonites.

"Seek out the lost and point them to Jesus. . . ." Elizabeth had good reason to indulge in reverie. She and her husband had done a courageous thing in working with "colored" people at the turn of the century in the first mission of Mennonites to blacks in the South.

What kind of woman would go with her husband into a hotbed of racial controversy? Someone consumed with activist zeal? Perhaps, but with Elizabeth's rural Mennonite upbringing her motives could hardly have been political. Her life's mainspring was a genuine love for all people, oiled with a dash of daring.

Elizabeth was born March 27, 1876, in South Russia to Bernhard and Maria Peters Pauls. Five older brothers and sisters greeted and spoiled her a little before she was joined by a younger brother and sister. That year the Pauls family joined a group of 21 families from Chortitza colony who planned to migrate to America. Having been influenced by the Baptists, the members of this group were fairly progressive in dress and education. Though most were landowners, their strong convictions about religious freedom compelled them to leave the good life for the rigors of pioneering on the Kansas plains.

The group headed for Ebenfeld, site of the first Mennonite Brethren church in North America. The Ebenfeld body which had recently arrived, was notoriously known for the sister-kiss and their "joyous" influences. Because the Paulses and most of their group felt uncomfortable with the Ebenfeld practices, they looked for another location and found it 120 miles away on land offered by the Missouri-Pacific Railroad, 12 miles northwest of Yates Center, Kansas.

When Elizabeth was about seven, her family moved to Lehigh, Kansas, where a number of Mennonite Brethren were congregating. Here her father opened a hardware store; and in 1884 he became the town's first mayor. As a child Elizabeth was given the diminutive "Lizzie" which she adopted all her life. At an early age she accepted Christ as Savior, and was baptized and accepted into the Lehigh Mennonite Brethren Church. As a teenager she left home to work for a Pettit family as a domestic servant. This brief exposure to life outside the Mennonite community broadened her knowledge of American life and language.

On June 16, 1898 Lizzie became the bride of Henry V. Wiebe, oldest child of minister P. A. Wiebe of the Springfield community, about five miles south of Lehigh. She was 22, and he, 27 years old.

Henry had migrated from Russia when he was three, so his entire youth, as the oldest child in a family of ten, had been devoted to helping his parents turn the virginal prairie into a productive farm. Despite the demands by the parental home, Henry managed to obtain an education. In the late 1800s higher education was looked upon with apprehension by Krimmer Mennonite Brethren parents. Young Henry had the advantage of having a first cousin from the neighboring farm as a role model, whom his father watched with interest. Cousin C. H. Wedel, who later became the first president of Bethel College in North Newton, Kansas, was 11 years older than Henry and broke many educational barriers for him. Henry was permitted to attend the preparatory school in Lehigh, where he boarded at the home of Lizzie's older sister. In his early twenties he attended McPherson College. Then, while his friends paired off in marriage, he continued to pursue education, graduating from Bethel College with a theology degree.

Henry's spiritual development coincided with his educational advancement. At 19 he was converted and asked for baptism by immersion in the cold of December. He accepted the covenant of faith and lifestyle of the Krimmer Mennonite Brethren Church and soon felt the call to mission work. After graduation from Bethel College, he was ready to share his life with a wife who shared his mission vision.

Lizzie was that person. But she didn't have the conservative "Krimmer" affiliation. Some of the marriageable young ladies in Henry's church fumed that he felt the need to go elsewhere for a wife. In retrospect, Lizzie found it amusing that one of the Krimmer Mennonite Brethren young ladies would not speak to her until she herself was finally married.

After their marriage Lizzie joined the Krimmer Mennonite Brethren Church at Springfield, and they were ready to become full-time Christian workers. But where should they go? Henry's younger brother Peter came home full of stories of his work in the Appalachian Mountains. He told of a field opening on the North Carolina border. Miss Emily Pruden, who was building segregated schools, had sent out a call for Christian teachers for schools for the Negro children, to be supported by their own church constituency. The newlyweds were willing to go to North Carolina but had to wait 18 months before the KMB Conference agreed to support and send them.

Several factors led to the slow response. Only a quarter century had elapsed since the group had settled on the open prairie of Kansas. Having met as a group of churches for the first time only in 1879, the conference — culturally distinct from American life in such things as dress and language — was struggling for a clear sense of mission. The members had managed to translate into action important spiritual concerns, such as an orphanage near Hillsboro and evangelization among the Hutterites — but such ministries were conducted in German. Teaching Negroes in the South in English was a revolutionary idea.

As the young couple "waited upon the Lord," Henry tutored at Bethel College. Following true Mennonite custom, Lizzie proudly presented Henry with a son after little more than nine months of marriage.

On an unusual date, New Year's Day 1900, they were both ordained to missionary work. In February Henry, Lizzie, and baby Bernard left for Elk Park, North Carolina, via Chicago and Flat Lick, Kentucky. They had never been far outside their home community before. These two stops enroute were their only preparation for the culture shock ahead. As they approached the South, they noticed obvious segregation: unlike the blacks they had no trouble finding night lodging, food, or restrooms.

That spring they spent enough time in Flat Lick, Kentucky, to gain the confidence of some of the poor people. They also soon encountered some very practical aspects of missionary life. Two white women, unable to care for their children, asked Lizzie to take their little girls with her. Lizzie agreed readily. The next summer she took the two girls to Kansas, where they were placed in permanent homes.

By late spring the enlarged family reached its destination in Elk Park, North Carolina. Lizzie was eager to unpack and settle into their new home. From the descriptions in Miss Pruden's letters, Lizzie had envisioned the mission house, which had been built on a hillside overlooking the community, as quite grand. She anticipated being "mistress of the hall." But as the Wiebes approached the site, their high hopes were dashed by reality — a white family was already living in the house.

What had happened? When the townspeople had learned that the beautiful building being erected by Miss Pruden was to house a white family engaged to teach blacks and that blacks might reside within its walls, hatred and jealousy overcame benevolent plans. The hostility frightened the first occupants away, and Miss Pruden despaired of finding teachers willing to take over under such threats. She had, therefore, leased the place to a white family and planned to place the Wiebes elsewhere, at least temporarily, hoping Elk Park community tempers would cool.

Miss Pruden suggested the Wiebes establish a summer school in the valley near Hudson, about seven miles from Lenoir. After becoming acquainted with the rural people, Lizzie and Henry opened a school in which they taught Bible and other subjects on weekdays and conducted a Sunday school and worship service on Sundays. Somehow Henry's calm, dignified manner of preaching was accepted by the usually exuberant blacks; of the services Lizzie said simply, "The work was blessed."

After some weeks of teaching Henry became ill. At first Lizzie relieved him in the schoolroom for part of the day to keep the school functioning while he rested at home. In time, she realized his illness was too serious for her to handle alone. Neighbors rumored he might have malaria. Her fears increased when she learned that the nearest doctor was miles away.

How could she get there? Vainly she wished for a horse from her father's stable in Kansas! Instead, she located a donkey. Though she was in the first trimester of pregnancy, she knew she must go for help. On the five-mile ride through the mountains the lazy animal stopped periodically to graze at the roadside. In spite of her prodding, she had to dismount repeatedly, pull the animal back onto the road, remount the broken saddle, and proceed again.

She finally reached the doctor, and from her description of Henry's symptoms, he confirmed the illness as malaria. She immediately started for home, the precious package of medicine he had given her like a spur in her side. She reached Henry in the evening, worn out, having been on the road ten hours. The malaria recurred, but with medical aid Henry finished the summer-school term.

By late summer Miss Pruden's building was available for the Wiebes. They hired a team of horses and a covered wagon to carry them across the Blue Ridge Mountains to Elk Park just inside the Tennessee-North Carolina border. The journey of 35 miles as the crow flies stretched to a 60-mile winding climb of several thousand feet. On the two-day trip, Lizzie, baby Bernard, and the two girls rode in the covered wagon while Henry walked most of the way to lighten the load.

The long-awaited home in Elk Park was a magnificent three-story building situated on eight acres of native flowers and white pine trees and overlooking the community they would serve, a coal-mining town cut out of the beautiful Appalachian Mountains at almost five thousand feet.

Though outward appearances were serene, ingrained hatreds and prejudices brewed, ready to surface, in the town where many blacks had settled to work in the white-owned mines. The Civil War was recent enough that nearly all black adults over age 35 had been born into slavery. Because of the large Negro population, whites feared that if the "coloreds" bettered themselves, they would lose control. They would have tolerated, but not encouraged a black teacher to instruct his own people; whites and blacks, however, were strictly segregated.

In spite of the community's repressive conventions, Lizzie and Henry opened their school for Negro children in September, 1900. Henry had found an empty building across the bridge and down the road a short distance from the mission house suitable for a schoolhouse. Sometime after Henry had left the house for the second day of school, Lizzie found a slip of paper on their small front porch. She read these threatening words:

> We the citizens of Elk Park will not allow for a white man to stoop so low as to teach the niggars, they have enough of their own color to teach them. Your time is up! After this day.

She retreated inside carrying the note, her heart crying, "Is this what our call from God has brought us into?" Alone and apprehensive, she waited for Henry's arrival for lunch, if indeed he would come home safely. When her husband entered the door, she gave him the slip. They prayed about the matter and then resumed their work.

The note was only the beginning of several years of harrassment. Though neither Lizzie nor Henry were ever actually hurt, he endured name-calling and dodged rocks aimed at him as he walked to and from school. Things could have been worse, for other white teachers of black children had their houses set ablaze or torn down, their wells contaminated with manure, and were faced by a boycott in grocery stores.

Lizzie learned how carefully God was watching over them.

After several months a black man said to her, "You see dis here gun? I keeps it and I watch wid it over your man all dis time since you come to dis here minin' town. Now don't tell the Rev'rend cause I knows he ain't got a mind fo guns, but I jes want you to know, I been watchin'." Lizzie looked in his eyes and, knowing he would have used the weapon to protect her husband, thanked God for preventing that use. Had the Negro used the gun on a white man the consequences to himself, his black brothers, and to the whole mission would have been disastrous.

The parents of the black pupils appreciated the fine teacher their children had. Having learned discipline by means of harsh physical punishment themselves, many parents said to Henry, "Now if my chile acts up, you just give him a whippin'." However, Lizzie and Henry felt that lovingkindness was more successful than the rod, and were gratified that parents soon agreed.

The women of the area loved Lizzie. One day that first winter an older woman, a former slave, showed Lizzie her souvenirs — ugly scars across her back from beatings. "Missus, dis what I git fo' crying' when they sol' my chil'un." As Charity relived the grief of her young children being sold and taken from her, Lizzie determined to remember the incident. If the child she was carrying would be a girl, she would name her Sara after Henry's mother and Charity after the former slave.

Meanwhile, the young white mother had to make the important decision of who, in lieu of a Mennonite midwife, would assist in delivering the baby. She decided to call Mrs. Carson, a black midwife popular among her people, who lived in the country. Mrs. Carson came to the fine white house, but barely in time — she had been delivering another baby at a neighbor's. Lizzie's wish for a girl named Sara Charity was realized. Over the next few years Mrs. Carson delivered two more of Lizzie's children.

Toward the end of the first year there was some hesitancy on the part of the Wiebes and the Krimmer Mennonite Brethren Conference concerning their work. In spring they were called home with the intention of sending them to a different field. But while they were in Kansas a petition arrived from Elk Park requesting them to come back to the work they had started. How could they refuse? After touring the conference to raise support for the work, they returned to North Carolina.

The school increased during the second year and became too

large for one teacher. Lizzie felt she had to take over the first three grades herself. She placed Sara Charity in the care of "Aunt" Betty, a black woman who lived nearby, and took young Bernard with her to the schoolhouse. From the age of three until he was old enough to be a pupil, he was a steady visitor in her classroom.

The Wiebes' gospel work also expanded the second year. In addition to Sunday worship service and Sunday school, they began Young People's Meetings every Sunday afternoon. Lizzie was the force behind these meetings. She taught the young people many songs and helped them organize trios and quartets. "Going Afar, Upon the Mountain" was one of her favorite gospel hymns. Once a group which wanted to perform that number was stumped because no bass singer was available to sing the melody which was in the bass part throughout the chorus. Lizzie solved the problem by singing the bass herself, an octave higher.

As if morning and afternoon services were not enough, every Sunday evening Lizzie and Henry held meetings alternately in the hamlets of Shell Creek and On Elk. They walked four miles to both places. Sometimes late Sunday night, after the children and Henry had gone to bed, Lizzie would sit alone in the dark in her chair. Only then did she acknowledge to herself she was weary.

One night when refreshing sleep was essential, she was awakened with a start by something that sounded like a cross between an explosion and a gun going off in the next room. "*Heinrich! Was war das?* (Henry! What was that?)" Only the German language could communicate at such a moment! They jumped out of bed, shivering. Below their second-story window they saw shadowy figures moving around. Suddenly a streak of fire whizzed through the air toward them and exploded against the house. Someone was trying to scare them away by bombarding their home with giant firecrackers. They soon knew the racket was harmless noise. But what would the gang of whites think of next? Was the worst yet to come? Lizzie hurried to quiet the children while Henry calmed himself in prayer.

One of the reasons for the continued harassment was that the Wiebes had started housing homeless black children in their home. The first one had arrived shortly after they had returned from Kansas. A 12-year-old boy had begged to stay with them. Lizzie could see that this sick, poorly dressed boy wouldn't live much longer without help. When she found out he was homeless, she felt that even though the consequences were unknown and possibly enormous, they must take the boy into their home. They fed him and nursed him back to robust health. Lizzie remembered all her life that he had said after a few days, "Ain't dis a nise place? I kin have all the oatmeal I wants."

Once they had taken in a child, the word spread. Before long Lizzie answered a timid knock at the door to find another child asking for shelter. Realizing she was starting a trend she might not be able to handle, the Wiebes wrote their sponsoring board for advice. As she waited for response, Lizzie knew she really couldn't consider turning any child away. She was relieved when the board affirmed their new ministry.

The animosity of local whites toward the young Krimmer Mennonite Brethren workers climaxed early in the third year. One evening when Henry was quietly reading the *Wahrheitsfreund* (the conference periodical), he heard noises outside. Lizzie came into the room as a voice called, "Wiebe, come outside! There's someone here who wants to see you!" Then more insistently, "Come on out, Wiebe; I want to talk with you." They couldn't tell how many others were waiting with the man. They recognized the speaker, and from his reputation surmised he had no good intentions.

Lizzie and Henry stood looking at each other, her usually confident eyes now pleading, "Don't go — not this time!" For Lizzie the clock stopped while she tried to make sense of the present in view of past promises and prayers. Time began again as her gentle husband slowly sank down into the chair.

After the harrassers had left, the incident seemed like a bad dream; and Lizzie wondered if she had been silly. Maybe she had just made Henry look cowardly. But in the morning she felt reassured. As they walked together across their front porch and descended the long flight of stairs down the little embankment in front of the house, they saw a pile of fist-sized rocks on the lower steps where the man had called and waited for Henry the night before. If he had gone out, he would have been trapped on the steep steps. That event was the last serious one.

As the work progressed, more workers were needed, so in 1903 the conference sent Rev. and Mrs. Jacob M. Tschetter to Elk Park. Lizzie continued teaching school and leading the youth work, but now she had a friend with whom to share the housekeeping chores of the growing orphanage. Lizzie kept responsibility for the sewing needs while Mrs. Tschetter took charge of the housework and cooking. She got a speedy initiation into orphanage affairs. She prided herself on being a good cook and once needed cream for a special recipe. When Mrs. Tschetter couldn't find any, Lizzie laughed to herself, brought her a bucketful of ordinary water, and said, "*Dies ist unsere Sahne!* (This is our cream!)"

The Wiebes acted as houseparents on the second floor for the girls and the Tschetters slept on the third floor, which also housed the boys. Mr. Tschetter supervised the boys' barn and fieldwork during the day while Henry continued as the upper-grades teacher at the schoolhouse and community spiritual leader. The Tschetters brought preschool children with them, but left their oldest child with grandparents in South Dakota. The Wiebes and the Tschetters learned to know each other as few friends do. They ate together every day for five years!

As the mission expanded the big white house was enlarged to double its size to include a good-sized chapel and living quarters for the two families and the orphans. A neatly lettered sign, "Salem Mission and Academy," hanging over the bay window, identified the buildings.

With the enlargement they were able to accept a maximum of 20 orphans ranging in age from three to 12. They kept them until they were 16 or 18. The Moore children were an example of the waifs they gathered in. Henry found them in the mountain living with an uncle, who motioned to a small exhausted patch of corn, indicating their sole source of food was spent. Most Negroes sent their children to the mill with little sacks of corn to be ground into meal for cornbread. Like many in the area, Zinny, Lilly, and Gaither Moore had had only cornbread and buttermilk to eat; so they, as well as the other children, enjoyed the good Mennonite cooking at the home. The large vegetable garden provided work for the orphans during the summer and yielded sufficient vegetables for table use throughout the year at a time when money was scarce.

Lizzie often chafed under the tight budgets. Once while on furlough, she told an interested group about her meager household finances, including the amount she spent for breakfast. When her listeners, among whom were church leaders, seemed to think the sum was a lot of money, Lizzie lost her patience. "Do you think *you* could fix breakfast for 30 people for this?'' she asked. They admitted they couldn't.

The mission philosophy of raising orphans was simply ''Train up a child in the way he should go; and when he is old he will not depart from it.'' Lizzie testified that eventually most of the orphans ''accepted Christ as their personal Savior.''

One of their boys left the mission sooner than planned. He was walking with a group of orphanage youths past the home of a local policeman's girlfriend. The lawman, who was visiting her, shouted a racial slur: ''I think it's going to rain; I see dark clouds coming.'' The boy retorted, ''And I think it's going to snow; I see white clouds.'' Before the night was over a warrant had been issued for the youth's arrest. The police came to the mission house to arrest the boy, Henry Shade. Was he in the house? Henry Wiebe calmly inquired what his offense was and stalled for time. Meanwhile Lizzie found the Shade boy in the third floor sleeping-room, hurriedly stuffing his things into a sack. Why was he leaving? He only had time to say, ''Missus Wiebe, I'm not runnin' away from *you*!'' With that he ran down the back stairs and over the mountain. It wasn't much of a good-bye from someone she had learned to love, but it was more than anyone else in the house got. She grasped he was running from the law, and she wasn't going to stop him. He wouldn't be safe until he'd made it out of the state. Fortunately, Tennessee was just one mile through the forest. The police, unable to find the boy on the premises, left in disgust. Later, Henry filled Lizzie in on details.

Through their work with children at school, the two white families were able to reach parents as well, and many adults were won to the Lord. Lizzie and Mrs. Tschetter visited countless area homes, often walking many miles together.

For five years Lizzie and Henry shared the house with their own small children (eventually four in a 6½-year spread), another family with small children, and 20 orphans. One handy way the two couples found to cope with constant sociality was the discreet use of High German. Some measure of privacy was thus insured.

Shortly after the beginning of the fourth school year, Henry Jr. was born, and at the start of the sixth school year Anna arrived. These were not convenient times for Lizzie to have babies, for she was still the only teacher for the primary grades. Sara, Henry, and Anna were all cared for during school hours by the Negro nurse,

''Aunt'' Betty, in her own small house close to the school. Lizzie was thankful the children loved the black woman who cared for them over the years. As long as a baby was being breast-fed, a determined Lizzie left school during recess to nurse the child. The relationship between Betty and Lizzie was much more than a babysitting-business arrangement. Evening meals as guests at Betty's table were times to be remembered by the Wiebes. Consequently the untimely death of Lizzie's trusted helper had a profound impact on the whole family.

There was always plenty of work to do at Elk Park and many occasions for sadness, but there were celebrations, too. During good weather, the Wiebes and the Tschetters planned special outings to a natural beauty spot with the people of school and church. For one of the last of these picnics the Wiebes engaged a professional photographer, who captured forever the grace of the occasion. The congregation of about 60 blacks were dressed in their best — the women and girls attired in long, full-skirted white dresses topped with stylish wide-brimmed hats and the men and boys in suits, ties, and hats. Lizzie, looking regal in a long black sweep of a dress with a fancy, broad-brimmed black hat, smiled approvingly at her charges.

When her oldest daughter reached school-age, Lizzie realized that community animosity would increase toward her children because they attended an integrated school. In fact, the law stated that white children couldn't go to school with Negroes. But the decision to leave was not prompted only by pressure from without. Lizzie felt her growing children needed friends of their own background. She and Henry were convinced that, after almost eight years, it was God's will they stop raising other people's children and concentrate on what was best for their own. They returned to their roots in Kansas where their family grew to nine children. Their call to God's service continued, Henry as an active minister and Lizzie in Sunday school and circle work.

The Depression and Dust Bowl years took their toll, but the capable wife and mother remained courageous, never failing to encourage and assist. She became head of the house when her husband was gone on trips. Though Henry, who was on the boards of numerous nonprofit organizations, often gave away funds needed for the family's use, she stood by him without complaining. She rejoiced with him when he received an honorary doctor of divinity degree several months before his death in 1943.

Twice Lizzie had the joy of going back to North Carolina. In 1923 Henry and she were sent by the Krimmer Mennonite Brethren Conference in recognition of their 25th wedding anniversary. Then, again, as a widow at age 73, she went with daughter Eunice for the 50th anniversary celebration of the North Carolina Krimmer Mennonite Brethren Churches.

After the last trip she wrote a lengthy report for the *Christian Witness* (March 15, 1950) entitled, "The Founding and Pioneer Work of the Krimmer Mennonite Brethren Mountain Mission in North Carolina." After reviewing their "mustard seed" beginnings in detail, she expressed disappointment that with the closing of the mines, their beautiful building had been sold and the orphanage discontinued. But she rejoiced that the work she and Henry had begun had grown into churches spread over the 35-mile area.

Eight years later her dynamic spirit was conquered by cancer. Her body was buried in the hilltop cemetery, next to Henry's, in the shadow of the Springfield Krimmer Mennonite Brethren Church.

Bibliography

Bergen, Eunice Wiebe. "A Visit to North Carolina," *The Christian Witness* (March 15, 1950).

Klassen, Anna Wiebe: Picture file.

Krimmer Mennonite Brethren Conference Yearbooks located at Center for Mennonite Brethren Studies, Fresno, Calif.

Wiebe, Elizabeth (Mrs. H. V.). "The Founding and Pioneer Work of the Krimmer Mennonite Brethren Mountain Mission in North Carolina," *The Christian Witness* (March 15, 1950).

______. "What It Means to Me to Be a Mother," unpublished manuscript.

Wiebe, D. V. *My Parents*. Hillsboro, Kan.: 1955

Wiebe, Joel A., Vernon R. Wiebe, Raymond F. Wiebe, editors. *The Groening-Wiebe Family, 1768-1974*. Hillsboro, Kan.: 1974.

Missionaries — Home and Abroad, 1869-1960. Published by Krimmer Mennonite Brethren Conference, 1960.

Interviews with Anna Wiebe Klassen, Sara Wiebe Heinrichs, Raymond F. Wiebe, Robert Heinrichs.

During the "settling-in" period of the Mennonites in Canada, many young women who worked in the cities needed a Big Sister to guide, to encourage, and to speak for them in this strange new land. Anna Thiessen became a sister, and sometimes a mother, to hundreds of young women as they tried to find a place in this new working world. Her ministry became a model for other congregations.

10

ANNA, SISTER TO MANY

Anna J. Thiessen (1892-1977)

By Neoma Jantz

As the train puffed its way towards Winnipeg the young girl stared bleakly at the October landscape. Leafless poplar trees fronted with high prairie grass and weeds formed a corridor through which she was being relentlessly carried to a foreboding destination. Occasionally the tracks ran near a pioneer homestead and the images of the family she had just left burst into her thoughts with intense poignancy and loss, making her even more miserable. If only she knew what was ahead. If only she knew where she would be next week and next month, and that she would be safe.

The one comfort in this dismal situation was the letter inside her shabby coat pocket. She pulled out the paper and read once more the message written in fine German script.

> Dear Mrs. Enns,
>
> I have received your letter of October 6 and I see from it that you are very anxious concerning your daughter who is to

come to Winnipeg to find work. In that regard I can certainly understand your fears, especially since she speaks little English.

I am most willing to meet her at the train station on October 17th in the afternoon. I will take her to stay with me until we find a suitable place of work.

To identify myself I will be carrying a book, and let her hold a handkerchief in her hand.

And now do not worry, dear Mrs. Enns. We will do our best for your daughter. She may also come to my place on her days off. There are a number of girls who meet here on Thursdays and Sundays. She will certainly find friends here. Put your trust in God. He will also watch over your child.

Hearty greetings,
Anna Thiessen.

It had been such a relief for her parents to read this letter, and the girl's own spirits had lifted.

But now with the train nearing Winnipeg, the fears returned. What if this Anna Thiessen would not be there? Whatever would she do?

True to her word, Anna Thiessen was there. Tall, dignified, friendly, reassuring. She moved with ease through the busy streets of the confusing city. By the time they reached the neatly painted two-story house on Mountain Avenue the girl knew she had found a trusted friend. And upon entering the house the girl became one of the hundreds to benefit from the care of this woman who had a unique "big-sister" ministry lasting 34 years. Perhaps Anna Thiessen would have agreed that she seemed born to the role of guardian and confidante.

* * *

She entered this world on January 26, 1892, as the first of 13 children born to Jacob W. and Helena (Siemens) Thiessen of Wassieljewka, Russia. Three died as infants. Anna held a lifelong spiritual and familial concern for her siblings.

Young Anna's Christian commitment came as a response to the example of her devout Mennonite Brethren parents. She developed a serious disposition and a receptive spirit. Once she settled on a course of action she followed it through. For example, as a small girl Anna talked of becoming a missionary to India. Her mother cautioned that the Indian climate was severely hot. One day while Mother napped, Anna sat bareheaded for some time in the garden in the hot sun without bad effects. That settled the question of climate for her.

The family emigrated to Manitoba in 1903, and settled in Herbert, Saskatchewan, in 1906. Anna led the other children in helping her parents establish a homestead on the inhospitable prairies. She was orderly, and expected her young brothers and sisters to copy her.

Home responsibilities ruled out an education, but she took seriously her involvement in Sunday school and youth work in the small church. Then a committee concerned about the spiritual nurture of the young people opened a local Bible school. It began with 14 students in October, 1913. Anna was one of these, and she spent two years in Bible school, especially encouraged by the teaching of Rev. John F. Harms.

Her modesty restrained her from directly approaching a mission board, so she waited for a call as God's sign of approval. The call came through Rev. William I. Bestvater who asked her to work for six months in the Winnipeg city mission. Anna accepted with joy and humility. In her diary on November 30, 1915, she wrote "I am on my way to Winnipeg. May the dear Lord give me much strength and grace . . . to be faithful to him. That is my deepest wish."

The job included door-to-door visitation, recruiting children for Sunday and weekday activities, bringing clothes and food to the poor, visiting the sick, and taking charge of the Sunday school. So Anna, 23, and strange to city ways, began an energetic ministry among the immigrants and transients who were settling in Winnipeg in the ongoing push to open the West. She found needy German-speaking families in food-bare homes, in cold apartments, in hospitals, and the sanitarium. The Mennonites who had come for treatment from outlying areas were grateful to be visited by someone who could speak their language.

By January 1918, Anna could report that in the past few months the children's meetings had been held on 16 Sunday afternoons with a total attendance of 578 children, and the girls' sewing class had met 16 Thursdays with 362 girls. Clothes were sewn for the poor; and when Anna distributed them, she took several girls along to see how the garments fitted and were received. The children in her classes did not respond to Anna because she was charming or flamboyant, for she was serious and could even be severe. They responded because they recognized her undisguised concern for them.

In July 1919 the young city worker was sent to report her activities to the MB General Conference in Mountain Lake, Minnesota. Then she spent a month in Minneapolis observing that mission. By 1923 her six-month assignment had extended to eight years, and Anna felt she needed more Bible training. She enrolled at the Los Angeles Bible Institute (later named the Bible Institute of Los Angeles) for Bible study and improvement of her English language skills. She helped to finance herself by working in private homes.

At the end of two years the invitation came again from Winnipeg and Anna responded with confidence. The C. N. Hieberts now directed the mission and they warmly offered her a room in their home. Very quickly she realized that this hospitable family was being crowded out of their house by the Mennonite immigrants who had escaped from Russia and were streaming into Canada. So Anna rented an upstairs room in a nearby house, a significant step in determining her future.

The mission now added to its agenda the responsibility of visiting the Immigration Center to see who might need help there. Refugees enroute to other destinations were often detained for various reasons and so found themselves stranded. It was a great comfort to them to be greeted in German and to hear warm words of exhortation from the Scriptures.

Weighing heavily on the spirits of many of these Mennonite newcomers was the knowledge that their travel debt (*Reiseschuld*) had to be paid as quickly as possible and by whatever means possible. Those settling in rural Manitoba thought it advantageous to leave their daughters in the city to work as live-in domestics. At first the girls were hired directly from the Immigration Center by employers who had become aware of this source of cheap labor.

But there were other girls. Girls who had already been through a lifetime's quota of tragedy. Orphaned girls whose parents had been murdered or exiled in Russia, or who had become separated from their families during the frantic flight from a once secure homeland. Without parents these girls now had to find their own way to survive. Anna was deeply moved by their plight. She consoled them, took their names and addresses and promised to visit them. She invited them to church. And if they arrived in the city and found no job, she gathered them into the shelter of her own rented room.

In a short while Anna secured a second bedroom, then the third and the fourth, and the girls filled these and overflowed onto the stairs. Almost overnight the upstairs apartment became refugee hostel, employment agency, and counseling center.

Anna had no opportunity to anticipate this situation for it just fell into her lap, and she was too conscientious to turn away. The girls responded by giving this shelter the name Mary-Martha Home (*Maria-Martha Heim*). Anna approved. Later in a booklet about the mission she wrote "A home . . . is a place where order, industry, and cleanliness is found, and where love abides. If love is absent, then all the others cannot make it a true home. That is why we have chosen the good name Mary-Martha Home, for Mary stands for worship and Martha for service."

So Anna quickly organized herself and the facilities. As each girl arrived, she was given a bed or floor space, and work possibilities were explored. The only job suitable for the untrained girl was housework, and this meant moving into the employer's home. At first Anna accompanied girls to the employment agency to advise and interpret for them, but then she decided to take another approach. She placed an ad in the newspaper, and, with the help of the neighbor's telephone, began her own negotiations.

Some women came to Anna's place to hire girls and "look them over," but this was too uncomfortable so Anna stopped this method. She made arrangements by phone and then personally escorted each girl to her work to make sure it was satisfactory. Many homes were Jewish and were accepted because the Yiddish-German similarities made at least a little communication possible.

As word reached the rural areas that the Mary-Martha Home existed, anxious parents soon wrote letters of enquiry. Thus Anna made trips to the train station with a book in her hand already knowing the name of the girl she was to meet. Years later an elderly woman remarked that perhaps the most welcome sight to any of those girls was this dignified lady in her dark neat clothes with her controlled warmth and serious eyes.

At that time the working girl was entitled to a half-day off each week plus every other Sunday afternoon. As part of the working agreement Anna designated Thursday afternoon as the day off for all the girls to allow them to meet for fellowship. She also insisted the employers provide a packed lunch for that day. Then on their first afternoon off Anna met as many girls as possible to escort them through the city. This whole process was very important to her.

By May 1927 Anna had rented the whole house, which gave her seven rooms. Finding adequate beds, linens, and dishes was in itself an act of faith. Anna was not one to campaign for these things. She committed her needs to God in prayer and waited for his response. The Mennonite Brethren Conference paid part of the rent, and hired a housekeeper to take charge of the cooking, cleaning, and laundry. The girls were charged a small fee for a bed and meals, and girls in residence were expected to pitch in and help with chores. Some girls stayed for only one night while others spent several weeks. Missionaries were guests, and those recovering from illness found a welcome there.

Anna's first concern for the young women was not their economic independence, but that they become spiritually and emotionally strong. She feared for their naiveté, and their vulnerability to "worldly" influences. She gave direct spiritual guidance in the daily morning and evening devotions, and planned the Thursday and Sunday meetings to that end. As girls crowded into the house on these days, Anna, with her amazing capacity for remembering names, greeted each one and drew aside for counsel those who seemed unhappy. Her sympathetic nature and devout spirit gave the girls confidence to unburden themselves.

The needs of the girls varied much. Some were barely into their teens, and others knew nothing about housework because they had grown up in wealthy homes in Russia. Some cringed at going into a house where children ridiculed them for not knowing English. Anna had to encourage and reason with them. She did not allow a girl to leave her post simply because she was depressed or didn't like housework. Of course, in many homes the girls were accepted and treated kindly.

Some arrived in the city in poor health, and coupled with inadequate clothing and the severe winter weather, easily succumbed to illness. Not infrequently Anna had to fetch a girl who was sick simply through overwork. There were natural tensions over wages and grumbling because some had much harder work than others. But the most demanding part for Anna was helping her girls overcome spiritual depression. The Russian Revolution and migration experiences had wounded some girls emotionally and they needed answers for their doubts and despair. Anna wept and prayed with them in these dark moments and lifted their eyes to Christ, the great Healer and Defender.

Because of these needs, the girls were eager to fill the house on free days. As many as seventy girls greeted each other with laughter and openness. There were letters to read as well as church papers, such as the *Rundschau* and *Zionsbote*. Some brought needlework and others played guitar and sang or borrowed books from the library in the home. Coffee was provided for the packed lunches.

At eight o'clock on Thursday it was time to leave for the *Tabea-Verein* (Dorcas Circle) meeting at the church, and if possible, stop enroute at a needy home here and there. Already in 1925 Anna saw a need to organize a fellowship for both her working girls and other interested women. She named it for the biblical model Tabitha, or Dorcas, to inspire the girls to service and good deeds. At the devotional and missionary programs the girls sang, recited, and shared experiences. Local and visiting ministers were invited to speak. These meetings were also the setting in which numerous girls became converted to Christ.

Since there was much coming and going, girls moving away with their families, going home, getting married, a need for some written link arose. So a monthly bulletin called *Tabea*, containing devotional items and news, was begun in 1927 and continued to 1930. Every issue carried a greeting from Anna. This excerpt is from the September 1930 column.

> Dear Sisters: "As thy day so shall thy strength be." How often we want to cross mountains before we get to them. In our daily work it is also not always easy. But the Lord gives strength for every new duty. Do not do Monday's work on Sunday. You have to wash the dishes for only one meal at a time, not for a whole day nor for a week. Do not become overwhelmed with tomorrow's work. . . . You must carry your load only one day at a time and for today there is strength, for the Lord is with you.

The pattern for Sunday's program was similar to Thursday's

with the addition of a five o'clock Sunday school class for the girls who could not attend a morning service. After the class Anna encouraged girls to attend the evening service at the church.

Several days were set aside during the year to celebrate birthdays with special food and favors. In this way Anna brought into the girls' lives a sense of family, festivity, and individual concern. Anna cherished the fact that while her own parents lived they never missed sending a special greeting on her birthday.

Christmas was a great highlight. For some girls it meant a rare visit home, and even those who were orphaned or had to stay at work looked forward to the event. In wealthy city homes the elaborate dinners and parties demanded even longer than usual hours, and so some girls spent years away from their families on this holiday. Anna provided as good a substitute as possible. A program by the *Tabea-Verein* was presented to friends on a Thursday shortly before Christmas. In the early years the celebration was quite simple, but later the older women of the church offered to prepare a banquet which was served to as many as one hundred girls. There was always a tree with lighted candles and a pile of small gifts for exchanging. Gifts, such as a crate of apples, a ham or turkey, also arrived for the home. On December 24, 1937, a surprise package containing 70 gifts arrived from the women students at Tabor College. Anna was delighted to see the pleasure of the girls and marvelled at the kindness of the givers.

Perhaps the most difficult day of the year was Mother's Day. For some the memories were painful, but the girls insisted on devoting a Thursday's program to their mothers. They made red and white paper flowers and invited the women of the church. Anna was deeply moved when she saw how many girls wore white flowers, which meant their mothers had died. Then, sometimes, only a wordless embrace could ease the pain.

Summers brought a change in the girls' routine. Some returned to their rural homes to help with gardening and field work while others accompanied their employer's family to lake resorts. For those who stayed in the city there were the usual church services and prayer meetings, and one grand picnic at a park.

Unfortunately, during these years, Anna had to relocate her Maria-Martha household several times when the rented houses were sold. This task was burdensome because of the additional cleaning and repairing that went with resettling. Anna became convinced that a permanent location was needed. The rent was $60 a month, of which the conference paid $20. One day a friend gave her 25 cents to launch a building fund and she made plans. In 1932 the opportunity came to buy a large, somewhat rundown house in the vicinity for $3,500. After renovations, it contained 16 rooms. So Anna could put down roots at 437 Mountain Avenue, and she stayed there for 27 years.

Anna did not worry about finances, but she kept meticulous records. Most of the operating costs were covered by the girls' room and board fees, but the home counted on contributions, and Anna was as grateful for the 12-cent donation as for the large check. Gifts came in a variety of ways. One day a mangle for ironing appeared on the verandah; farmers brought vegetables in the fall. These gifts were not to be taken for granted, for the Depression was spreading its pall over the country. Anna was herself many times an anonymous donor. A penniless girl who had to tramp through bitter-cold streets woke up in the morning to find streetcar tickets on her table.

Anna's one luxury was a yearly trip to Saskatchewan to visit home and family. This trip included attending the Canadian Mennonite Brethren Conference where she was expected to give a report. In 1931 she told the conference delegates that 440 jobs had been accepted by girls. In 1932 approximately 275 girls answered 500 requests, and in 1937 295 girls had registered at the home.

The legwork and negotiations represented by these figures was enormous. Each job was given the same scrutiny, and Anna's concern did not ease over the years. In a lengthy report to the conference in 1933 she confessed, "When a girl has found a satisfactory place of work and is at the point where she can find her own way back to the home, then I feel literally like a mother who observes that her child is strong enough to walk."

During the first years employers were somewhat reluctant to hire these young immigrants, but the girls quickly proved themselves. Anna received calls from the employers praising the servants for their high ethical standards. This reaction pleased her greatly because she had challenged the girls to make their jobs a place of witness.

Anna was always quick to intervene on behalf of a girl. The one complaint that brought instant action was harassment by a male member of the house. Then Anna withdrew her girl and vowed never to send another. Perhaps Anna was overly suspicious in that regard and may have been taken advantage of by a girl, but she felt it was much too serious a risk. If Anna had a fault it was that of a parent. She believed the girl, sided with the girl, overlooked the bad, and took personal blame for disappointing behavior.

On one occasion she sent a girl to work for an Archbishop and then discovered he had another servant who smoked. When she confronted him, he was startled by her protests. After she had explained her concern, she won his respect and friendship.

She had strong convictions but she was not a crusader. She stood her ground with dignity and humility. Recently a friend remarked "I was surprised when I stood beside her to realize we were the same height. Anna always seemed taller."

For some girls the independence of the city was a heady adventure and threatened to sweep them off their feet. Then Anna stepped in sternly, a move that was not always appreciated. At times she seemed prying and possessive. Why, rebelled a headstrong girl, should Anna have to approve a boyfriend? Anna would reply that she was responsible to God and to the girl's parents.

In some ways she remained behind the times and was rather inflexible. But the fact that so many hundreds of young women returned again and again and kept in touch when they left proved their gratitude for her influence. Today her old friends still refer to her as "sister Anna who was like a mother."

As the years passed, the positions of the girls changed considerably. The *Reiseschuld* (travel debt from Russia) had been paid long ago and parents no longer counted on the extra income sent home by their daughters. Girls were able to afford their own apartments and worked as domestics by the day. Some boarded at the home while they attended schools or worked in factories. Post-war refugees benefited from Anna's help. Yet in 1950 about 250 girls still signed in and out.

Anna had hoped to continue the home as a retirement center but the Manitoba Conference did not think the idea practical. She was disappointed, yet she probably did not realize her physical strength was diminishing. The home was sold and Anna together with her friend, Tina Friesen, who had been the housekeeper for so many years, moved into an apartment. So she was bereft of her work, but she was not robbed of her calling. She visited, entertained, and participated in the life of the congregation.

She also turned to writing, a pastime she had always enjoyed. She had already written a 130-page booklet called *Die Stadtmission in Winnipeg,* which recounted the history of activity from 1913 to 1955. In it Anna described in detail her experiences, and included financial statements and tributes to her coworkers and helpers.

Anna also wrote poetry, but mainly she wrote letters. Her correspondence had always been extensive, but now it flourished. Her own biological family received her attention just as she had enjoyed theirs over the years. Later, when she disposed of her memorabilia, her relatives were surprised to find that she had kept letters from nephews and nieces written when they were small children. She cherished her family ties, and became a great prayer intercessor.

Anna's last years were spent in a nursing home and here, too, "her girls" continued to visit, and sometimes brought their lunches as in the old days.

She died on April 1, 1977 at the age of 85. At the funeral about one hundred women who had at one time been in her care gathered to sing the German theme song of the home. After each of the four stanzas they sang this chorus:

> O Home, we truly love you
> O Home, beloved house
> O Home, you grow dearer year by year.

Anna had never borne her own children, but her family had nevertheless grown year by year.

Katharina Zacharias Martens, like so many other women, began her life in Russia and was transplanted to America after the shattering experiences of World War I. She left all daughters a legacy in the advice she gave her own: "Plant trees wherever you go. You may not be there to enjoy the fruit, but today you are eating what someone else has planted." As an elder's wife, her spiritual concern strengthened her husband's ministry. Five of eight children survived childbirth. An only son was killed by the Makhno revolutionaries. Two foster children grew up in her home. Despite failing health, she helped forge a new life in Canada and start a Mennonite Brethren church in southern Saskatchewan.

11

PLANT TREES WHEREVER YOU GO

Katharina Zacharias Martens (1867-1929)

By Hilda J. Born

Mid-summer heat settled on the Sagradowka Colony in the Ukraine. In Orloff everyone arose early to get the important outdoor work done before the blistering sun overheated the village. The hard-packed dirt road between the two rows of houses became too hot for bare feet to cross. Sudden dusty wind-twisters reddened the eyes if one ventured outdoors. To keep both the searing heat and the dust from entering the house, solid wooden shutters were hinged to the window frames. Each morning these shutters were carefully latched in the center of the window. By keeping the shutters closed, the wood and mud homes in Village

No. 6 stayed cool and dark.

This darkness bothered Katharina. She wanted to read. Each time she opened the shutters to get a little light, her sisters quickly closed them again. They knew that the proper thing for Mennonite girls to do on a hot summer afternoon was to shell peas or stem gooseberries. This certainly was not the time to sit around and read — even if it was the Bible!

But she persisted. The New Testament was there to be read. She was determined to read it for herself. Eventually she got through it. But her inner uneasiness was not stilled. If only she could find a way to talk privately with someone who really believed Christ's words in John 3. She only knew of two people in the Mennonite villages in the Ukraine who ever talked of being saved and acted as if they meant it. One was the young people's choir leader, and the other, their minister, Johann Kroeker. He spoke with such an inner glow you were certain that he had something extra in his life. But how could a young Mennonite woman ever meet either of these men to talk to them? What would her family think of her?

Katharina did the only thing she could do. She prayed. Faithfully, earnestly, she pleaded for a way to meet someone who could help unload her burden of sin and guilt.

The busy harvest month of July arrived at the Zacharias farm. While Katharina helped her mother cook and care for the little children, the men were out in the fields pitching oat sheaves into the ladder wagons. Horses provided the power to pull the heavy telescoping grain wagons to the threshing floor. At such times each horse on the farm was urgently needed. One afternoon the strongest horse, the big black Oldenburger, started to shiver. Gerhard Zacharias, Katharina's father, couldn't get along without this horse because disease had already robbed him of two good workhorses that spring. He knew of only one quick thing to do. Send his *Katreen*. Let her go to Preacher Kroeker's place, and dear brother Johann could sell her the healing oil and herbs needed for horse medication. He didn't have time to go himself and *Katreen* knew where Kroekers lived.

Hurriedly Katharina smoothed down her hair, slipped into an embroidered apron, and dashed away for the horse medicine. But she prayed as she panted in her quick runover. Her spirits rose as she spotted *Onkel* Kroeker in the yard. Yes, he had the necessary medicine for the sick horse. Katharina took it, thanked him, but lingered near him.

"Is there anything else I can help you with, for your soul, perhaps?" he asked.

"Please, Pastor Kroeker, I want what you've been preaching about; I want to be converted."

It did not take Kroeker long to point the troubled girl to the passages of Scripture that could cure her soul's disease. After prayer and reassurance, she took the medicine and hurried home. Her soul was cleansed, and she hoped Papa would forgive her for the tardiness in bringing the cure for the horse.

She had reason to feel concern. Papa Zacharias was prompt, punctual, and particular. If he reached for a tool, or for a broom in the corner, it had better be there. This time when *Katreen* explained her delay, he did not scold.

The relief to be free of all her sin cheered Katharina. She resolved to keep this purity of spirit all her days. Sadly she remembered the slights and grudges she had carried since childhood. How she regretted the scorn she had held, even for helpful uncles! Whenever the Zachariases rode out to visit relatives, her uncles would lift the young girls in and out of the wagon. She hated that. Especially she resented the teasing she always got when they told her, "You've a pretty face, but lead in your legs." However, now that she had been newly forgiven by Christ, Katharina felt a loving warmth toward everyone.

All bitterness was washed away by her spiritual rebirth. Desperately poor, that's what she had always been — but it didn't matter anymore. During Katharina's early years, the Zacharias family had barely survived on their meager acreage at Friedensruh, Molotschna. One terrible spring all her father's horses had died. However, his honest reputation had encouraged Zacharias' neighbors to lend him some horses on credit. New hope had come to the family when Katharina's older sister, Liese, and her husband, got permission to move to a new settlement at Alexanderfeld started by the Molotschna Colony for poor landless Mennonites. The excitement of moving had worn off readily during the weary hundred-mile trek from Friedensruh to Alexanderfeld No. 1, Sagradowka. Because her brothers were all younger, 12-year-old Katharina had been chosen for the task of herding cattle behind the wagons. Katharina always maintained she had walked double the distance because she had to constantly backtrack for those ornery animals. The tears she had shed along that trail were far behind her now. A year and a half later, she had joined her parents again when the Zachariases, too, were able to move to a homestead in Sagradowka.

After her conversion Katharina resolved never again to allow herself to fall into self-pity and sin. Instead, she determined to prepare herself for the Christian young man whom she had asked God to lead into her life. And there was a great deal of work to do every day looking after the animals, garden, and house. She still found time to study God's Word and learned to sew well. Everyone knew that to be a good wife a young girl should be able to handsew a shirt neatly in a day. She had plenty of opportunity to practice sewing. All the clothing of her family was handsewn at home.

Every Thursday Katharina went to choir practice and enjoyed the company of the village young people. Her thick brown hair and kind blue eyes were noticed by the young men. Repeatedly she turned down their marriage proposals. It wasn't the personality or appearance of a suitor that bothered her; it was simply that she wasn't sure of the young man's faith in Christ. She felt sorry for a young widower, who, knowing of her fondness for children, brought his own little ones with him when he came to propose. But she could not accept him either.

Across the village street in Orloff, Sagradowka, lived the Wilhelm Martens family. They had moved here from Huettertal in 1872. Most of the family was grown and gone from home except the youngest surviving twin, Franz. He was now a handsome young man with thoughtful grey eyes and a neatly pointed beard. On completion of the local schools, Franz began tutoring. Evenings, Saturdays, and summer holidays he spent at Russian lessons in preparation for his pedagogical examinations. He passed these exams with honors in 1886. Because he was so studious, he paid very little attention to the village girls. There wasn't too much point in looking for a wife anyway, because as soon as he turned 21 he would be eligible for military service. Only after two years of faraway duty could he possibly consider setting up a home. In the meantime he was teaching in Neu Schoensee, and Katharina Zacharias always noticed when he came home to visit his parents. The discussions at the young people's choir evenings were so much better when he was around. She could tell that he really loved the Lord and studied his Bible thoroughly. Since his conversion in 1883, Franz even prayed aloud in public.

On November 1, 1890, Franz had to report to the military headquarters in Kherson. Military regulations required the recruits to draw lots for the number of open positions. A wonderful miracle happened! Franz drew lot No. 498. This meant that 497 men would be called before he became eligible for military duty. Franz was free. Freed by God to go on teaching and to begin courting the girl who was waiting for him.

A formal engagement was announced in church and celebrated at the Zacharias' home on December 22, 1890. For the January 3rd evening wedding, Gerhard and Justina Zacharias' house was filled with guests. Their much-loved minister used John 2:11 as his wedding text. Then Jakob Martens, the youth leader, filled the rest of that long evening with enthusiastic singing by the young people. Katharina and Franz both shared the joy and confidence that their decision to marry was God-directed. Franz was 22 and Katharina 24.

Because Franz had rented a room at Frank Enns's house while he was teaching in Neu Schoensee, he took his bride there on January 5, 1891. With happy hearts and great hopes for their future together, the young couple settled in with the Ennses. Here they lived until after seeding time when the teacherage adjoining the school was available.

Baby Tina brightened their home soon after their first anniversary. Next spring jolly Justina was born. In 1895, a son, Wilhelm, received a royal welcome. But the births were not easy.

Katharina cared gently for their little ones and tried to keep the children happy and quiet while Franz prepared for his teaching and preaching assignments. His sermons were well-liked, and in September, 1894, the big Nikolaifeld Mennonite Church elected him as one of their regular speakers. A month later, on October 23, this action was followed by ordination to a ministry that extended to several villages.

Franz's early passion for study seemed to accelerate after marriage. Katharina shared his evangelistic zeal. Together they pored over sermons and textbooks. Eagerly they listened to traveling ministers and invited missionaries into their home. With no biblical seminary nearby, they prepared to attend the highly esteemed Bielefeld School in Germany by selling their superfluous household goods.

But Katharina knew she was pregnant. They weren't sure the Lord would want them to leave with four little children. Franz was optimistic; if Gideon could put out a fleece, so could he. He believed that a normal birth and Katharina's good recovery afterwards, would clearly indicate the Lord's approval of their study plans. Katharina cringed at his words. Her confinements were always difficult; now this indecision would add to the strain. Soon after the turn of the century, little Maria arrived. But it took many weeks before her mother recovered. Roads were impassable at the height of winter, and no trained nurse lived nearby. Puerpural fever (*Blutvergiftung*) drained much strength from Katharina. Five-year-old Willie almost succumbed to dysentery. Then the dreaded typhoid fever kept Franz at the brink of death from August 27 to November 6 following a spiritual visit to the forestry camp (*Forstei*) of the young men in alternate service. Of course, the young couple gave up their plans for study abroad and Franz continued teaching.

The teaching honors that came to Franz Martens in 1900 greatly encouraged the family. After 15 years in teaching he was presented with the silver medallion for merit by the Russian Department of Education at Alexanderbande on May 6. This was the first time such recognition had been given a teacher in Sagradowka. The inscription read: "Awarded to you with highest honors for your outstanding service." His teaching career had begun at age 16 as a private tutor. He was now 31 years old.

Despite the civil recognition Franz and Katharina were still considering his resignation from the teaching profession to concentrate more fully on the gospel ministry. To support their growing family they would try to build up a thriving farm. At the end of the school year they reluctantly left Neu Schoensee. In that same year, 1901, shortly before little Maria's first birthday, Katharina gave birth to her last living child, Elise. She and Franz now had five children.

The seven members of the Martens family moved into Grandmother Wilhelm Martens' "summer room" temporarily. By October their little home in Altonau Village No. 9 was livable. This small structure was just the beginning of a yearly building program that continued until, finally, their stately home, barns, and orchards became a showplace.

When the new home was completed in 1904 it became one of the largest in the village. The thick walls of cut stone had large double windows for adequate lighting. The lower wooden window frames made fine window seats or shelves for houseplants. Cement tiles covered the roof and heavy wooden shutters kept out sun and storm. A steel grate over the pantry window discouraged thieves. Central heating was provided by the brick stove and heater built into the chimneys. An iron cauldron and a stovetop with ringed lids topped the brick stove located in the central hallway. Although the house followed the usual Mennonite layout of rooms, all seven rooms and hall were roomy and well-furnished. Instead of the customary foldaway *Himmel-bed* in the summer room, Franz had built in a wardrobe for good clothes and a study area. Tall acacia trees shaded the house and a neat front garden bordered the driveway. A steel four-post hitching rail (*Vollim*) was installed in the front yard for the convenience of visitors. When this rail was not used by guests' horses, the women used it for sunning the bedding before the next guests arrived.

In those pre-motel days the Martens' home was an obvious place for travelers to spend the night. They always received a gracious welcome. One year when the Martenses found time to keep a record, they discovered that they had had an overnight guest every third night of the year. Some guests, like missionary Bekking from India, stayed three months.

Not only were the children growing and the farm expanding, but Franz's spiritual responsibilities became greater as well. At a well-attended church business meeting on June 15, 1902, he was elected as *Aeltester* (Elder) of the Nikolaifeld Mennonite Church by 166 male votes. The responsibility of the position of *Aeltester* was an awesome spiritual task for such a young couple. The comforting words of Jeremiah 15:19 strengthened them for their work throughout life.

They sorely needed another kind of comfort during the next five years. Three babies were born to Katharina, but each in turn could not survive the trauma of delivery. Near Altonau was located a cement roof-tile factory which also manufactured rectangular frames for funeral plots. In the graveyard behind the village school, Franz sadly placed a cement frame around the plot of Gerhard, then Agnes, and lastly little Franz.

The Martens' personal sorrow, however, was softened by the spiritual rebirths within the church. The revival was particularly evident among the youth and the large lay ministry. The enthusiasm of the newly revived brought them into serious conflict with the established churchgoers. Not only did the converts recognize the falsehood in their own lives, but they also were appalled by the hypocrisy within the church. To them it was evident that the biblical pattern of church discipline was lacking in the local congregation. The apathy and loose conduct of fellow members disturbed them. Moreover, they believed Scripture indicated the apostolic practice of baptism by immersion of believers only.

Stormy days followed for the church, and high waves of discontent arose within its ranks. The ministry urged greater adherence to the confession of faith. Hard feelings arose, too, over the request to baptize at another time in addition to Pentecost. However, the majority of male members who were eligible to vote objected strongly to any changes in tradition. Franz's attempts at reconciliation of brethren with such widely varying viewpoints were futile. After much inner probing, he resigned from his position as *Aeltester* of the large Nikolaifeld Mennonite Church on February 7, 1907. The comforting words of Franz's aged father, "The truth remains, it cannot be buried," soothed Katharina's and Franz's lacerated hearts.

Instead of spelling the end of their public Christian duties, this climactic experience gained them an even wider area of service. Twenty-eight brethren, including Franz's brother, Preacher Peter Martens, left the established church and began meeting in schools for church services. On May 14, 1907, the group of 75 members organized under the name of Altonau Evangelical Mennonite Church with Franz Martens as leader. A remodeled store, owned by Peter and Helena Martens of Orloff, served as meetingplace until a meetinghouse was built nearby; hence the name change to Orloff Church. Because Helena was Katharina's sister, these Sunday trips to Orloff gave their children a happy meeting of Zacharias-Martens double-cousins. The church progressed in loving unity. Brother Martin Hamm baptized both Katharina and Franz by immersion in 1911.

Gradually, Katharina had to look after the increasing farm business and the family by herself. Franz was a popular speaker at missionary conferences, weddings, and so forth in his own church (*Kirchliche*), and in Mennonite Brethren churches in the Ukraine. For 17 consecutive years, 1902-19, he also served as chairman of the ministerial association. Two equally important and time-consuming committees were the local elementary school board and the Neu Schoensee high school board. At home the family was never sure of his arrival times.

Growing things gave Katharina great pleasure from girlhood to grandmother years. In the teacherage her windows were full of flowers. Then Franz's classroom windows overflowed with them. On the farm she took great pride to see that the tree trunks were always whitewashed before Easter. The family's food supply depended on the vegetables that were carefully cultivated and canned in summer. Cherries and plums were bottled and apricots, apples, pears, and plums dried patiently on the nine-tier outdoor dryer. However, grafting roses was Katharina's specialty. She taught her girls how to build a trellis and train perfumed roses to grow over it.

All living things appealed to her. As a young matron she was never afraid of the horses or long-horned cattle. She could hitch a team quickly and taught the children and hired helpers to handle the threshing teams, a needed skill because Franz was away so much.

The pressure of all this responsibility wore heavily on Katharina. Beginning with ulcer surgery in 1904 she required medical treatment from time to time for various ailments. In 1912, even though war had been declared, Franz took her to the Crimea for treatment costing 100 rubles. She came back eager to work harder than ever. But her work-worn knees found difficulty in bending.

World War 1 raged furiously by 1915. The government land liquidation seriously affected the Mennonites. Tribute to the government had always been required in the form of special services by young men of military age. Now one mobilization followed another. Daughter Justina's husband, Peter Bahnmann, started as a medical aide and was put in charge of a munitions warehouse. Katharina's only son, Wilhelm, also a conscientious objector to war, worked in the Crimea. Requisition orders were sent to the villages for horses, wagons, drivers, and provisions to be delivered to the warfront.

During the war years the girls became of marriageable age. Gratefully Katharina took out her worn guest linens and gave them to her daughters for their dowry. Nothing could be bought in the shops except the rare occasion when someone was willing to trade a shawl for a cow.

Thievery and arson increased. Many homes were gutted by fire or their owners wracked with disease. Grandmothers Martens and Zacharias both died of influenza during the 1916 Christmas season. Many women were widowed and children orphaned. Katharina had always been noted for her love of children. Even during peaceful times, when Franz went to conferences, the youngsters there would check to see if *Tante* Martens had come along. If she had, they would invariably receive a handful of dried fruit from her knitting bag. Katharina's heart had not changed with the times. For many years she kept a hatbox with baby things ready to care for an infant. Then, suddenly, a tiny orphan was brought to them, but sadly, after six months, she had to give up the little one. Her swollen arthritic hands could no longer hold an active baby. But three-year-old Hedwig Schroeder needed a home. She stayed with the Martenses for eight years. When 13-year-old Ben Epp lost his parents, his grandfather asked the Martenses to accept him; they did so gladly. He lived with them as long as Katharina lived.

The women and girls worked hard in the fields, garden, and home. Each time the troops passed through the area, they had to be fed. Each time she heard the soldiers approaching, Katharina sent her daughters into hiding in the attic or a cellar by the hedge. Then she handed out the food. Once a soldier chided her for her generosity. He suggested she give each man only one peppernut bun so she'd be able to feed even more hungry men. When nothing was left at the big house, the troops demanded she ''borrow'' from the poorest family in the village.

In 1919, during the Revolution, Mr. Peelman, a prisoner of war, shared the household. On November 28, he rode to a Russian village to get his shoes repaired and returned in the evening on a little black horse. He told of a large ruthless band of men who had taken his good horse and left him with the weak one he had ridden home on. Much worse was the news that the bandits were heading this way and planned to plunder Altonau tomorrow. Immediately the four girls were told to dress warmly, and the best transportation left on the estate was prepared for their hasty departure. Tina, Maria, Elise, and Hedwig were sent off to the remote little village where Hedwig's poor widowed mother lived.

Franz and Katharina waited. Tensely they lay in bed in their overcoats, expecting at any time to flee or face the firing squad. At last the grim foggy dawn of the 29th arrived. To relieve the tension during the day, young boys and their grandfathers would climb to the top of the roof or strawstack and report the fires in nearby villages. They soon lost count because at least 75 homes with attached barns were burned that dreadful day.

At precisely two-thirty in the afternoon, the tightly packed, dark-clothed horsemen rode into Orloff. Boldly they waved their black flags proclaiming death to the rich and the Germans! Every householder knew instantly that this was the infamous deadly gang of Nestor Makhno. All clocks were stopped on entering the home, and for two grim hours, until four-thirty, these lawless men carried out their most wicked, blood-thirsty, bestial cravings. Men were bludgeoned, women abused, and those who struggled died also. Lastly the torch was put to the house. Then, suddenly, the Makhnovites left, carrying with them anything that pleased their fancy, and headed toward the next village looking for more prey and booty.

Darkness fell early and the air was heavy with smoke and fog. At nightfall Mrs. Gerhard Siemens dashed breathlessly into the Martens home with her little one wrapped in her skirt. Her father-in-law had been murdered and her husband forced to chauffeur the bandits. The killers' arrival in Altonau was imminent.

That evening anyone who dared go outdoors saw a strange, eerie light in the smoke-filled sky. The Makhno gang saw it, too, and changed direction — they rode into the forest.

In the early morning, neighbor David Friesen brought the sad news that Wilhelm, Katharina's only son, had been shot, and Peter Bahnmann, Justina's husband, hacked to death. Friesen took a message to the girls in hiding to rendezvous with their parents at Uncle Henry Zacharias' place in Village No. 5 and they would all hide with Russian friends in one of their villages. Franz and Katharina rushed to get the distraught widows and their five terrorized grandchildren. But who would bury the dead? The sorrow-stunned family stayed in Mechajlowka for about a week until news arrived that the Makhno gang had moved on.

A month later a union memorial service was held at the once-beautiful church in Orloff. Every family was in mourning. More than two hundred loved ones had been murdered in Sagradowka! At planting time in May, the Martens family had buried Franz's 100-year-old father, and now, half a year later, in late fall, a host of relatives joined him in glory.

Although the war was officially over by 1920, the bloodbath in the Crimea continued and anarchy and looting continued throughout the land. The government continued to demand men, horses, and wagons. Thieving gangs roved everywhere. Katharina and Franz had previously lost choice animals and that summer thieves took all the horses from the premises. Franz's hand was wounded by gunshot. The threat of cholera hovered over the community and claimed even Mrs. Koop next door.

In 1921 and 1922, when the men and machinery were gone and no rains fell, times were hard. It seemed as if even the land was mourning. The icy silver thaw in the spring of 1921 coated the few struggling winter wheat shoots that dared peek out of the earth and killed them off, too. And who was left to properly till the little portion of land that the government left the farmers?

The glory of the large Martens estate had departed. Only a few cows and a plow was left. Each morning Katharina kneaded seasoned cottage cheese into balls and set a platter on the pantry shelf to have something to give each beggar who came to the door. If there was bread in the house, she added a slice also. When that was gone, she could only draw the curtains and pray for food for the next day. Because the Friesens living next door had young children, and their cow was dry, Katharina suggested they milk one of the Martens' cows. The ever-hungry granddaughters were taught to take very tiny bites to make the food morsels last longer.

In 1922, the first reports arrived of food being sent from America. Food kitchens were set up in the Mennonite villages and saved many lives. Christians from across the sea (American Mennonite Relief Association) sent flour, rice, and milk that strengthened both body and spirit of the starving Mennonites. At last the children could be told to eat as much as they liked. But after two good bites they felt full, for their stomachs had shrunk. For some the nightmares of these ordeals continued through life.

But even in such trying times the youngest daughter, Elise,

fell in love with a dark-eyed handsome young musician, John Funk. He gave new hope to the family as an aspiring preacher. They celebrated this wedding on April 25, 1922, in the Altonau school. The young lovers dreamt of someday finding freedom in Canada. Daughter Tina, who had married a widower with two girls, wanted to move to Canada. How Katharina longed to go, too! This land that had swallowed the blood of her children was not the land in which she wanted to be buried.

Preparations for immigration were begun in 1923. It was a long, slow process requiring many trips to officials as far away as Moscow. Each interview was approached with anxiety. Mercifully the extended family all passed the medical examination. The health official's chief concern was that the emigrants carry no lice. Lice infestation was not a problem for Katharina because the Martens clan prided themselves on personal cleanliness. On February 25 farm implements and household goods were auctioned. The farm and once-stately home sold for 7,000 *pud* winter wheat. Permission to leave the area was not granted until June 9, 1924. Tearfully Katharina gave a farewell hug to Wilhelm's widow, grandson Willi, and dear Hedwig, who chose to stay with their mothers in Russia.

After numerous delays enroute, the Martenses reached Quebec safely on the *Minnedosa*. At three-thirty in the afternoon, July 21, 1924, Franz and Katharina Martens, daughter Maria, foster son Ben Epp, widowed daughter Justina Bahnmann, and her four tired little girls stepped off the train at Herbert, Saskatchewan. After renting a place for a while, Franz and Katharina bought a farm in the middle of Blumenort village, 20 miles south of Swift Current. In time the children married and established their own homes.

As always, worship and prayer services were held under any circumstances. The Mennonite Brethren Church of Blumenort was organized. While Franz went around the neighborhood contacting people for Christ, Katharina prayed at home amid her arthritic pain. Granddaughter Katherine cleaned the lamp chimneys, milked the cow, and combed her grandmother's long brown hair. Not long after her 60th birthday, Katharina's diabetic condition worsened and she was forced to remain in bed. One hot June day in 1929, Maria held a feather before her mother's nostrils — and it no longer moved. The girls wanted to weep but Franz insisted:

"First we will praise God for such a wife and mother!"

Today only a prairie mound marks the grave. Gone are the yellow irises and purple stone placed lovingly by her daughters. But the fruit of her witness remains. "We mocked the gospel then, but now we, too, believe," a neighbor testifies.

During the Russian Revolution of 1917-19, many communities in the Ukraine experienced the tragic consequences of war. The following story is the personal account of Mrs. Franz Bargen, formerly of Tiege, in the Molotschna. Her experience is representative of many women during that period of anarchy and bloodshed. The Bargens later migrated to Canada. The original account appeared in Sagradowka, Die Geschichte einer mennonitischen Ansiedlung in Sueden Russlands, *edited by Gerhard Lohrenz, and is used with permission of the editor and the Bargen family.*

12

A TIME OF TERROR

Elizabeth Regehr Bargen (1897-1976)

Translated by Esther Jost

On November 28, 1919, we had butchered two hogs, which gave us a good supply of lard, cracklings, sausages, and other meat. Our parents from both sides and our neighbors helped with the butchering. While we were working there was much talk about the murders and rapes which were occurring daily. I was so emotionally upset by this talk I felt sick and weak.

My parents, the K. Regehrs, drove home for the night; but my husband's parents decided to spend the night with us, for they thought they would be safer here in Tiege than in Altonau. During the day suspicious riders on horseback had appeared and said that Altonau would be attacked that night. Before my parents left for their home, we read Psalm 91 and prayed together.

We had a quiet night. However, the next day, November 29,

we experienced the most horrible day of our lives.

That morning I took a liverwurst and some spareribs to our neighbors. Mrs. Martens looked very frightened when she met me at the door. She told me she had not slept during the night and that Mr. Martens hadn't even taken off his clothes. When I entered the room, Uncle Martens cried as he said, "Today is my birthday, and I am going to be murdered before the day is over. They will come and kill me." I advised him to call Minister Frank Klassen who would comfort and pray with him. (Klassen came to see him that afternoon.)

As I returned home, many of our neighbors were standing on the street, talking and looking very terrified. Father Bargen went home but Mother Bargen decided to stay with us. My husband changed into old workclothes, so that the robbers would not assume he was the owner of the estate. He even put on some wooden shoes which he had not worn for years. Mother Bargen and I cleaned up the meat from yesterday's butchering while Rosa, our 15-year-old maid, played with our children, and our other housemaid, Pauline, brewed some coffee.

My husband, who had gone outside, came back into the house and told us that in Gnadenfeld people were being murdered and buildings burned. How anxious we became! We cried for protection and help for the people in Gnadenfeld and also for us. Towards evening, I undressed our children and put them to bed. Our son, Franz, was two years old and Liese, our daughter, was nine months. Pauline, our servant, went to do the milking and the children's maid was about to set the table when a man burst into our house and exclaimed, "Now they are here! They have come from Orloff, which they left in flames."

He had just finished speaking when our yard and house filled with bandits to the extent they had to crowd close behind each other. They looked like living devils, for they were all covered with blood and filth. Many carried unsheathed blood-stained swords in their hands.

The David Wiens family from Steinfeld lived by us in our summer house. Wiens was looking for his wife and maneuvered his way among the robbers into our kitchen. The bandits thought he was the owner of the estate. He was very frightened and said, "I'm not the owner; there he is," and pointed to my husband, Franz.

Immediately the bandits tore my husband from my side and swung their blood-stained swords at him. One drunken man screamed, "I'll cut off your head." He aimed at my husband's head but missed and cut a big hole in the wall instead. Franz was silent. I was holding our baby Liese dressed in her nightgown in my arms and held our little son's hand as I watched the terrible sight, the like I had never seen in my life.

Our son Franz approached one of the bandits and said, "Give me the gun. It is my father's." The bandit jabbed our son in the back and said to his comrade, the bandit next to him, "Kill that child. He'll only grow up to be our enemy." However, the other bandit only stroked little Franz's head and said, "Let the little one live."

During this incident, my husband had left the room. Because of his shabby dress, he was taken for a hired hand and was able to walk through the mob. One bandit had even suggested that he hide himself because everyone in sight would be murdered. So Franz removed his wooden shoes and crept on stocking feet to the back of our garden and towards Nikolaifeld.

The bandits demanded I give them money and gold, and with their bloody swords pushed me from one room to the next. Suddenly, one of them tore my baby from my arms and hurled her from one end of the room to the other. She gave one anguished cry and then lay quiet and still. In the meantime I had lost sight of our little son.

Cursing and hitting, the bandits demanded that I allow myself to be raped or else they would hack me to pieces. I begged them to leave me alone; but if they wouldn't, to kill my children first. Then my husband's mother intervened and begged them to let me go, for I was pregnant as well as sick. They began hitting her and forgot about me. Immediately I picked up the baby, who was blue and limp, and pushed toward the front of the house. One of the bandits steered our little son to me and winked at the door for me to escape. I pressed my way through the cursing, shouting mob to the door and finally got outside into the open yard. (Before I left the house and while being mistreated by the robbers, I glanced through the window and saw a bandit hit our neighbor Johann Martens' breast with a long stick and pull a pistol from his pocket and kill him.)

Our two servant girls saw me and called me to come to them.

They were hiding in the pigpen, which was a small shed built onto our barn. I went to them and we hid midst the pigs and muck. We were up to our knees in filth. Here my baby regained consciousness and began to cry pitifully.

Through a small window between the pigpen and the barn, we saw that the barn had filled with bandits searching for my husband. Fortunately, God held his hand over the window on the bandits' side so that they didn't discover us.

The cold was so intense that the muck in the pigpen froze solid. I took off my dress and petticoat and wrapped my crying baby in them. Both children and the servant girls were crying loudly, but the noise in the barn was so much more intense that the bandits did not hear us even though we were just a few feet from them. We cried to God for help. Finally the children fell asleep, but the three of us sat wakeful, cold, shivering, and depressed.

Suddenly I heard loud swearing and banging of stones in the barn. I was afraid the bandits were hurting my husband, but as I peeked through the window, I saw the bandits were mistreating a lovely young girl and raping her. There were about 40 men in the barn. Next, people were running wildly on our yard, for someone had called saying he had caught a pretty girl. The bandits dashed out of the barn into the yard. Their previous victim was left lying on the straw, so I called to her to come to us. She had barely enough strength to come to the window, so the two servant girls pulled her into the pigpen where she collapsed. She escaped just in time, for the bandits returned to the barn and searched for her. Fortunately, they missed looking through the window and seeing us. We thanked God for protecting us.

We heard someone suggesting that the entire village should be burned, so we crept from our hiding place. Contrary to all our expectations, we were alive! We escaped to the fields; and as we looked back to our village, we saw many farms in flames. The animals stood in the fire, stomping and bellowing. When we stopped to rest, the girl we had rescued told me that my husband had been killed. I was so overcome with grief I couldn't cry.

We fled the entire night. We had lost our shoes, so we walked on stocking feet over the frozen plowed ground. I was dressed only in underclothing. At times, we heard people walking or running near us; but we didn't know whether they were friends or enemies, so we kept quiet.

As we neared the village of Blumenort, we couldn't see a soul, which made us feel very uncomfortable. We had to cross a body of water (which was frozen over) to get into the village. I was carrying the baby and the servant girls took turns carrying our boy. As I crossed the ice, I broke through and sank up to my armpits in the water. The baby and I were soaked. The girls pulled us out of the water and helped us to the nearest house where we could see faintly gleaming light. The owners, Peter Friesens, were ready to flee from their home, but first they gave me and my children some dry clothes. Then they took me to Jacob Janzens in Neu Schoensee. Mrs. Janzen put me into a warm bed and cared for me as best she could. I needed a doctor for I had had a miscarriage and it seemed I would die. I wasn't afraid to die; for then, I thought, I would see my husband again.

News came in the afternoon that the bandits were on their way to this village, so everyone fled except Mrs. Janzen, who stayed with me. Fortunately, the people who arrived were not bandits but refugees, and among them was my husband! What a reunion! We shed tears which up to now both of us hadn't been able to do. We had experienced so much!

We all had to leave Schoensee, for an upheaval in the village was feared; so we drove to Neu Halbstadt. Here I was taken in by Minister Janzen, whose wife cared for me as a mother cares for a child.

After five days all the bandits left and we were able to return to our home. What a sight! Our clothes, beds, and anything valuable had been taken. Jars of fruit and jam had been smashed, and all the rooms were full of filth and human excrement. Nothing edible remained. Regardless of the loss, we were fortunate, for we were all alive and our house was still standing. Many could not say this.

It was clear after these terrible experiences that our people should leave Russia but we could not expect help from anyone, so it was not possible to emigrate.

There were many small upheavals in the villages, and larger ones could be expected to happen any day. One December evening Abraham Quiring was walking on the street when someone who had been hiding behind a lamp post shot him. No police could investigate this shooting incident for there were no policemen.

One thing was certain, what had happened to Quiring could happen to anyone in the near future.

In February of 1920, someone knocked on Franz Wiens' window. (He was the mayor of Neu Schoensee.) When he answered the knock, soldiers demanded he go with them. As they neared Jacob Janzen's yard, the men insisted that they stop and take Janzen along, also. Wiens had to awaken Janzen and tell him to come with them. As soon as Janzen opened the door, the bandits entered the house and took whatever they pleased. They loaded it on Janzen's wagons which they had previously driven in front of the house. When the bandits had stolen all they wanted, they lined up Janzen, his son and Wiens, one in front of the other. They shot Janzen, hoping that the same bullet would kill all three. This would have happened if the bandits hadn't used a sawed-off shot gun which lessened the impact of the bullet after hitting Janzen. With the words, "I am hit," Janzen fell down and died. His son was slightly wounded and Wiens was not hurt at all. In the meantime, the bandits had blown out the lamp and run out of the room. Then they sprang onto the vehicles in front of the house and drove away.

Much blood flowed, also, in Alexanderfeld and Nikolaifeld. No one whether rich or poor, German, Russian, or Jew was spared. No women, whether young or old, beautiful or homely, well or sick, were immune to rape. The atmosphere of the time we lived in was one of plunder, rape, and murder.

A forced journey from one's homeland, even with friends and neighbors, is never welcome. After World War 2 hundreds of German-speaking settlers in the Ukraine were driven before the German army as it retreated. Their flight was in winter; and, as this journal describes, sometimes under almost impossible conditions. In wartime, the frequent plight of women and children is to struggle for survival apart from husbands and fathers. Anna Loewen and her husband later made their home in British Columbia, Canada.

13

A FLIGHT IN WINTER*

Anna Falk Loewen (1902-)

Translated by Katie Funk Wiebe

The last Sunday in Adelsheim, October 3, 1943. We have received notice that the men must leave tomorrow to begin the trek with horses. Women and children are to follow them several days later. So we came together in the schoolhouse to say farewell once again. Minister Peter Guenther preached the farewell sermon. He used the text: "Hitherto hath the Lord helped us" (1 Sam. 7:12). Then Minister David Penner spoke using Psalm 23:1: "The Lord is my shepherd, I shall not want."

If the Lord has helped us until now and promises to be our shepherd, why should we doubt that he will provide grace for the journey? Because of all the terror we have experienced, our houses do not mean as much to us as they once did. We live only six kilometers from the Dnjepr* River and several times the front has

*Original spelling of place names has been used in this writing.

come to the river. For days we have heard the reverberations during the waking hours and at night. The sounds of shooting and shelling carry clearly from the front. At night the parachute flares hang over the neighboring villages of Dnjepropetrowsk, Saporoshje or Dnjeportroij like lit candles on a Christmas tree. Soon after, many enemy airplanes fly over our peaceful villages to unload their bombs, and the sites where searchlights are situated respond with fire. So much fire is belched forth, it would seem that everything will be destroyed. But instead, as the German says, "Not every bomb hits its mark." One night we heard the thunder of cannons close by and machine guns crackling. We dressed quickly and rushed outside to learn that the Russians were attempting to cross the river in boats. The Germans were defending the other shore, and that was the reason for the battle. The constant fear and turmoil have exhausted us.

October 4. Today our men left by wagon. The cattle and sheep were herded behind them. They hoped to go as far as Apostolowo, where we are to meet them. How empty everything seems since the men left, in spite of the fact that houses and barns are full of the German military. How we miss our husbands, sons, and the livestock. We feel uneasy, for the enemy planes dropped many bombs on our beloved Adelsheim last night. Thank God they were not accurate hits, though they were aimed at the village. Someone probably had allowed a little light to gleam through. That was the reason for the disturbance. "May the Lord lift up his countenance upon us and give us peace."

October 7. Yesterday the neighboring villages received notice to drive their wagons to our yards and take us to the little railway station at Kanzerowka. We were allowed to take some bedding, clothing, flour, and lard with us. We gathered at the edge of the village. As we waited for several stragglers I remembered that I had kept the key to the piano in my purse. I ran back, for it would have been unfortunate if someone had broken the lid. I unlocked the instrument and said good-bye once more while I slid my hand lovingly over the wood. The house felt strangely empty. But I could not stay. Back to the station where the wagons wait, where my children wait.

I sit down by my dear children, who have so little understanding of what is going on or what it means to lose one's home. We start out slowly. The heavily loaded farm wagons groan under the weight of several families. The sun rises higher, the dust whirls in the air. For a long time our tear-filled eyes gaze at the village. There lies our beloved hometown, so peaceful and quiet, as if it wants to say, "Please, don't leave me behind alone. Life was so pleasant within these walls." But the village disappears behind the horizon. Farewell, dear Adelsheim! Dear homeland, though we may be far away, we will always think of you.

October 8. Yesterday evening our train started for Apostolowo where our men are. After traveling a short stretch, we experienced our first air attack at the Nikopol railway station. Yet the Lord heard our prayers and cries for help and the train came through unharmed. After the attack we traveled farther and came successfully to Apostolowo, where we remained standing. Toward evening, finally, some of our men arrived to tell us that they were located in the neighboring village of Nowo-Alexandrowka with the wagons and cattle and had to travel another 20 kilometers the next day to get to the Russian village Oljenowka where they were to be lodged. We had to stay behind on our train and await whatever lay ahead.

October 10. Yesterday evening we and our belongings were unloaded from the train and taken to Nowo-Alexandrowka. There I met my dear husband, who was happy to be able to supply us with milk, for he had taken a cow with him, tied to the wagon. This morning we took to the poorly maintained, dusty roads of Oljenowka. Here the poor Russians in their shabby huts were commanded to lodge us. We lived together in one room with my sister Maria Schapansky and her daughter, Mrs. Epp (widow of Elder Heinrich Epp), and my husband's mother in a very miserable mud hut. Still, we had some straw to sleep on and we had brought bedding with us. We didn't have enough food to eat, so we butchered a sheep. But why have we been brought here so far away from the railway? If the Russians move in, what will become of us? How little these huts seem like home. The other transport trains drove through to Litzmannstadt; only our transport was not allowed to go on. We have been told the railways are overburdened; we will have to wait. This transport includes the people from the villages of Adelsheim, Einlage, Kronsweide, Neuenburg, Nieder-Chortitza, Chortitza, and Burwalde. But not all the villagers are present.

October 19. I haven't written since October 10, because life became monotonous. Each day was the same. Yesterday we were told that our husbands must move on to Proskurow on the Polish border. The men do not want to leave before our train leaves, because the front is so close. But no questioning was allowed. Orders were orders. With heavy hearts we let them go and now I am alone again with my mother-in-law and my children. She is weak, about ready to collapse, and can hardly walk. At times I have to plead with someone to help me carry her. The trip has been dreadfully hard on this poor woman thus far. How she fears the long journey ahead.

October 22. Today we were ordered to get to the railway station quickly, this very night if possible. Everyone rushed, as if without heads. Our belongings were quickly packed. O God, give grace for this journey.

October 23. We have lived through a good night. We packed and baked feverishly. At 3 a.m. we left, but without enough vehicles, so that again we had to leave behind some of the few things we carried with us. To journey into the unknown, not knowing what lies ahead, and to leave some food behind cuts through the heart like a knife. I left behind a few sacks of flour, meat, kitchen utensils, and a variety of other things. Bedding, clothing, lard, and some flour I could take along. "Behold the fowls of the air — for they sow not, neither do they reap, yet our heavenly father feeds them."

October 24. Yesterday we arrived in Apostolowo, but because the station is a target for air attacks, we had to drive four kilometers to an outlying village. That was our first night under the open sky. I had found lodging for Mother in a Russian home. I laid the children close to the house to protect them from the wind. I sat on the wagon the whole night to guard our belongings.

The day before I had walked much of the time and had become overheated, and now the night air was cold. I became chilled through, and my body ached. I felt feverish and my voice hoarse. The night seemed as if it would never end. No sleep refreshed my weary body and in the morning we had to return to the railway station.

Then came the order to leave everything behind and to go 12 kilometers on foot to the next railway station. The officer hollered to the people, "If you walk, we can perhaps help you. Tomorrow it may be too late.'' We stood there as if paralyzed. First hesitantly, then deliberately, we prepared to leave. One wagon was brought to the street and the old people and small children placed in it. We got ready to carry what we could and were about to leave. But before we left, another order came to stay. Wagons to take us were on the way.

You hear, yes, you hear our prayers;
Before we ask, you answer.

October 25. We have lived through another long night and are still here at the railway station. The night air was bitterly cold. We sit and wait longingly for the morning. We fear air attacks, which we can expect at any time. How many prayers are sent to God! This night we were spared. This morning our train cars actually arrived. Even though they are coal cars, open at the top, they are not as cold as sitting on the ground. With everyone and their belongings inside, the cars are very full, and we are tightly cramped. But we can't leave as yet, for we are waiting for some more refugees and we have to stay here another night. We are told this is the last transport train.

October 26. This afternoon we finally left this horrible Apostolowo. This morning a child was buried which a mother had accidentally suffocated yesterday during an air attack. We haven't gone far and already we're standing at the Beresinowataja station.

October 27. We are still at the same spot and our locomotive has deserted us. The sky is dark and it looks as if it might rain. My brother and Gerhard Quiring are trying to cover the cars with blankets. Yesterday they dragged some boards from the shelled houses. Outside it's dark; inside it's dark. God, be merciful to me. . . . ''Mine enemies would daily swallow me up: for they be many that fight against me'' (Ps. 56:2).

October 28. We are still at the same place. It did not rain yesterday and the weather has changed. Wind and frost have moved in. The children walk around with stiffly frozen hands, the grandmothers are tired and sick, and the men are quite discouraged that we have simply been left standing in the open. We have no provisions, except for a fire we have made outside on which we cook a few things. Last night a little earth pilgrim was born in an open traincar. It will soon be evening and nothing changes. The roar of cannons sounds again in the distance. If only we were so far away we didn't need to listen to that. I drew a Scripture verse: "Rest in the Lord and wait patiently for him." We want to continue to trust him.

October 29. The weather has become warmer. It froze considerably last night, but the sun's rays are warm. This morning we had a service in the open air. Minister Neufeld spoke, using Exodus 14:14: "The Lord shall fight for you, and ye shall hold your peace." He stressed we should not complain about our misfortune so that God would have to take us into even deeper experiences. He drew our attention to the fact that we had much to be thankful for. God had wonderfully protected us during the bombing. — An order has come that we are to leave at four o'clock. May God protect us!

October 30. We did not leave yesterday. We have been stranded in this cold weather out in the open. If only God would have mercy on us. The train conductor is much concerned about us, but he has no locomotive. More children die each day. "Lord, rebuke me not in thy anger, nor chasten me in thy wrath."

October 31. Early this morning we were sent a locomotive and have been traveling about an hour. Our train crossed the Inguletz River, and now we are standing again because there is only one track and that one has been scheduled for another train. "He who keeps thee does not sleep."

November 1. Yesterday we covered a long stretch and drove until late in the evening. Then the train stopped. In the morning we learned that we were ten kilometers from Nikolajew. At night another child died and Minister Neufeld spoke using the text, "For me to live is Christ and to die is gain." In the afternoon we started off again, but this time we went backwards because all the tracks are full and it is difficult to move forward. The Germans have control of the railway in Kriwoj Rog, so that we will travel on that line.

November 2. We traveled from yesterday noon almost without a break. In the night we almost had an accident when another train hit us, specifically our car. Fortunately the train was going slowly and could stop. We were very frightened because our car was shoved sideways and the wooden walls are broken. Now we are traveling through the area where the Russians have broken through. The sight is horrible. Tank after tank lies scattered, either burned or disabled. Many houses have been shelled and dead soldiers lie here and there. The Russians were here for four days. In the morning we were at the Kuzewka station and now we are on the way to Snamenka. That is supposed to be a dangerous place because of air attacks. "Until now the Lord has helped through his great goodness."

November 3. Yesterday we traveled a long distance and reached Snamenka at noon. There we were given two freight cars for the sick. We brought Mother to one. She didn't want to go — she would rather have stayed with us in the train. But the whole time she had been sitting squeezed between our baggage. She said everything hurt and she was dead tired. At night she was very sick. So I fashioned a simple bed for her in the car for the sick. She lay down in the featherbed and rested like a child. If only her health were restored and she would not die on the journey. Today three children were buried. Yesterday we came to the Bobrinskaja station and at eleven o'clock in the evening we were given some barley broth. During the day we were able to cook some food for ourselves out in the open, for, finally, we have to eat.

November 4. We left Bobrinskaja yesterday and arrived this morning at the Kasatin station, where we will probably remain the whole day. Our condition in these open cars is getting more precarious each day. The blankets which cover the roof protect us from the wind, but not from the rain. The children had to stay in bed under covers all day. Mother is quite sick and can hardly eat anything. Yesterday my feet were cold all day, and I worried about my husband. Will we see each other again? Have the men and their wagons perhaps fallen into the hands of the Russians? Soon it will be evening, and we are to move on tonight. We were told the partisans dynamited a train on this stretch. — "Father, watch over us and keep us."

November 5. Yesterday it rained very little, but today it is very cold. The children have to stay in bed again. Last night we traveled a long distance, past Fastow. This morning we stood for a short while at the Winitiza station where we could buy some apples. We haven't had such a luxury for a long time, and I bought a few. Mother will be happy for them, and I will take them to her when the train stops.

November 6. We traveled during the night without a break.

We had hoped to reach Proskurow but have found out we are already past it. A request has come not to discharge us at Proskurow, but to take us to Litzmannstadt. In two hours we will be in Lemberg where we should receive some provisions. We are traveling through much forest. The thought of the partisans makes us uneasy. "You will protect us; you can protect us; you are all powerful."

November 7. Today is Sunday, welcome Sunday, which used to make us so happy. But today everything has changed. After I fell asleep yesterday, I awoke suddenly because the rain was leaking through on me. Quickly I got up and covered the children some more. But it continued to rain and snow. The children woke up and the littlest one cried: "Mama, we're wet." I didn't know what to do. I pulled them out of their beds, but where to now? It was raining through all over, because the blankets on the roof were heavily covered with snow. The train stopped. I grabbed both children by their hands and ran out. I ran to several freight wagons near the front of the train. They took me in, and so now we were at least dry even if our belongings are wet.

At ten o'clock we arrived in Lemberg and were given some soup made with flour. Today the snow which fell on the roof yesterday is melting, and so we have to struggle with water again. The weather looks ugly. If only we were at our destination. We have been told we should be at Litzmannstadt soon. Where will we meet our husbands again, and how much farther have we traveled than was originally planned?

November 8. We are still traveling through Poland, a country which has no end. Last night it froze considerably, and our feet haven't gotten warm all day. On top of that we can't cook any food because the train hasn't stopped. Other than the flour soup we received in Lemberg we have had no provisions. The children beg for food all day. We have been told we will soon be there — perhaps by evening. I can't see us spending another night in the train. Our bedding is wet and cold from yesterday. Perhaps we will get some soup. If only we were given some kind of dry shelter, even if only a barn or a shed. We are completely exhausted, hungry, and chilled through. We long for rest and room to stretch our arms and legs. I am very weary and my knees ache from arthritis. How long have we been sitting in this fashion among our belongings? Who would have believed that we would travel in open cars in freezing temperatures? The water outside is frozen solid, whereas formerly our grandmother was accustomed to sitting in a warm easy chair. I have thought often of the words, "Pray that your flight may not be in winter."

November 10. Yesterday I never wrote anything. We arrived late in the evening and then we still had to drive another 16 kilometers to Pabianitze. There we had to go to an exit camp (*Entlassungslager*), as it was called. We could not take Mother with us, because the sick were to go the hospital. So I stayed until I had brought her to the hospital. Then I followed my children. We finally received some soup and a piece of bread. What a joy after waiting so long!

In the morning we were taken immediately to the showers. We were told that our journey is to continue today. Our baggage is already being reloaded. We are to travel in passenger cars so that we will arrive at our destination like human beings. I visited Mother in the hospital. She is resting so well in her bed that she begged me to leave her there and go on without her. She can't imagine getting out of bed again and traveling farther. Yet I can't decide to leave her here. What if she were to die here alone? I spoke to the Sister about the matter. She said all the patients have to leave. Mrs. Wiebe, nee Penner, is dying but has to go along.

November 12. Our situation has changed. We are sitting in a closed-in section of the car and are traveling toward our new home — to Oberschlesien. We received some food today: bread, a dab of butter, sausage, and marmalade. We were overjoyed. If only our husbands were here with us. Where are all the exiles and refugees? How many are buried in the forests of Siberia? No loving eye watches over their graves. Branded as enemies of the state, they have slowly been offered to death. What they endure is a worse trial than sword and fire. It is a slow martyrdom because of their faith. We still hope that our men will come, sooner or later, even though many wives have waited many, many years without hope.

The word has just arrived that Mrs. Wiebe has died. She was taken to the hospital yesterday together with Mother and died shortly after being returned to the train. No lamp could be lit. It was hard for her relatives not to be able to see her die. Because of the airplanes we have to travel without light. But she has finished her suffering. How much she endured! She was sick five years.

She spent the winters in bed, and usually felt a little better in summer so that she could get up. Four sons, one daughter, three grandchildren, one son-in-law, and numerous relatives were banished. God alone knows what that poor mother's heart has suffered. How much she wanted to see one of her children again, but it never happened. Now she is finally free of her suffering and we don't want to deny her her rest. She died last night, never having reached the destination of this journey. Today we are supposed to arrive there.

November 13. Yesterday about three o'clock in the afternoon we arrived in Lissick, which is to be our home for the time being. We are being lodged in a large monastery with many small rooms and three quite large ones in which about 50 persons live. Each family has been allocated some beds, which stand close together. Each morning and evening we are given a piece of bread, and some soup at noon.

November 16. Because Mother is still not getting well, I had to bathe her today and take her to the hospital. She wanted to stay with us in our room, but we had to take her to the hospital. She is resting there in a nice bed, and we are both agreed that this is better than staying with us in our noisy room, which has seven children. On top of that, those in the next room always have to walk through ours.

November 29. We are still at the same place. At first when we were told that we were to stay here five weeks, everything seemed gloomy. Now one day follows the other, and we are resigned to our situation. We have been directed to stay in our rooms. The outside doors have been locked. We can go out into the yard, but we are to be quarantined for five weeks. Otherwise everything is much the same and our men have still not arrived. We will have much to talk about regarding all the suffering we have gone through. May God grant that we can soon share joy and sorrows.

December 29. Because each day is the same as the next, I am writing only seldom. Mother's strength is waning. She has little appetite. She has stomach problems, but her feet are healing. She is waiting anxiously for her son, my husband, and for her youngest boy, Jakob Falk, who is also in the trek. If only they would come while she is still alive.

December 30. I hardly know how to write today. My feelings are mixed. Our dear mother and grandmother died peacefully in the Lord today. She never got well again after the difficult journey, even though she wanted to see her sons again badly. She became at peace about the matter at the end, committed her sons to the Lord and asked him to take over. The last day she asked me, wide-eyed, "Anna, have you seen Julius yet?" "No," I replied. "I have seen him," she said. "He is in the field, well-dressed and not even thin. . . ." She had seen him as she dozed and now was convinced the men were coming. Then she begged, "Anna, let me die. Don't keep me here." Yesterday evening she couldn't speak anymore, and fell asleep. Today at eight o'clock in the morning she died, and at four o'clock in the evening her youngest son, Jakob Falk, stood at the door. I cannot describe my feelings at that moment. I felt as if I should run to Mother with the words, "Mother, rejoice, they have arrived!" But I couldn't give her the news for she was dead and couldn't hear me.

The wave of excitement which spread through the camp cannot be described. Finally someone from the trek had come. I was also glad, for I knew that soon my husband would come also. But my joy was mixed with much concern: our men had arrived in Hindenburg just before New Year's Day and had to stay there for a whole week, when they would be released to join their families. They had met some acquaintances there who had told them that we were in Lissick near Ribnik. So two men had come to see for themselves. If only they had come one day earlier, then Mother would have experienced this joy also.

What God does, is well done;
His will is best for us.

January 1, 1944. My husband arrived today at three o'clock. We had sent the bad news to him at Hindenburg and so he was allowed to come. Thank God he is here. We were waiting for him very much, for today his mother is to be buried. Because it is already so late, she will be buried in the morning. Then he has to go back and come again on January 8.

August 16, 1944. I have written nothing for eight months. Our life was so monotonous during this time, that it seemed hardly worthwhile. Today something unusual happened, so I must record it. Tomorrow we are to leave this camp which has been our home for nine months. Many good and many difficult experiences have been ours during this time. We had one big advantage: we who came from Adelsheim could live under one roof. During this time we felt drawn even closer to one another. Who knows where we will be scattered to now? Where will we find a little spot again which we can call home?

Someone asked me, what burdens you so heavily?

I can't go home, for I no longer have a home.

August 19. At two o'clock in the afternoon we left Lissick. At noon on August 18 we came to Loewenstadt. Here our train stopped. The rain was pouring, but in spite of this we had to get out with the children and baggage. We were divided among the waiting wagons and taken 12 kilometers to the outlying camp Schimanischka. Here, in spite of the apparent poverty, we were received with warmth. We were soaked through. Today the sun is shining and we want to dry out bedding and clothing. Nearly everything we own is wet, for it rained the entire time.

August 26. We are still in this camp and feel quite comfortable, even though we have no beds and are sleeping on straw on the floor. But why have we been brought here? Not far away we can hear the roar of cannons. At night airplaines bombed the neighboring area. Why have we been sent so far east? We can't understand it.

August 30. On August 28 we were taken from the Schimanischka camp and divided among the villages. We were to help bring in the harvest. We would rather have stayed in the camp, but yet we have to submit. We are 120 kilometers from Warshau where the front is. Should the Russians break through the front, where can we go? Furthermore, winter is approaching. Yet no hair can fall from our heads without God's knowledge.

April 15, 1945. It will soon be eight months since I last wrote. Today life has become more peaceful, so I will try to describe the last terrible months. I recall these events unwillingly, yet the story of our wandering should not have any omissions. So I must write it down.

On January 17, 1945, we received the sudden order to pack up again, for danger was near. They had waited too long to notify us. Women and children were to travel by train and the men in the trek. Suddenly the Russians broke through the front, so that flight by rail was out of the question. The railway stations were being shelled, for the Russians were only a few kilometers away. All telephone communications were cut off, and everyone lost his head.

We had seen this coming and had baked and packed ahead of time. Quickly we loaded our baggage on wagons, and so we left at one-thirty on the night of January 18. The air was cold and the snow gleamed under the bright moonlight. The streets were slippery, and the horses had a hard time getting their footing. The wagons tended to slide around, and so we drove into the cold night and into an uncertain and unknown future.

We were to travel over Litzmannstadt, but after we had gone half the distance, the order came to travel by Kirschberg and Pabianitza because the Russians had already pushed through by Loewenstadt and were shelling Litzmannstadt. This detour took much of our precious time. Just as we reached Pabianitza, it was heavily shelled. We left the wagons standing and ran into the houses. To go any farther was out of the question. The streets were blocked with the military, heavy cannons, tanks, refugees — everything mixed up. The street on which we drove was wide, so that often three or four rows of traffic drove alongside each other. We walked alongside our wagons and had to watch that we didn't slide into the trenches in the streets.

When darkness fell, the road was overrun with fleeing military personnel, so that we poor refugees had no chance. So we and a few others stood nearly the whole night. The wind blew icy cold. How I froze that night. Tired and without strength, I clung to the back of the wagon. Each moment I wanted to sink to my knees. Fear gripped my entire body. Fire flashed out of the dark night behind us from the front and before us from the air attack. As morning dawned our trek got moving again. So we drove through Pabianitza early in the morning. But what a sight confronted us! The whole street was terribly disrupted: before us were shelled houses, military automobiles, dead soldiers, and refugees, whose wagons were stalled. Dead horses, chests, and bicycles were strewn about. Fear and dread overwhelmed us.

Inwardly we cried, "Keep going, keep going." At the same time the first dive bombers were over us. We left the wagons standing and threw ourselves into the trenches in the streets. The bomber's deadly weapons exploded over us and their bombs shrieked. After they had left, we drove as quickly as possible to Lask. But the dive bombers didn't go away and attacked us five times that day. Each time we lay down in the forest or crawled into trenches on the road. The machine guns crackled so close that at each moment we were sure we would be killed. How we prayed. And God heard us. We were not harmed. We and the poor children lived through much terror that day. Our little one begged repeatedly, "Don't leave me on the wagon when you run away!" The air attacks came so suddenly that we hardly had time to jump out. What a blessing that Mother didn't have to experience this. She was at peace. By evening we had left behind a dangerous stretch and had come to the Warthe River spanned by a long wooden bridge. Again we had to wait nearly the whole night, for all traffic was stopped. At the first grey glimmer of dawn we crossed the bridge and came to the town of Schieratz.

Everywhere we looked people were fleeing or had already left. By evening we came to Kalisch, a large city. The sight was disquieting. The Germans had covered everything with a smokescreen, so that it was frightfully dark and we could not see the road. The wagons of some women and children had fallen into the trenches on the streets and the women begged for help, but who could help? Everyone had to stay in the line of traffic, for if one dropped out, one never got back in again; wagon followed wagon closely, and no driver made room for the one who wanted to get in. Even though the street was dark we couldn't wait. Always the word was "Keep moving, keep moving." Because the people had no time to eat or sleep and were living in constant fear, some no longer acted rationally. They couldn't think clearly and lost their wagons and families. When a street was blocked, we stopped to feed the horses.

In Kalisch the soldiers gave us a horse. Up until now our two families had been driving with one horse. With a second horse we would be able to keep up better. We already had discarded all kinds of belongings. As we drove through Kalisch in the night, all was deathly quiet, but the next day the street was shelled by Russian tanks again. Many of our people were still in the city. Jakob Woelk lost his life there. As he was holding the hands of his two daughters, ages 9 and 11, he was torn to pieces. One daughter was killed immediately and the other so seriously wounded that she bled to death. The dead child was laid beside her father in the trench and the journey renewed. His wife was lying in the wagon with an infant born three days earlier and was seriously wounded, so that she was hemorrhaging. She begged them to stop long enough so she could die. Her relatives were with her on the wagon, so they stopped — and let her die. In between, the second daughter also died. So the mother and the other daughter were also laid in one of the trenches in the road.

That done, they tried to make up for lost time. The three-day-old daughter and little three-year-old Peter were still alive. As they traveled, the horses of Johann Janzen were hit. He grabbed his children from the wagon and ran. After they had run a few meters, along came a grenade and blew his wagon into the air. He lost everything. Not a purse or piece of paper was saved. Three children of Heinrich Schulz were also wounded; all were from Adelsheim. How many from other villages were hit we don't know.

We made it through Kalisch where we had received the horse. However, after traveling a short distance, we noticed that the horse couldn't keep up. He always fell out of line, so that we were slowed down. My husband had a few horseshoe nails in his pocket, but no blacksmith was working. Finally one blacksmith was persuaded to shoe the horse for a high fee. But we didn't have enough nails for all four hooves, and we couldn't keep going without having the horse shod. The Lord saw our need. As we stood on the street in a little village and fed the horses, two little girls came near us pulling a small sled on which stood a small chest. As they passed by, the sled swerved and the chest fell off. Part of its contents fell near our wagon. And what do you think it was? Horseshoe nails and calking. They left them lying and drove off. We, however, looked on with amazement at our sudden riches. We gathered them together, used some for our horses, and let others have some also.

At five o'clock in the evening we drove through Ostrowo. The Adelsheim people were up ahead. Because our shoeless horses had caused us to fall behind, we were now among strangers. But our horses were making better progress, so we decided to rest about 2 a.m. My husband could hardly keep going, for this was about the fifth or sixth night without rest. He was so tired that the reins and whip fell out of his hands. He slept in a house from two until five, we drank some warm coffee, and the journey began again.

The next day we drove through Pleschen. There we had to

trade wagons because the wheels on ours were dragging. Our journey took us through Lissa, where we stayed in a large castle. We met Helen Regier (nee Harder) there. She was very discouraged for she had lost her husband and daughter-in-law. Her grandchildren were with her. Here we cooked some supper, rested, and drove off again early the next morning. We kept going for five days without seeing any Adelsheimer.

One day as we were feeding the horses, we were overtaken by Jakob Falks and Schellenbergs. What a joy! We had lost Mr. Schellenberg earlier. From then on we took pains to stay together and to rest at night. Early in the morning, however, we set out again on the crisp snow. Soon we arrived at the Oder but always we saw the same sights: empty houses and barns full of cattle. The cows bellowed in pain, their udders swollen, and the pigs clamored for feed. A picture of desolation! At Neusalz we drove over the Oder River and rejoiced to find people living in their houses on the other side. The bakeries were in operation. Now we could trade flour for bread.

But here a different kind of need surfaced. Where before we had simply driven onto the empty farmyards, fed the horses, cooked some food, and slept on the premises, now things were different. People were living in their homes, with beautiful furnished rooms, and didn't want dirty refugees soiling them. When we arrived at Sagan it was snowing heavily and the poor horses struggled with all their might to keep going. Going uphill we got out and shoved. Anni's feet froze and she moaned day and night.

On February 6, after many hardships, we came to Leuben, where we were surprised to see many dear friends from Adelsheim already there. The joy at seeing each other again was wonderful. Each one had a story to tell. Here many people who had been separated found each other again, including Mr. Schellenberg. The difficult part was that my relatives and my mother were not there. No one had seen them after the first days. Had they fallen into the hands of the Russians? Our friends encouraged us by saying they might still catch up.

Everyone was registered here in order to bring families together. Then we were divided among the villages in the area. We were sent to Leibchel, where we were lodged in a large room in a children's home to which children from Berlin were sent. The staff, mostly Berliners, were friendly. But we were shocked to hear the thunder of war close by. At first we comforted ourselves by saying that probably there were military bases close at hand and the noise was from practice runs. After asking some questions we learned that we were 47 kilometers from Frankfurt on the Oder where the Russians were engaged in a serious attack. At night the enemy planes flew overhead and bombed the neighboring village.

On February 17 we were sent out to various farms. We came to a farmer named Lehnieger who was good to us although others did not fare as well. On February 20 Jakob Falks' 1½-year-old son died after a short but painful illness. We buried him, and on the 24th we received orders to move on.

On February 25 we moved on again after a nearly 20-day rest. This journey was not so rushed, because the Russians were not close as yet and the landowners had all remained in their homes. Only the refugees left. The roads were not as full as before, so that we drove without stopping and rested at night. Even though the alarm sounded often for an air attack, we were never in real danger.

On March 9 we drove as far as Roecken. On the tenth we came to Unterwerschen to an inn. We wanted to stay until the 11th in the area. We visited some of them and they visited us. I shed many tears, for so many had found their relatives but my relatives and mother were not among them. No one had seen them. Was it possible that they had actually had the serious misfortune to fall into the hands of the enemy?

We thank God that we have endured the rigors of the journey. . . . On April 13, early in the morning, the first American tanks rolled through our village and in an instant it was taken. They drove through the village and lined themselves up at the edge of the village in long rows. Many stood near our houses, the others to the left, on the pasture. Then some terrible shooting broke forth and we ran for the cellar. Clouds of smoke rose from many houses. At noon everything was quiet. We remained in the cellar. Suddenly we heard footsteps at the cellar door coming toward us.

We saw our first American soldiers. One said in German: "You can come out of the cellar. We have quit shooting." He said a few friendly words to the children, asked if we had any weapons, and left. How thankful we were to God that we had crossed over the front and had fallen into the hands of the Americans as we had hoped. We have had peace now for two days.

The thundering grows fainter all the time. We hope it will never return. We have soldiers lodged with us in the houses, yet they don't bother us. The last few weeks we have had hardly any rest at night. Repeatedly we have had to pull the children out of their beds and rush into the cellar because of the airplanes.

August 13. Again considerable time has passed since I last wrote in April how we fell into American hands. Once again something has happened of which we had no inkling. After two months under American control we heard now and then that after the division Sachsen and Thueringen would be given to the Russians. We were very upset. We couldn't move away because zone boundaries had been established. Many people no longer owned horses and no trains were operating. We prayed and hoped that the rumor was not true.

One day as we returned from work we heard over the radio that Middle Germany (Sachsen and Thueringen) would be given to the Russians. We stood there dumbfounded, unable to believe our ears. Perplexed and uneasy, we ran from one person to the next asking: What now? The men asked the military authorities to allow us to move out. But they denied the request. We prayed and hoped for help. From time to time we approached the military authorities again. One day we learned that the Lord can soften the hearts of people until they are streams of water. Our men returned with the documents permitting us to go west into the English zone. We rejoiced at the news and prepared for the journey. Many people believed, however, that the Americans would demand the territory and wanted to wait for more news over the radio. Because the West was so devastated, some feared they wouldn't find food and lodging there. As a result we had to separate from our beloved Adelsheimer. During the whole flight we had tried to stay together, and now, during peaceful times, we were separating.

Only two wagons left the Zeitz district. Even today we thank the Lord that he gave us no peace of mind until we were on the road again. More families set forth out of the Wissenfels district, where many Adelsheimer lived also. The others wanted to wait. Unfortunately no more news came through, and one day the district was occupied by the Russians. The poorest people were returned to Russia and are in exile today. Only a few escaped secretly across the border and brought us the sad news regarding what had happened.

Our new flight led from Sachsen via Thueringen and Hessen to Westfalen, where we are today. We left on June 19 and traveled two weeks with horses and wagon. We saw many, many ruins the farther westward we drove. The once flourishing cities of Germany now lay in ruins and ashes — a place of horror and desolation.

January 13, 1946. Christmas has come and gone again — the third time since we left our beloved Adelsheim. In 1943 we were in a camp in Lager. Christmas 1944 was celebrated in Poland. In 1945 we were here in Westfalen. Where will we spend the next Christmas?

Since dear Brother C. F. Klassen has found us here, we aren't nearly as downcast. Hope that we will find a home again has so inspired us that it feels as if new life is surging through our bodies. We are confident that our overseas brothers and sisters in the Lord with God's help will see that we get out of here. But where are my relatives and my mother? Our search until today has been fruitless.

What God does is done well;
His will is always the best.

A physical deformity closed the door to marriage and a family of her own for Anna Baerg, but created the opportunity for literary expression. Anna left extensive journals which record her observations of life in Russia during troubled times. This sketch deals primarily with her attempts to be true to her poetic gifts as her response to God's call to service.

14

THE POET OF APANLEE

Anna Baerg (1897-1972)

By Betty Suderman Klassen

She straightened up a little, to ease the curvature of her spine into the leather brace. Deftly her pencil formed the up and down strokes of German Gothic script. "Apanlee, November 14, 1916. My name is Anna Baerg. Apanlee is a large estate in the Molotschna Mennonite colony in south Russia, where my father is the manager. That should be sufficient introduction, I think." The idea of keeping a journal made her heart beat a bit faster, even if it would only be "a small mirror" of what life would bring her.

Since the day had passed without deviation from routine, she described the weather: "Outside, the restless solitary November wind sweeps through the vast countryside. Sitting inside, a person listens to its whispering tones without knowing where they come from or whither they go. And high above the earthly ordinariness shines the restful universe of stars, the silent preachers of eternal truth. There is something wonderful about the starry heavens."

Because her education had been interrupted by ill health, Anna took private lessons with Miss Schotter, the governess who tutored the children of the David Dicks, the estate owners (Dec. 16, 1916).* Noticing Anna's interest in writing, Miss Schotter urged her to try a short story. Anna complied, but after she reread her creation, she disposed of it in the kitchen stove. Rhymes seemed more natural to her. When she had been in the Crimea for medical treatments for her back, Uncle Abraham had encouraged her to express her feelings in words instead of tears. Now she showed Miss Schotter what she considered to be her first "real" poem, entitled "Evening Rest."

"Read it to me aloud," Miss Schotter suggested.

Anna straightened up and began:

Evening star so bright and lovely,
Silently I look aloft,
Field and forest rest so calmly,
All I hear are whispers soft.
One small cloud is drifting slowly
'Cross the purple evening sky,
Silently it makes its journey
As my muted thoughts flow by.

And the moon so brightly shining
Comfortingly says, "Don't weep.
The Creator is so loving,
You, my child, He too will keep.
He your prayer will surely answer
That you murmured for your child,
And He safely soon will lead her
To her mother's hand so mild."

"That's a fair poem, Anna," Miss Schotter began. "The vocabulary is quite ordinary, and the imagery in the last part, confusing. You'll never become another Goethe, but keep writing anyway. You express some universal feelings, and turn a person's thoughts to God. That's good."

In her journal Anna confessed that her dream of becoming a poet would probably never be realized. But hope still flickered. "When I think of the words I wrote several years ago, I am overcome by a happy feeling that it has not all been in vain!" (Dec.

---

* Dates of journal entries

19, 1916). Perhaps Miss Schotter would be proven wrong.

As she approached her 20th birthday, Anna struggled with big thoughts about life: ''Will you find the way to true happiness? Oh that you could rise above the earthly and temporary to Him who said, 'I am the way, the truth and the life.' Then your life would not be purposeless; then you too would find and fill your little niche in the vast universe'' (Jan. 8, 1917).

Though she never complained to the family about her hunched back, her frustrations were real. ''Oh God, why did you let me become like this? Why can't I be like other girls? Sometimes the future looks so dark and black that one would despair. But thank God, such hours don't come often, and this is God's grace. Oh that one could always quietly, in faith, submit to one's fate!'' (Jan. 27, 1917). When she took her first teaching assignment, she commented, ''It's almost humorous that someone should think of hiring Anna Baerg as a teacher. Fortunately for her, the three students aren't making great demands on her scientific knowledge'' (Dec. 6, 1917).

Occasionally, Anna and her sister Nela (short for Cornelia), who was one year her junior, went for a walk through the well-groomed estate gardens and meadow. Nela bent down and picked violets for Anna to press and add to her growing collection of south Russian flora and fauna. Often Anna was too tired for an extended walk. Could her weakness be due to tuberculosis? Only her journal knew of those fears.

When winter approached in 1917, and the convulsions of the Russian revolution and World War 1 spread through the Molotschna colony. Anna reneged on her earlier resolve to leave politics to the men. She asked herself difficult questions like: ''For whom should one harbor patriotism? For Russia, which would like to deprive us of rights and homes (through collectivization) because we are Germans?'' (Nov. 13, 1917). As the pressures increased, she tried to correct her own attitude toward the Russian people. ''And if, as you say, they are dumb Russians, you still have no right to despise them, Anna Baerg. For they are people, and as such God has put them all on one level, without exception'' (Dec. 22, 1917).

Upon rereading her entries recounting robberies, illness, deaths, as well as miraculous escapes in the colony during that tense period, she comments, ''Who would have thought when I began to keep a journal, that it would have such weighty matters to report. I myself am in suspense as to what the next pages will record. Oh that it were enough of the horrors!'' (Feb. 14, 1918).

As the Makhno bandits plundered Mennonite villages and raped the women, the men organized self-defense units. On December 22, 1918, as Anna sat beside the kitchen window, she observed four men marching down the street, guns on their shoulders, and pockets bulging with hand grenades. Because they lacked military uniforms, she concluded they were Mennonites. ''Exactly the opposite of what one calls nonresistance,'' she noted. ''I don't want to say anything more about it — each one shall act according to his conscience. And in this case, dire distress threatens. Yet, I think God would have been able to deal with the robbers without this little band of Mennonites. I can't help wondering what our forefathers would have said in response to all this.''

The following year, Mennonite men were drafted into the Russian army. As in many other homes, the question of emigration was discussed at the Baerg supper table. Would it be possible to go to North America? To Africa?

''My cousins seem content in America,'' Mother Baerg admitted. ''But the thought of crossing the ocean terrifies me.''

''For my part,'' Anna spoke up, ''I'd like to see more of the world. Yet when I think of leaving, my heart gets heavy, for I would never again see many whom I regard highly'' (Jan. 22, 1919).

Long-range plans, however, gave way to immediate needs. When the Bolsheviks approached the Apanlee estate, the Baerg family, along with others, fled to the neighboring village of Wassilewka. By March 18 they had found refuge in Alexanderkrone.

Several weeks later, Anna's father became ill with spotted typhus. Since the disease was highly contagious, her mother didn't allow the children into the sickroom. Anna, along with seven younger brothers and sisters, had to go out into the garden and look in through the window to catch a glimpse of father. They couldn't see much, but the motto on the wall above the bed was clear: ''God, your way is holy.'' One evening as they sat in the kitchen, they heard singing outside the bedroom window. ''Commit thy way, confiding/When trials here arise/To him whose hand is guiding/The tumult of the skies.'' How they hoped and prayed that father would recover. But he died on Good Friday, April 18, 1919.

Anna watched her mother struggle with providing food and a future for eight children: herself, Nela, Abram, Hans, Mariechen, Gerhard, Willi, and Henry. ''Oh why did it have to be father? Why not I? It's so hard for poor mother!'' Anna wrote (May 16, 1919). But life had to go on. Then Nela was engaged. Anna threw herself wholeheartedly into the wedding preparations. The Concordia choir, in which she sang, used green garlands and boughs to decorate the shed where the wedding was to be held. One of the men lettered the words ''With God,'' on a piece of linen, and Anna outlined the words with pressed flowers. The motto was hung above the bridal couple (May 27, 1919).

After the wedding, the reality of her father's death seemed to descend anew. Her mother said she wanted to die, and cried so much that it seemed to distort her vision. One Sunday afternoon in July, brother Willi lay on the couch, crying and complaining, ''I haven't seen father for such a long time.''

Noticing how his grief added to her mother's distress, Anna took Willi and little Henry for a walk. At the cemetery she showed them father's grave. Henry turned his little face up toward hers, saying, ''Let's dig him up.''

''Go ahead,'' Anna replied.

The small hands began to scoop away the dirt. But Henry soon gave up. ''I can't do it. They closed it all up.''

She had helped the boys to understand what had happened. Anna comforted herself that ''God is the father of the orphans, and he will not forsake us, no matter how dark it seems.'' But her question remained, ''Good father, why did you have to leave us so soon?'' (July 23, 1919).

Anna wished she could contribute to the family income by teaching. But there was no school in summer, and she seemed too weak to handle a job if it should become available. ''You, Anna Baerg,'' she wrote in her journal, ''are not so weak that you are good for nothing. You would like to make an independent contribution, would like to have a vocation, in order not to be dependent on the good graces of others. You often feel such a strong urge to work, but have to suppress it repeatedly, conscious that you lack the strength and knowledge to bring it to realization.

But one can also tell that to the Lord'' (Aug. 2, 1919).

Reading the works of such authors as Uhland, Emerson, Schreimer, Sturmfels, and Schiller, alone or in the company of others, was one of Anna's favorite evening pastimes. Since she couldn't attend school because of her health, teacher Gerhard Peters of the Alexanderkrone high school tutored her and his sister, Tina, privately. Anna wrote essays on topics such as ''War: its influence on the development and progress of human society'' (Jan. 16, 1920).

Anna contributed to her family's welfare through music. At the end of a year of hardship, sorrow, and upheaval, she wrote, ''The old year was hard and dark, and the future seems dark too. — Nevertheless, this day came to a beautiful close. The sun had disappeared, and the last glow of evening lay pensively on roofs and gables. Then dusk descended. We all sat together in the corner room. I played the zither and the others sang along, each probably thinking of father. Meanwhile, one little star after another appeared on the heavenly dome and beamed its marvelous light into the New Year's night'' (Dec. 31, 1919).

She loved the ''beautiful times'' when the Concordia choir rehearsed on Sunday afternoons. Following a period of singing, conductor Isaac Regehr would call a recess. But this was not a time for idle gossip. At one session, Heinrich Kornelsen spoke on ''The Origin and Development of the Scriptures.'' Anna took her turn by reciting some of her poetry. When she read an essay on ''Mennonite Youth in General and the Feminine in Particular,'' she noticed some of the girls exchanging strange glances. Later one of them confessed that their doubts about her essay had been dispelled during the course of her presentation (Mar. 2, 1920). Anna concurred wholeheartedly when the son of the director articulated the purpose of the choir: to be the voice of conscience in Mennonite society. She, too, wished to help ''restrain evil and foster enthusiasm for the truly good and beautiful'' (Jan. 12, 1922).

Frequently, as on April 19, 1920, the choir went to sing for the sick. They lined up under the sickroom window and conductor Regehr hummed the pitch. Then four-part harmony rang through the night: ''We're going home, no more to roam/No more to sin and sorrow.'' In her journal Anna commented, ''The return walk was especially beautiful. The moon shone brightly across the wide green meadow and the silent cemetery. Yes, so it is: effervescent life on the one hand, and the silent graves on the other. How close together death and life are! But that's how it must be, otherwise the heart would never come to rest, for what is the longing in one's breast other than the homesickness of the soul? And how would it find the way home if death did not open the gate to the beyond? And yet, one wouldn't like to die'' (Apr. 19, 1920).

The Russian revolution continued unabated, with Anna observing from her limited perspective. Her first reaction to the sight of Russian reconnaissance airplanes was ''Majestic! They swooped over, so sure of themselves that I thought: What an exalted feeling that must be, to fly so high above the earth to greet the morning sun!'' (June 16, 1920). But her appraisal of the ''technological birds'' changed when, two days later, one circled suspiciously over Alexanderkrone. Groups of soldiers standing in the street assured the villagers that the planes were ''from our side.'' Then – crash! A bomb exploded. Anna grabbed Willi and Henry and ran inside. Quickly Mother opened the trap door into the cellar and they stumbled down the ladder into the damp darkness. Another crash. A soldier followed them into the cellar. They waited. Hearts pounding.

''I'll never forget those minutes in the cellar as long as I live,'' Anna wrote later. Habitually, she looked for a moral in the situation. ''When imminent death approaches, one begins to see life in the right light. How futile everything earthly is. How necessary it is to be prepared for death at any time'' (June 21, 1920).

After the unrest subsided, Anna set to work anew learning from other writers. She, her sisters and four other girls, including the local elementary school teacher, met for a ''reading hour.'' Tina Peters brought a volume by Ufer Hold. Anna read the first essay on character development aloud. Her voice rose like that of a preacher as she reached the concluding paragraph: ''Do you want to become whole and firm, a mature person, who is happy and becomes a blessing to others? Would you get out of your distress, your wavering and uncertainty? Then come to Jesus, the great character builder! He made whole persons out of the men and women that surrounded him'' (Jan. 15, 1922).

''What's the next chapter about?'' Tina ventured after a few minutes' silence. The other girls waited for an answer.

Anna turned to the table of contents and read, "The True Essence of Life," "The Role of a Woman," "Quiet Women — Mighty Women," "Struggle and Victory in the Life of a Woman," and "True Pleasures of Youth."

Anna's ideals of a woman's personhood and role in the home came to the fore one day when she delivered a note about emigration to the newlywed neighbors. The young wife had begun to read the note when her husband walked in. He demanded that she give it to him at once. She complied with a meek, "I only wanted to see who was on the emigration list." "Smart Alec," he retorted as he stomped out.

Anna was indignant, but knew better than to tell him what she thought. Instead, she confided in her journal. "What does he think of his wife anyway? Isn't she entitled to keep herself informed on current questions? Otherwise, how can she understand what her husband is talking about? How can she be his helpmeet? But the new husband probably believed his dignity to be threatened if he didn't force his wife into the subordinate position. He doesn't know that the ruling position consists of protecting and not tyrannizing his wife, and that the former is much more appropriate!" (June 15, 1922).

Anna also observed people in other situations. When she noticed that persons frequently passed one another in silence, without communicating, she wrote: "How much more we should have to share with one another. How much more receptive we would be if we didn't live unto ourselves, for that is the reason one is dissatisfied and unhappy. It is in the other that we find ourselves" (May 8, 1922). She once outlined the essence of true friendship in an essay. She pinpointed its characteristics as selfless love, unlimited faith and trust, honesty, involvement in the interests of the other, chaste reserve in interpersonal communication, and faithfulness that is unaltered by separation or death (Jan. 28, 1922).

During those days, physical concerns again pressured the Baerg family. In the aftermath of the revolution, the authorities had confiscated not only property and money, but also food supplies, which had already been shrivelled by drought. Mother Baerg parcelled out daily rations to her children, to stretch the supplies through the winter. Potatoes and other vegetables were planted in late February, 1922, considerably earlier than usual. And when her mother baked bread, Anna noticed that she used only half the usual amount of flour, adding bran and the grounds from their cereal beverage to make up the difference.

"Mother," Anna commented, "you would never have served bread like that three years ago. We would have shoved it aside in disgust." Mother nodded, wiping a tear on her sleeve as she kneaded the dough. "But we're thankful," Anna added. "It doesn't matter whether it tastes good, as long as it is edible. We may feel hungry, but we are not starving yet, and food is on the way from the Mennonites in America."

The village waited long weeks for the food. Then on March 1, 1922, Anna wrote, "The bread has finally arrived, thank God." But it was rationed only to children and those in ill health. Within three weeks, she and her brothers Willi and Henry were declared eligible for one meal a day from the Mennonite Central Committee "American kitchen" in the basement of the Alexanderkrone trade school. Thankfully, Anna took her little brothers to get their helping of boiled rice, bean soup, or cocoa. They didn't eat their pieces of white bread there, however; Anna wrapped them in her handkerchief and carried them home to add to their meager supper (Mar. 23, 1922).

When the supplies from America were depleted, Dutch Mennonites provided food, administered by Mr. Willig. So grateful was Anna that she wrote a 45-line poem dedicated to him. She described their plight: revolution, illness, crop failure, and famine. The joy that the relief food brought was like the joy at Christmas (May 1, 1922).

In spite of the relief, the Baerg family budget became tighter as the local economy worsened. Mother traded the parental wedding bands and their cream separator for maize and wheat flour. Anna couldn't understand how her mother could part with these last "heirlooms" from father. She concluded that love for the children must have been the motivation (May 1, 4, 1922).

During this time, Anna received a letter from David Epp, the youth leader at Berdjansk. He reported that the poems she had sent at their request had earned her "the warmest sympathy of our young people." They hoped to enjoy more "children of her muse" in the future. Further, they had printed some of her pieces in their collection of "Mennonite Poetry." Anna still wondered whether

her poems were good enough for publication. But when she recovered from the awesome responsibility of having opened her thoughts to the public, she wrote, "One is glad when what one did found understanding and a friendly reception with others" (May 22, 1922).

That year's spring concert of the Concordia choir gave Anna the haunting feeling that it might be their last time together. They decorated the assembly room of the tradeschool with garlands and bouquets of roses. In addition to the choir music, the program included two sermons and educational presentations. Only the refreshments, a plate of rice, and a few sprinkles of salt, betrayed the dire straits of those who participated (May 23, 1922).

Meanwhile, Anna found a new avenue of fulfillment: teaching a kindergarten of some 20 students, aged four to seven, for two hours each day. The weekly tuition of one-quarter pound of butter, four eggs, or other food products, provided a tangible contribution to the family income. She prepared lessons suitable for the various personalities, and used the little songs and finger plays she had learned in the Froebel course in Halbstadt. But even after adequate preparation, she prayed that God would help her be a faithful teacher and leader. She observed that things didn't go well if she didn't approach her work with prayer (Mar. 9, 1923). When the children shoved and pushed in order to hold her hand at playtime, she remarked, "How thankful a child is. It repays every kindness with the best it has to offer: with love" (Mar. 23, 1923).

When Uncle Abraham came from the Crimea, he visited Anna's kindergarten and also encouraged her to have "the children of her muse" printed when more prosperous times would come. He told her that the poems she had sent to her grandmother last year had been forwarded to him in prison. His cell-mates, two Lutherans, had been complaining bitterly about their lot as political prisoners. When he had read them her poems, they became quiet, and later copied them and sent them home. "You unknowingly ministered to those strangers in their dark, dreary hours. Continue to use your God-given gifts," he told her.

"How good that feels, and how it encourages," Anna later admitted in her journal (Oct. 12, 1922).

During this time, the Baerg family, along with many others, applied for emigration to America, and underwent the appropriate medical examination. Several of the boys, as well as Anna, had trachoma, a disease of the eyes, which had to be cauterized with bluestone (copper sulphate), without anesthesia (July 6, 1922). They waited for emigration proceedings to take their course.

Meanwhile, Anna enjoyed the simple things of life. "While outside, the night spreads its black wings over the earth, and frost threatens to snuff out tender life, we are sitting in the warm kitchen, dimly lit by a small oil lamp. Mother is knitting, Nela is sewing, Mariechen is mending Henry's pants, Abram is fixing Hans' sandals while the latter is reading. Gerhard and the youngest two are in bed. To be at home is better than anything else! Who knows how long we will enjoy this comfortable togetherness, and where the next winter will find us" (Oct. 7, 1922).

A year after the first health inspection, the Baergs had to see Dr. Buettner for another emigration checkup. "Anna has tuberculosis," was his diagnosis.

"Now the whole family will have to stay here because of me," Anna lamented.

Her mother chided her, "Don't feel bad about it. That will only make matters worse."

Anna tried to be cheerful, but when she was alone, despair almost overwhelmed her. "Fear creeps up my throat as though it would choke me," she wrote. Again she took refuge in God. "If you could believe! I want to believe. I believe. Lord, help my unbelief and make me totally quiet and glad."

Two days later, David Matties brought them word that the doctor had reviewed their case. He had declared Anna well! Mother Baerg took the news as a divine indication that they should move. But Anna wondered what would happen at the final health inspection.

When she saw others enjoying health, love, and happiness, she admitted her own desire to love and be loved. It was never realized in marriage. In a poem, "Unrequited Love," she suggests that rejected love should be redirected to the elderly and poor, instead of turning into bitterness. In her journal she wrote, "The foolish heart has so many wishes and hopes that cannot be fulfilled. Lord, I ask for one thing: Give me a strong clean heart that can rejoice in the good fortune of others and be content" (Dec. 31, 1923). A few days later she added, "Lord, help me to bear my cross (hunchback) with honor. Oh, it sometimes gets almost too heavy for me'' (Jan. 4, 1924).

Five months later the family went for a final health check, all harboring the silent fear that Anna might be barred from emigration. But she passed! On the way home in the ladder wagon, Hans led out in one song after another, praising God for answered prayer.

Even then, the time of parting on June 23, 1924, was hard. As the strains of ''God be with you till we meet again,'' died away, the train moved out of Lichtenau and the family had begun the journey to Canada. Anna's innate curiosity helped her adjust to life with an (Old) Mennonite host family in Waterloo, Ontario. ''I find it very interesting to study the worldviews, customs, and manners of people. There isn't such a class distinction here as in Russia. Yet a nobility is evident, one that all can attain: honest labor'' (Aug. 7, 1924). Six months later she wrote, ''I still speak English pitifully, but communication with the lady for whom I work gets a bit better every day'' (Feb. 13, 1925).

In the fall of 1925 the Baerg family acquired a farm at Dominion City, near Arnaud, Manitoba. When other emigrants arrived from Russia, the Baergs opened their home to strangers. Anna wrote, ''How wonderfully our fate has changed. After being dependent on the goodness and mercy of others for years, the hour has come where we are in a position to help others'' (Feb. 7, 1926).

The Baergs attended the worship services of a group of Mennonite Brethren and General Conference Mennonites who met in the Arnaud United Church. Abraham Nachtigall, whom Anna had learned to appreciate in Russia, was one of the preachers. After the harvest, Anna began to write again, though not in her journal. In a school exercise book she began a collection of poetry, her own as well as short favorites by other authors. Neatly she penned her motto: ''Whatsoever things are true, honest, just, pure, lovely, of good report, think on these things'' (Phil. 4:8). She tried to make each page a balanced picture and sketched a few tiny leaves, berries or flowers at the end of shorter poems. On December 24, 1926, her Sunday school class presented a question-and-answer narration of the Christmas story which she had written.

During the next year she wrote numerous dialogues and poems that were presented at the local *Jugendverein*. Subsequently, she produced several sermon-style essays, not only for the Arnaud youth meetings, but even for a visit to the group in Gretna. When she received word of the passing of Isaac Regehr, she wrote a three-page memorial to the former director of the Concordia choir. As young men began to preach at the youth meetings, the demand for Anna's essays slacked off, and her emphasis turned to poems for special occasions. For her sister Mariechen's marriage to Aron Isaak, she created an acrostic, spelling out the names of the bridal couple. Her Christmas gift to Nela's family in 1932 was a collection of her poems, including a sparkling description of the snowy "Christmas at Waldesruh." The recitation of her 17-stanza poem at the dedication of the Mennonite Brethren Church in Arnaud must have been the highlight of 1935 for Anna.

Besides teaching Sunday school, Anna found another niche: she organized a *Maedchenverein* (girls club). When a Sunday afternoon business meeting, or a break between the morning and afternoon services of the harvest festival left the teen-age girls with time on their hands, Anna got them together for singing and Bible study. She lectured to them on walking with the Lord, working in his vineyard, and being a testimony through one's life. Her conservatism became evident in lectures on etiquette. Many of the girls got the impression that associating with boys spelled trouble, that talking to boys was sin, and that it was better to stay single than to get married.

One day, after she had expounded the dangers of being too free and forward with boys, the girls stood around, visiting.

"How does she know so much about boys when she isn't even married?" one of them whispered. They all giggled.

Anna looked in their direction sternly. Hadn't she taught them to suppress joking and laughter? Though they met only sporadically, the 25 girls in the club at its zenith appreciated Anna's sincerity and friendliness.

In 1940, when Anna's brother Gerhard married one of the girls who had been in her club, she wrote a poem for Hilda entitled, "From the *Maedchenverein.*" She also wrote "Brotherly Advice" for Gerhard. It must have been a bit disconcerting to Anna when the girl she asked to recite it thought she couldn't give such words of counsel to a man. Fortunately, Anna found another girl who didn't have such scruples and recited the piece with a flourish. Anna was satisfied.

During World War 2, Anna's interest in world affairs, so evident in her earlier journal, sparked anew. While her brothers, dressed in the blue overalls she had sewed, went to the barn to milk cows and feed horses, hogs, and poultry, Anna kept abreast of current events. The dishes had to wait while she went into the living room and turned on the battery-operated cabinet radio. She tuned in the BBC news from London and sat down on her little throw rug, with her ear next to the speaker. Her attention was focused on the news, so that she could recite all the significant details to her brothers when they returned from doing the chores.

After the Baerg brothers left the farm, Anna and her mother moved to Nela's home in Winnipeg. The relocation from the sparsely populated rural countryside to the city raised Anna's hopes for a new area of service. Perhaps she could begin another kindergarten like the one in Alexanderkrone. But Winnipeg already had well-established kindergartens, and the neighbors objected to her request for a permit to open a nursery school. So she and her mother took in boarders. At the Elmwood Mennonite Brethren Church she met the editor of the *Mennonitische Rundschau* and the *Christliche Jugendfreund*. Between January, 1947 and June, 1953, poems and fingerplays of her own composition and from her collection appeared in these periodicals. And again, she wrote poems for special occasions like women's meetings, and the C. A. DeFehrs' return from their MCC mission to South America.

When her mother died in November, 1954, Anna went to stay with Nela, who had remarried and now lived in Saskatchewan. After her brother Abram became ill with Parkinson's disease, Anna moved to their home in Coaldale, Alberta. She enjoyed her stay there, especially since several of her friends from the Concordia choir resided in the area. Here she took up her journal again. Though prayer had always been an important ingredient in her Christian life, it now took on new meaning.

One Sunday morning in November, 1963, Anna got a violent headache. Later, in the hospital, she lapsed into unconsciousness due to a brain hemorrhage. Her life hung in the balance for several weeks. Then she wrote, "The Lord gave me the gift of life once more, thanks to the many prayers on my behalf" (Nov. 29, 1963). On January 4, when she returned to the hospital because of recurring kidney infection, the doctor asked, "Aren't you tired of the hospital yet?"

"No."

"Not tired yet, after six weeks?"

"Well, a little," Anna admitted, "but I was home for a spell in between. If I had my own home, it would be different; but as it is, I'd rather be in the hospital longer."

After her release, she took up residence in Clearbrook, British Columbia, with Nela and her husband, who received her graciously. But it was a new beginning for Anna. "I'll have to pray much, so I'll be able to feel at home here," she wrote on January 29, 1964. If meeting old friends could have created that feeling, it should have come about quickly. But depression was hard to shake off. "I am mostly quiet. It has become different than it used to be," she admitted.

Occasionally, the Anna of happier days shone through. She criticized Susie, her protege of *Maedchenverein* days, for not living with her parents, saying, "It is different now than it used to be. She is a teacher and can have her own house and a car in addition." However, when Susie entertained her one Saturday afternoon, Anna's appraisal changed. "Does she ever have a nice house, and so roomy! I had a good time there and hopefully it won't be the last time" (Feb. 29, 1964).

Not all the church services in Clearbrook met with Anna's approval. If a preacher told a lot of jokes, she felt he was too lighthearted. But when Henry Born preached about intercession and prayer, she commented, "Never before have I heard it preached about like that! Too bad one forgets so easily. I'll have to bring paper and pencil in the future and take notes" (Mar. 10, 1964).

On March 20, Nela asked Anna to write a poem on intercession for their women's meeting. Anna declined. She hadn't written any poetry since her illness. However, prayer was her favorite topic, and Nela persisted. So Anna consented, saying, "It will have to come as an answer to prayer." Less than two weeks later, the poem entitled "Faithfulness" was finished. "It took quite a long time," she commented. "I always have to pray about it, otherwise it doesn't turn out to be anything worthwhile" (Mar. 31, 1964). When the poem was recited on April 19, Anna was disappointed with the "timid" interpretation, which made it sound mediocre.

Later, in early summer, she confessed to her journal that she had "more or less" lost the urge to write. In July she admitted that "thinking is getting slower, even if you don't want to perceive it" (July 4, 1964). Even letter-writing became a chore. "Since I now write so poorly, I prayed that the Lord might help me — and then I was able to write much more legibly," she noted (Aug. 29, 1964). She passed away on February 16, 1972, at the age of 75.

PRAYER

That in life's battle I will not despair,
Lord, stay with me!
So that with patience I my lot may bear,
Be Thou my strength!
That outward joy and fortune not my thoughts perturb
By their appearance,
The day's confusion not my faith disturb,
Stay Thou with me!
Prove Thou my heart, uncover my offenses,
That not a word
Condemns me, bared of false pretenses.
Cleanse me from sin!
The worlds rest at Thy feet alone,
Creator, Lord,
Not swayed by beggar's staff nor lofty thrones,
O hear Thou me!
And when my day of life draws to an end,
Lord, stay with me!
And bear my spirit in Thine own strong hand
To where Thou art!

—published in *Mennonitische Rundschau,* November 8, 1950

BIBLIOGRAPHY

Arnaud Through the Years. Arnaud: Arnaud Historical Committee, 1974.

Baerg, Anna. Collection of poetry, dialogues, essays, but not journals. Mennonite Library and Archives, Bethel College, North Newton, Kansas.

Baerg, Anna. Journal (1916-1926). Transcribed from the Gothic into the Latin script by Clara K. Dyck under the auspices of MCC (Canada), 1978.

________. Journal (1963-1964). Courtesy of her sister, Cornelia Baerg Jantzen.

Dyck, Clara K. "Biography of Anna Baerg," preface to the journal serialization in *Der Bote* and *Mennonitsche Post* (1978).

Dyck, Peter J. "The Diary of Anna Baerg," *Mennonite Life* (Dec., 1973), 121-125.

Personal letters and/or interviews: Martha Boese Suderman, Martha Neufeld Baerg, Gertrude Boese Enns, Agatha Boese Schimpky, Lydia Suderman Fast, Cornelia Baerg Jantzen, Clara K. Dyck, Anne Kornelsen.

Mary J. Regier Hiebert believed in the education of women. She gave her money, her energy, her time, and her love to Christian higher education. She provided $15,000 toward the construction of the first Ladies Home at Tabor College, Hillsboro, Kansas, and became its first matron, a position she held for two decades.

15

THE FIRST MATRON OF THE LADIES HOME

Mary J. Regier Hiebert (1884-1970)

By Wanda Frye Horn

"Tabor is burning!"

The alarm cry spread quickly across the small Kansas town of Hillsboro in the early hours of that April morning in 1918. Townspeople who rushed to help found they could do nothing but join the crowd of quiet, weeping students and faculty members watching fire engulf the frame building that was Tabor College in those days. The building was consumed in less than an hour. Almost nothing was saved.

At first it seemed as if the college, then in its tenth year of operation, could not continue. But sacrifice and determination became the watchwords of faculty, students, and Hillsboro residents. They considered it a privilege to begrime themselves with cleanup chores. Classes resumed in temporary quarters. School administrators went to the people in Mennonite Brethren churches to ask for money to rebuild Tabor. And within days came an announcement that Tabor alumna Mary J. Regier would donate, on an annuity plan, $15,000 toward the construction of a girls' dormitory. Tabor would survive, and the affairs of Tabor College and Mary J. Regier would be closely intertwined for years to come.

Mary Joan Regier. Her background was similar to that of hundreds of other American Mennonites: the family came from Russia (in this case the Molotschna Colony) in the 1870s to settle in the rich wheat country of the central United States. It was in the summer of 1879 that the Johann Regier family migrated to this country, five years before Mary (Maria) J. was born. Johann J. Regier was at that time 40 years of age. His first wife had died in 1875, leaving him with four daughters. Now he and his second wife, Maria Schellenberg Regier, had an infant son, Johann, whose name was later anglicized to John S. Regier. The family settled first in Boone County, Nebraska, but soon moved to York County, near Henderson, and the father became the first elder of the Henderson Mennonite Brethren Church.

Elder Regier was a staunch leader in the church, and one who wielded a great deal of influence. His deep dedication to his church and to Christianity as a whole was transmitted to his children, surfacing in their adult years in the selfless manner in which daughter Mary J. devoted herself to Christian activities, and in son John S. Regier's Bible teaching ministry.

On the Regier farm, three miles north of Henderson, Mary J. was born on September 4, 1884. She received the dual education usual for a Mennonite child of her time: German *Vereinschule* (located on the country church yard of the Mennonite Brethren church) and the American public school. Mary J.'s education took on an international flavor, however, when in 1895 the family made a year-long trip back to Russia to visit relatives. There, in the village of Rueckenau, Mary J. attended the village school and finished first and second grades in German and Russian.

The happy visit to Russia nearly had a tragic ending. On the return trip, three-year-old Abe became very ill, and in Berlin, Germany, his illness was diagnosed as smallpox. The next stop on their journey was Ruleben, and there the entire family was quarantined inside a seven-foot-high fence. ''We were shut off from the world,'' Mary J. wrote many years later, ''but our upward look could not be shut off.''

John, a teenager at the time, also fell ill with smallpox, and he and Mary J., neither of whom had yet come to a personal acceptance of Christ, both began to see their spiritual needs.

The day came when John's illness had progressed to the point that his mother felt he could not live. She raised her son up from his bed and said, "John, you are dying, and where are you going?" His reply: "Jesus is with me." At that the mother laid him back down and said, "Now you can die; I am satisfied." But he did not die. Almost from that moment he began to recover, and six weeks later the family was released from quarantine to go on home to Henderson. This incident of John's illness and conversion made such an impression on Mary J. that she looked back to it later in her life as the beginning of her own quest for salvation.

The assurance of forgiveness of sin did not come easily, however, for Mary J. Regier. Although she continued to pray for such assurance, it was not until some time after the family returned to Henderson that God spoke to the girl through the words of Romans 5:1 — "Therefore being justified by faith, we have peace with God through our Lord Jesus Christ." Then came the peace, the joy, the assurance she had been seeking. She was later baptized by her father in the Big Blue River, and she became a member of the Henderson Mennonite Brethren Church.

July, 1902. The death of Elder Johann Regier left Mary J. and her brother John with the burden of gathering in a plentiful harvest. Mary J. was almost 18, John a young married man in his early twenties, already becoming well-known in Mennonite Brethren circles as an evangelist and Bible lecturer. One morning, before going out to work, Mary J. read the 11th chapter of John from her Bible. In this chapter, which recounts the death and resurrection of Lazarus, Martha says to her sister Mary, "The Master is come, and calleth for thee." These words impressed themselves deeply into the mind of Mary J., and through them she realized God had work for her to do. She wrote later, "All day the many shocks of wheat seemed to be souls calling for help to find the way of life."

Mary J. remained in Henderson another four years, and for at least part of that time she taught the *Vereinschule* on the churchyard. Despite her lack of advanced education, Mary J. was a good teacher. A Henderson man who was one of her students in 1906 remembers her as "strict but loving." This boy, a shy and frightened six-year-old, was soon put at ease by Mary J.'s kindness. She insisted that her students learn, but through her encouragement she gave them the desire to learn. She also used an incentive method: she gave "head marks" for good performance, and sometimes an accumulation of head marks even meant a small gift from teacher to student. Mary J. enjoyed watching her students meet an academic challenge; she enjoyed watching their games at recess time. If Mary J. did not enjoy sweeping out the schoolhouse or stoking the fire in the coal stove, no one heard much about it.

Serving God in the way Mary J. wanted, however, required further education for herself. Thus, in 1906, she enrolled in the Bible institute at Fort Wayne, Indiana. In 1908, when her own denomination opened a college in Kansas, Mary J. went to Hillsboro and became a student at Tabor College. There she spent the next four years, completing what was called the "Preparatory and Academic Course," the equivalent of today's high school education. When she graduated from Tabor in May, 1912, Mary J. was four months away from her 28th birthday.

The training she had received qualified her for a "second grade State certificate for Kansas." This certification for teaching, however, was not good in her home state of Nebraska; and the next year she attended York College in York, Nebraska. The one-year normal-training course she took there gave her a "first grade York County Nebraska certificate."

Mary J. spent the next few years teaching in country schools in the area around Henderson. But her education, while giving her the qualifications for teaching, had not satisfied her desire for Bible knowledge. She decided to go to California and study at the Bible Institute of Los Angeles (Biola).

In April, 1918, when Mary J. was in school in California, the Mennonite Brethren constituency was rocked by the news of the near-destruction of Tabor College by fire. In the Tabor disaster, Mary J. Regier saw an opportunity to express her love for her Lord, her church, and her college. Mary J.'s niece, Anna Regier, writes, "She [Mary] sold 80 acres of land that she had inherited from her father, valued at $20,000, and gave $15,000 as an annuity to build a girls' dormitory at Tabor College." The agreement was that the college would pay Miss Regier four per cent interest on the $15,000 "during her natural life." Mary J.'s gift covered approximately one-half the cost of construction of the dormitory.

Mary J. was well-acquainted with the need for dormitories at Tabor. In her student days, living and eating arrangements were the problem of the individual student. Some students rented "housekeeping rooms" where they could do their own cooking. If these students were fortunate enough to live within easy traveling distance of Hillsboro, they went home every weekend and returned to their rented rooms with ample provender for the coming week. Other students boarded in faculty homes, and many a faculty wife could expect ten to twenty hungry students at her table three times a day. One faculty wife from those early days says, "Any year a faculty wife was not pregnant, she was expected to board students." One of her counterparts laughed at hearing this statement and said she wasn't sure even pregnancy gave any exemption from the boarding chores.

However, the new Ladies' Home (later the Music Building) to be constructed at Tabor would provide living quarters for women students and dining facilities for both men and women.

The Ladies' Home was begun in March, 1919, less than a year after the fire, and in a month the foundation was completed. By mid-September the brick work and the roof — essentially all the exterior work — were finished. By the following February (1920) the last of the interior work was being done, and at 6 p.m. on March 4, 1920, the Tabor Dining Hall (located in the basement level of the Ladies' Home) served its first meal. Slightly less than two years had elapsed since the fire.

The dormitory building faced the west and fronted on what is now South Jefferson Street in Hillsboro. Above the building's main entrance, embossed in large letters, were the words "The Ladies' Home." The brick structure, rising two stories above the basement level, was large for this small 1920 prairie town but was somewhat overshadowed by the even larger and more ornate Administration Building which was under construction slightly to the south and farther back from the road. The open fields around the buildings accentuated their massive appearance — "built as though they're to last for eternity," some people said. The cost staggered some of the brethren — somewhere in the neighborhood of $100,000.

After the opening of the dining hall in March, 1920, plans progressed for the opening of the dormitory itself in the fall. The Tabor administration invited Mary J., then still a student at Biola, to become the first matron of the Ladies' Home. She accepted the invitation and moved into the large brick building that would be her home for 20 years.

Many of the students in Mary J.'s early years as matron were much like she had been when she first enrolled at Tabor in 1908. Students in their twenties, denied a high school education by the press of farm duties, now made up for lost time with a singular dedication to the Academic (high school level) course, or even pre-high-school work to prepare them for the Academic course. Many had missions or the ministry as their goal.

Mary J. appears often in the Tabor College yearbooks chronicling those years from 1920 to 1940. She was a member of the YWCA cabinet, a member of the graduating class of 1924 (when she received her A.B. degree), secretary-treasurer of the mission band, a member of the Anti-Tobacco Association, a teacher of German, advisor to the *Bonne Amite* organization of dormitory students. But primarily she was the matron, or housemother, and the reigning lady in the college dining room.

The 20 years treated Mary J. kindly. By 1930 she was wearing glasses, but in her photograph for that year, the eyes behind the glasses still hold the familiar expression of a quiet, amused enjoyment of life. Smile wrinkles frame the eyes. The 1937 photograph shows her sitting in a wicker rocking chair in the dormitory. In her dark dress with its white collar, she looks a bit like "Whistler's Mother," but her smile has not changed from the earliest pictures. Her hair grayed gradually over the years, but her light-colored hair did not show the gray readily. The hair style remained much the same — pulled neatly into a bun at the nape of the neck, yet with just a touch of softness about the face. The styling of her hair was probably her one concession to primping, for she wore no cosmetics. She did, however, take good care of her skin, which remained firm and youthful throughout most of her life. Her beauty advice: wash the face with snow whenever possible.

Mary J. took the mothering of her girls seriously. She saw to it that they checked in and out of the dorm, and she imposed a strict ten o'clock curfew. She conducted room checks at night to be sure the girls were settled and had their lights out. Undoubtedly some of the young ladies chafed under these restrictions; but time has a way of erasing any unpleasantness of a situation, and the now-gray-haired women who were dormitory residents during the

Regier years speak primarily of her devotion and dedication. It was not at all unusual for Mary J. to sit up all night with a sick girl, giving whatever help she could. On her bulletin board was the poem, "Others." "Others, Lord, yes others, let this my motto be. . . ." And this truly was her motto.

Above all, Miss Regier desired that her girls learn to do things "properly." One of those girls (now a grandmother of college-age young people) tells how she asked to use Mary J.'s sewing machine for a quick repair job on a garment. Since it was a short seam, the girl stood on one foot and pedaled with the other — until Miss Regier insisted she sit down and do it properly.

Sinks for the girls' use were located at both ends of the long dormitory corridor. Beside each sink hung a rag, and the girls had instructions to always wipe out the sink properly after using, leaving it ready for the next user.

And Miss Regier worried about the students — both girls and fellows. She worried over the naughtiness of students who raided the college pantry at night trying to appease ever-present adolescent hunger. She worried about whether it would be modest for her girls to don those new-fangled bloomers to take part in the physical education classes which came into more and more prominence at Tabor over the years. Not that Mary J. had anything against physical activity. She thrived on it. She was a wiry woman who moved most of the time at a run; and even when she was well into her seventies she demonstrated to a friend some of the rigorous exercises she did to keep her muscles in good tone. But she was concerned that the girls be dressed modestly and properly at all times.

Mary Regier's duties at Tabor were legion. Her supervision of the college dining operation included planning meals, purchasing food, keeping meticulous, detailed records of these purchases, sometimes even rolling up her sleeves to help the kitchen staff when such help was needed. She and a crew of helpers spent many summer hours canning food for use during the next school year.

And she did all this without receiving any salary, according to an early president of Tabor. Miss Regier received the interest on her annuity gift to Tabor, and she received free room and board in return for her dormitory and dining hall duties, but the only work for which she was paid an actual salary was her teaching of German. However, Mary J. did not suffer financially. Her personal needs were modest; she did not dress lavishly or travel a great deal. She contributed to religious groups and shared her resources. The college yearbooks over the years tell of occasional special treats she gave the students: a social with ice cream and cake; pears at vespers. Small gifts, but undoubtedly important to young people away from home.

Miss Regier stayed at Tabor College until 1940. During her 20-year residence, a deep concern for education had grown up within the Mennonite Brethren Conference. In earlier years, even high school training was not emphasized among the Mennonite Brethren. Most of the young people remained on the farms, and advanced education was not needed for farming at that time. But during the 1920's and early 1930's, men with a vision of what education could mean to the church worked for years to persuade leaders of the conference to underwrite Tabor College as a conference institution. This came to pass in the mid-1930's. Mary J. Regier must have shared that vision of the worth of education. Not only was she herself well educated for a Mennonite woman of her day, but she also considered higher education worthy of her financial support.

In 1940 the Tabor administration decided to revamp the dormitory system and put some of the senior students in charge of dormitory management. It was time for Mary J. to leave Tabor. Maybe it was just as well. The older, serious students who had made up a large portion of the student body 20 years earlier had been generally replaced by a much younger group — typically adolescent, typically boisterous — and Mary J. was by now almost 56 years old.

However, her mothering days were not over. From Hillsboro, Miss Regier moved to Emporia, Kansas; and there, seeing the need for living facilities for girls attending the state teachers' college, she rented a house and began making a home for college girls once more. When Mary J. asked God for his will about this project, he spoke to her again, as he had so many times before, through his Word: "The earth is the Lord's and the fullness thereof; the world, and they that dwell therein." Mary J. wrote later, "So I was still in God's territory and served the people he had created." After two years, she bought a ten-room house and continued mothering her girls (some from Mennonite Brethren churches around the area, but others from foreign countries —

Japan, China, Korea) for another 19 years.

Miss Regier maintained her ties with Tabor, even after moving to Emporia. In 1955, when the college announced plans for a new library, Mary J. donated $15,000 for the purchase of books. This increase in library holdings enabled Tabor to comply with standards set up by the North Central Accrediting Association, and thus helped the college along its way toward accreditation.

Mary J. kept up her church activities, too, after leaving Hillsboro. She transferred her church membership to the First Baptist Church of Emporia, attended there faithfully, and taught the Women's Sunday School Class for many years.

Probably no one among Mary J. Regier's large number of friends and acquaintances ever thought she would marry, but in 1961, such an event did indeed take place. The gentleman was Mr. J. J. Hiebert, whom Mary J. had known for many years. He was twice-widowed, and his first wife had been Mary J.'s niece, Mary Schmidt Hiebert, daughter of Mary J.'s older half-sister. The two Marys were nearly the same age; and down through the years, whenever Mary J. traveled to California, she and her niece had enjoyed visiting together.

In July, 1961, Widower Hiebert passed through Kansas on his way to visit his son in Illinois, and stopped off in Emporia to see Mary J., now nearly 77 years of age. This brief visit resulted in the setting of a wedding date for the following month. The arrangements were not taken lightly. A Hiebert daughter-in-law tells how, when informing his family of his forthcoming marriage, Mr. Hiebert produced a copy of Mary J.'s health record, duly signed by her doctor in Emporia. (The family is "still wondering if she required one of him.") Mary J., as usual, had sought God's leading through his Word, and the Lord spoke to her through Psalm 37:23: "The steps of a good man are ordered by the Lord: and he delighteth in his way."

Mary J., who had watched so many of her girls become brides, was radiant with excitement as she planned her own wedding. Friends from her early years at Tabor helped her with preparations.

The wedding took place on August 24, 1961, in the Hillsboro Mennonite Brethren Church. Mary J., wearing a pale green dress and a small white feather hat, was given in marriage by her younger brother, A. J. J. Regier. One friend describes the bride as "glowing with joy and happiness" and "exuberant in expressing her delight."

The newlyweds made their home in Dinuba, California. Moving halfway across the country means a great deal of adjustment under any circumstances, and especially so for a woman of Mary J.'s age. Her activities were greatly changed, after more than 40 years of managing and mothering college students. But although she slowed down, idleness was still a stranger to Mary J. Regier Hiebert. She corresponded with many friends, and she read. At one time she subscribed to 36 periodicals and magazines.

On June 2, 1966, Mr. Hiebert died suddenly, and it seemed wise to Mary J. to leave California and return to Hillsboro, Kansas. There she settled at the Parkside retirement home to spend the remainder of her life. The woman who had given so many years in the service of others was gearing down, though still praising God for his goodness, and preparing for her face-to-face meeting with Christ.

That meeting took place on January 31, 1970. The eyes with the laugh-crinkles at the corners closed; the busy hands rested. Mary J. had lived 85 years, four months, and 27 days.

The accomplishments of a woman such as Mary J. Regier Hiebert are beyond the realm of measurement. There is no scale. In the early years of this century, Mary J. saw the need for education for herself at a time when most women were staying home. Even after education became readily available and acceptable for Mennonite Brethren men, many young women used college only to fill the gap between high school and marriage. There is no way to number the young women who took education seriously because of what they saw in Mary J. Regier's life. There is no way to number the Mennonite Brethren families who felt easier in those earlier years about sending their daughters to college because Mary J.'s gift had made possible a good dormitory setting where daughters could be well supervised. Mary J.'s financial contributions to the Lord's work can be measured in dollars, but such measurement falls woefully short of accounting for the multiplied effect of those dollars as they filtered down through several generations into the present-day educational system within the Mennonite Brethren Conference.

What was once the Ladies' Home still stands at Tabor

College, although the words are gone from above the door. The interior of the building has been completely remodeled to provide practice facilities, classrooms and offices for the Music Department. The Art Department occupies the basement area, where Mary J. fed so many hungry Tabor students. Most students today do not know how the building was financed, but whether or not they know the source, they collect the interest on a life invested in the service of God and "others."

Acknowledgments

The bulk of the material for this biography was gathered through interviews and correspondence with the following persons: Esther Ebel, Hillsboro, Kansas; J. C. Ediger, Henderson, Nebraska; Helen Franz, Hillsboro, Kansas; Kathleen Hiebert, Fresno, California; A. E. Janzen, Hillsboro, Kansas; H. B. Kliewer, Hillsboro, Kansas; Hulda Langhofer, Dinuba, California; Dr. and Mrs. S. L. Loewen, Hillsboro, Kansas; Anna Regier, Hillsboro, Kansas; Mariana Rempel, Lawrence, Kansas; Mr. and Mrs. H. C. Richert, Hillsboro, Kansas; Mrs. Herbert E. Richert, Reedley, California; Viola Bergthold Wiebe, Hillsboro, Kansas.

Other sources: the *Christian Leader;* Hillsboro Mennonite Brethren Church records; Hillsboro *Star Journal; The Mennonite Encyclopedia*; Tabor College *View*; Tabor College yearbooks, courtesy of Tabor College Historical Library.

THE WRITERS

Elizabeth Regehr Bargen, wife of Frank Peter Bargen, migrated to Canada in 1930 just before the heavy Iron Gate of the Soviet Union slammed shut. In Canada she and her husband took up farming and raised their four children. Both died in 1976. Her experiences and those of her husband's during the Russian Revolution are being produced as a movie in Canada.

Hilda J. Born, homemaker and free lance writer from Matsqui, British Columbia, writes about her maternal grandmother, Katharina Zacharias Martens. She and her husband Jacob have five children and are active in the Central Heights Mennonite Brethren Church of Abbotsford.

Wanda Frye Horn is a free lance writer from Topeka, Kansas. Her articles have appeared in *REJOICE!* and the *Christian Leader*. She and her husband Charles are members of the Fairlawn Mennonite Brethren Church. They have four children.

Connie Wiebe Isaac is the niece of Elizabeth Pauls Wiebe, of whom she writes. Connie is active in researching and publicly promoting the heritage of the Russian Mennonites through original songs and translations of German folk hymns. Her album *Sing Alleluia . . . A Century of Mennonite Experience* appeared in 1974. She and her husband Don have two children and live in Fresno, California, where they are members of the Clovis College Community Church.

Neoma Jantz is a homemaker from Winnipeg, Manitoba, where she and her husband Harold are members of the River East Mennonite Brethren Church. She enjoys volunteer work in community, school, and church. The Jantzes have three children.

Esther Jost, free lance writer, homemaker, and former teacher, is the grandniece of Justina Friesen Wiebe. She and her husband Arthur are active in the Reedley, California, Mennonite Brethren Church. They have three sons.

Betty Suderman Klassen enjoys historical research and writing. Her first book *Trailblazer for the Brethren*, a full-length fictionalized biography of Johann Claassen, husband of Katharina, was published in 1978. She and her husband A. J. Klassen are members of the Butler Avenue Mennonite Brethren Church in Fresno. They have four children.

Anna Loewen continued her journal, which is excerpted here, until the family reached Canada in 1950. Soon thereafter she and her husband Julius bought a farm in Clearbrook, British Columbia, and made this their home for the next 21 years. The Loewens have two daughters and are members of the King Road Mennonite Brethren Church.

Luetta Reimer teaches literature and composition at Fresno Pacific College. Magdalena Becker's husband, A. J. Becker, was the brother of her maternal grandmother. Luetta and her husband Wilbert are active in the Butler Avenue Mennonite Brethren Church. They have two children.

Esther Loewen Vogt is a prolific writer of juvenile and adult fiction with more than ten books published. Sara Block Eitzen, about whom she writes, was the grandmother of numerous friends and acquaintances. Esther's husband died in 1975 leaving her with three adult children. She is a member of the Hillsboro, Kansas, Mennonite Brethren Church.

Katie Funk Wiebe, free lance writer, teaches English at Tabor College in Hillsboro, Kansas. Among her books are *Alone: A Widow's Search for Joy* and *Good Times with Old Times: How to Write Your Memoirs*. This book is the fulfillment of a long-standing dream that her four children and all children separated from their past by time and distance may learn to cherish the kind of spirit which indwelt earlier women among the brethren.